LaTeX
For
Everyone

A Reference Guide and Tutorial
for Typesetting Documents Using a Computer

Jane Hahn

Prentice Hall PTR, Upper Saddle River, New Jersey 07458

Library of Congress Cataloging-in-Publication Data

Hahn, Jane.
   LATEX for everyone : a reference guide and tutorial for
typesetting documents using a computer / Jane Hahn.
      p.   cm.
   Includes bibliographical references (p.) and index.
   ISBN 0-13-605908-2
   1. LaTeX (Computer system) 2. Computerized typesetting.
I. Title.
Z253.4.L38H35 1993
686.2'2544--dc20   93-16767
                                                        CIP

About the author: Jane Hahn lives in Santa Barbara, California, and is employed by Mission Research Corporation, a physics research firm. She has been an expert in the TeX and LaTeX software systems since 1987, when MRC began using LaTeX to produce its main product, technical reports. Since that time, besides her scientific programming duties, Ms. Hahn has been responsible for training and consulting in all aspects of electronic document preparation for all of MRC's branch offices country-wide, as well as for the headquarters in Santa Barbara. When she is not working for Mission Research, Ms. Hahn enjoys spending time with her family, singing and choral conducting.

This book was prepared with LaTeX and PC TeX using Computer Modern Fonts. It was published from TeX .dvi files prepared by the author, and printed from camera-ready pages typeset at 2000dpi.

Personal TeX, Inc.
12 Madrona Avenue
Mill Valley, CA 94941
Phone: (415) 388-8853
Fax: (415) 388-8865
Internet: pti@well.sf.ca.us
Personal TeX BBS: (415) 388-1708
TeX Users Group: (805) 963-1338

Copyright © 1993, 1991 by Personal TeX, Inc. All rights reserved. Printed in the United States of America. TeX is a trademark of the American Mathematical Society. PC TeX and Personal TeX are registered trademarks of Personal TeX, Inc. All other trade names are trademarks of their respective owners.

No part of this publication may be reproduced or distributed in any form or by any means, or stored in a data base or retrieval system, without the prior written permission of the publisher. Personal TeX, Inc. makes no representations, express or implied, with respect to this documentation or the software it describes, including without limitations, any implied warranties of merchantability or fitness for a particular purpose, all of which are expressly disclaimed. Personal TeX, Inc. shall in no way be liable for any indirect, incidental or consequential damages.

© Published by Prentice Hall PTR
Prentice-Hall, Inc.
A Simon & Schuster Company
Upper Saddle River, New Jersey 07458

All rights reserved. No part of this book may be
reproduced, in any form or by any means,
without permission in writing from the publisher.

Printed in the United States of America

10 9 8 7 6 5 4

ISBN 0-13-605908-2

Prentice-Hall International (UK) Limited, *London*
Prentice-Hall of Australia Pty. Limited, *Sydney*
Prentice-Hall Canada, Inc., *Toronto*
Prentice-Hall Hispanoamericana, S.A., *Mexico*
Prentice-Hall of India Private Limited, *New Delhi*
Prentice-Hall of Japan, Inc., *Tokyo*
Simon & Schuster Asia Pte. Ltd., *Singapore*
Editora Prentice-Hall do Brasil, Ltda., *Rio de Janeiro*

Contents

1 Introduction   **1**
   1.1 What Are TEX and LATEX? 1
   1.2 Typesetting versus Word Processing 3
      1.2.1 Word Processing 3
      1.2.2 Typesetting 3
   1.3 LATEX Input and Output Files 4
      1.3.1 ASCII Files 4
      1.3.2 Input Files 5
      1.3.3 Output Files 5
      1.3.4 File Names 6
   1.4 Printing a LATEX Document 7
   1.5 What LATEX Does for You 7
   1.6 Customization 8

2 The Very Beginning   **9**
   2.1 Basic Ingredients 9
   2.2 LATEX Commands 11
   2.3 The Document Style 13
   2.4 Sentences 13
      2.4.1 Special Cases 14
      2.4.2 Adjusting Margins and Line Spacing 15
   2.5 Paragraphs 16
      2.5.1 Avoiding Paragraph Indentation 17
      2.5.2 Adjusting Paragraph Indentation 17
   2.6 Punctuation 18
      2.6.1 Quotes 18
      2.6.2 Dashes 19

i

2.7   Special Symbols   20
2.8   Footnotes   21
      2.8.1   Adjusting Spacing Between Footnotes   23
2.9   Marginal Notes   23
2.10 Simple Formulas   25
2.11 The Comment Character   26
2.12 Moving Arguments   27
      2.12.1 Fragile Commands   28
      2.12.2 The \protect Command   28
2.13 Verbatim Text   29

3   Matters of Style   31
3.1   The Document Style Command   31
      3.1.1   Document Style Options   32
3.2   Letter Style   36
3.3   Title Page   39
3.4   Typestyles   41
      3.4.1   Type Sizes   42
      3.4.2   Using Braces to Form Groups   44
3.5   Sectioning Commands   46
      3.5.1   Appendices   47
      3.5.2   Unnumbered Sections   48
      3.5.3   The Table of Contents   49
      3.5.4   Changing an Entry in the Table of Contents . . .   49
      3.5.5   Adding a Line to the Table of Contents   50
      3.5.6   Extra Control over Sectional Numbering   51
3.6   Symbolic Referencing   53
      3.6.1   Labelling and Referencing Pages   55
3.7   User-Specified Hyphenation   57
3.8   LaTeX Environments   59
3.9   Quotations   60
3.10 Lists   61
      3.10.1 Itemized List   61
      3.10.2 Enumerated List   65
      3.10.3 References to List Items   66
      3.10.4 Descriptive List   68
      3.10.5 Spacing Between Items   69

3.11 Displayed Formulas 70

    3.11.1 Referring to Numbered Equations 72

    3.11.2 Integrals and Summations 72

    3.11.3 Text Mode versus Display Mode 73

    3.11.4 Other Math Typestyles 74

    3.11.5 Left-Justified Equation Numbers 75

    3.11.6 Left-Justified Equations 75

    3.11.7 Customization of Displayed Equations 76

3.12 Foreign Symbols and Accents 77

3.13 Page-Numbering Style 78

3.14 Headers and Footers 80

    3.14.1 Myheadings Page Style 82

    3.14.2 Adjusting the Height of Headers and
Footers 83

4 Typesetting Mathematics   **85**

4.1 Superscripts and Subscripts 86

4.2 Fractions 88

4.3 Roots 91

    4.3.1 Cube Roots, Etc. 91

4.4 Ellipses 92

4.5 Greek and Calligraphic Letters 94

    4.5.1 Greek Letters 94

    4.5.2 Calligraphic Letters 94

4.6 Math Symbols 95

    4.6.1 Special Functions 98

    4.6.2 Delimiters 98

4.7 Words as Part of a Formula 101

4.8 Fancy Details 102

    4.8.1 Math Mode Accents 102

    4.8.2 Horizontal Braces and Bars 102

    4.8.3 Dotless i and j 104

    4.8.4 Stacking Two Symbols 104

    4.8.5 Customizing Spacing in Math Mode 105

    4.8.6 Bolding in Math Mode 105

5 Rows and Columns   **109**

  5.1 Tabbing Environment 109

  5.2 Tabular Environment 111

       5.2.1 Normal Tabular Spacing 112

       5.2.2 Added Vertical Space 113

       5.2.3 Horizontal Lines 113

       5.2.4 Vertical Lines 114

       5.2.5 Headings over More than One Column 114

       5.2.6 Paragraph Columns 116

       5.2.7 Inserting an Expression into Each Row 118

       5.2.8 Tables as Paragraphs 120

       5.2.9 Aligning Tables with Surrounding Text 120

  5.3 Array Environment 128

       5.3.1 Adjusting Array Spacing 131

  5.4 Eqnarray Environment 133

       5.4.1 Eqnarray* Environment 134

       5.4.2 Breaking Lines in Formulas 134

       5.4.3 Extra Space Between Eqnarray Rows 135

6 Customization   **137**

  6.1 Page Breaks 137

       6.1.1 Forcing a Page Break 137

       6.1.2 Suggesting a Page Break 138

       6.1.3 Keeping Text Together on a Page 139

  6.2 Line Breaks 141

       6.2.1 Inhibiting Line Breaks: Special Cases 142

  6.3 Centering 144

  6.4 Making Text Flush 145

  6.5 Vertical and Horizontal Space 146

  6.6 Lengths 148

       6.6.1 Expandable Lengths 149

       6.6.2 Length Commands 149

  6.7 Boxes 152

       6.7.1 One Line of Text Inside a Box 153

       6.7.2 Adjusting Frame Thickness and Spacing 155

       6.7.3 Wrapping Text Inside a Box 155

       6.7.4 Boxes Filled In with Ink 157

        6.7.5   Raising a Box Full of Text 158
        6.7.6   Saving a Box of Text for Later Use 158
    6.8 Margins 163
    6.9 Underlining Text 166

7 **Floating Objects**   **169**
    7.1 What Is a Float? 169
    7.2 Figures 170
        7.2.1   Captions and Figure Numbering 171
        7.2.2   Labelling and Referencing Figures 172
        7.2.3   The List of Figures 172
        7.2.4   Alternate Entry to the List of Figures 173
        7.2.5   Adding a Line to the List of Figures 173
    7.3 Tables 177
        7.3.1   Captions and Table Numbering 177
        7.3.2   Labelling and Referencing Tables 178
        7.3.3   The List of Tables 179
        7.3.4   Alternate Entry in the List of Tables 179
        7.3.5   Adding a Line to the List of Tables 180
    7.4 Floats in Two-Column Format 183
    7.5 Rules for Float Placement 183

8 **Preparing Large Documents**   **185**
    8.1 Splitting the Document into Small Files 185
    8.2 The Root File 185
        8.2.1   The Input Command 188
    8.3 The Text of the Document 190
    8.4 The Index 192
        8.4.1   Creating the Index Entries 194
        8.4.2   From .idx Entries to Actual Index 196
    8.5 The Bibliography 198
    8.6 Preventing Output To Auxiliary Files 201

A **Defining Your Own Commands**   **203**
    A.1 Defining New Commands 203
        A.1.1   Simple Text 203
        A.1.2   A Series of LaTeX Commands 204

    A.1.3 Abbreviations for LATEX Commands 205
  A.2 Redefining Old Commands 206
  A.3 Defining Commands That Take Arguments 207
  A.4 Defining New Environments 209
  A.5 The list Environment 211

B Customizing Counters   215
  B.1 What is a Counter? 215
  B.2 Setting a Counter 216
    B.2.1 Adding to a Counter 217
  B.3 Printing a Counter 218
  B.4 Styles of Counters 219
    B.4.1 Marking Footnotes with Symbols 221
  B.5 Creating Your Own Counter 221

C Style Parameters   223
  C.1 Length Parameters 223
  C.2 Counter Parameters 224
  C.3 Default Settings for Parameters 224
  C.4 Rubber Lengths 224
  C.5 When to Change a Parameter 227
  C.6 Parameter Definitions 227

D The Picture Environment   239
  D.1 Defining the Picture Area 239
  D.2 Putting Objects in the Picture 240
    D.2.1 Putting Text in the Picture 242
    D.2.2 Putting Shapes into the Picture 247

E Errors   261
  E.1 When LATEX Encounters an Error 261
    E.1.1 Continuing On With the Run 262
    E.1.2 Inserting Text and Continuing 263
    E.1.3 Writing as Much s Possible to the .DVI File . . . 263
    E.1.4 Missing \ end{document} 263
    E.1.5 File Not Found 264
  E.2 Interpreting Error Messages 264

        E.2.1   The Error Indicator 265
        E.2.2   The Error Locator 265
        E.2.3   Examples of Error Messages 266
   E.3   The .log File 268
   E.4   Helpful Hints for Finding Errors 271
        E.4.1   Look Before the Indicated Line 271
        E.4.2   Incidental Error? 272
        E.4.3   Which Input File? 273
        E.4.4   Checking Output for Anomalies 278
        E.4.5   Isolate the Error 279
   E.5   LATEX's Error Messages 280
   E.6   Some of TEX's Error Messages 296

F Examples   **299**
   F.1   Eqnarray and Array 299
   F.2   General Math 304
   F.3   Footnotes 306
   F.4   Table of Contents, Lists of Figures and Tables 307
   F.5   Style 308
   F.6   Tabular Environment 311
   F.7   Floats 316
   F.8   Page Breaks 317

G Making Slides with SLITEX   **319**

Bibliography   **321**

Index   **323**

List of Figures

7.1   This is the caption of the figure. 172

2.D This is a sample figure with a customized number including a period. 220

D.1 Sample grid. 241
D.2 Text-placing commands in the Picture environment. . . . 242
D.3 Sample horizontal and vertical lines. 248
D.4 Illustration of length argument to line command. 250
D.5 More examples of lines. 251
D.6 All possible line slopes in the first quadrant. 252
D.7 All possible line slopes in the second quadrant. 252
D.8 All possible line slopes in the third quadrant. 253
D.9 All possible line slopes in the fourth quadrant. 253
D.10 Sample arrows. 254
D.11 Sample circles and disks. 256
D.12 Sample oval shapes. 258
D.13 Multiple circles drawn with the multiput command. . . . 259
D.14 Multiple frameboxes drawn with the multiput command. 259

List of Tables

3.1 Document style Options 34
3.2 Examples of usage of some document style options 35
3.3 Foreign Symbols and Accents 77

4.1 Greek Letters 94
4.2 Binary Operation Symbols 96
4.3 Relation Symbols 96
4.4 Arrow Symbols 97
4.5 Miscellaneous Symbols 97
4.6 Variable-sized Symbols 97
4.7 Trigonometric Functions, Etc. 98
4.8 Delimiters 98
4.9 Math Mode Accents 102

7.1 This is the caption of the table. 178

C.1 Default values for style parameters in Report, Book, Article, and Letter styles, assuming the default point size of 12 points. 225
C.1 *(Continued)* Default values for style parameters in Report, Book, Article, and Letter styles, assuming the default point size of 12 points. 226

Chapter 1

Introduction

1.1 What Are TeX and LaTeX?

In the beginning was the word. And for a Stanford math professor named Donald Knuth, the word was difficult to manage. Difficult, that is, whenever Dr. Knuth had to communicate to his publishers exactly how a formula in one of his textbooks was to be typeset. So the computer program named TeX was written to do the job of describing and typesetting formulas. In time, it developed into a complete document formatting system, sufficient for producing entire textbooks or other technical documents.

To prepare a document with TeX, you type your text into an ASCII file, seasoning it with TeX *commands* wherever special formatting or non-ASCII symbols are desired. For example, the TeX command to produce the greek letter α is `$\alpha$`. So your file might read

```
The cosine of angle $\alpha$ is 0. Therefore $\alpha$ = 90
degrees.
```

This would give

The cosine of angle α is 0. Therefore $\alpha = 90$ degrees.

Now, you may be thinking, "There are so many different symbols and formatting possibilities—there must be millions of TeX commands!" Imagine what is needed in producing a chapter or section header:

1

1. Leave vertical space before the header; perhaps start a new page.

2. Turn on a large, bold font.

3. Figure out the appropriate section number.

4. Enter the section number, some horizontal space, and the heading.

5. Create an entry in the Table of Contents.

6. Switch back to the regular font.

7. Leave a little vertical space after the header.

Now, do all that every time you start a new section?! Don't panic! Here's where LaTeX comes to the rescue.

Each of the steps described above requires at least one TeX command—some more than one. But that same sequence of commands is going to be used over and over again in your document. So, why not combine them all together into one new command? In fact, that's what Leslie Lamport, the writer of the LaTeX program, has done for you. LaTeX gives you a complete set of commands—sufficient for producing your document—by combining frequently used or convenient *sequences* of TeX commands.

You do not need to know TeX to use LaTeX. However, TeX must be present on your computer for LaTeX to work. If you need or prefer simplicity in preparing your documents, and you do not insist on control over every minute detail, then LaTeX is a good choice for you.

However, for rare instances where you need fine control over formatting, you can use most TeX commands within a LaTeX document.

Summary

- TeX is a software program that does document typesetting.

- LaTeX is a program like TeX, but with fewer and simpler commands for typesetting.

- TeX must be present for LaTeX to work.

- You do not have to know TEX to learn and use LATEX.

1.2 Typesetting versus Word Processing

LATEX is a typesetting system, *not* a word processor. The difference is subtle, but important. Typesetting has many advantages over word processing.

1.2.1 Word Processing

You are probably familiar with the idea of word processing. You may have used one of the popular word processing programs to prepare a paper or report. You type your words into a computer, and they are formatted for you. Typical features of a word processor can be put into two categories:

- The first category is *editing*, which includes functions like text entry, cursor movement, search and replace, block and move, delete, save to disk and retrieve from disk—in other words things that allow you to enter and change your text.

- The second category is *formatting*; that is, all of the operations that enhance the appearance of your document, such as text justification; margins; using bold, italic or other fonts; spacing; centering of text; tabbing; and underlining.

There is more that can be done, however, to make a document look its best.

1.2.2 Typesetting

Typesetting provides all of the formatting features of word processing, plus a lot more logic for enhancing the appearance of your document.

Typesetting would

- Make sure that a line with large word spaces (due to justification) would not fall next to a line with small word spaces

- Make sure that a page of text does not have too many hyphenated words

- Perform kerning to bring combinations of characters such as "A" and "V" closer together for easy reading

- Replace combinations of characters such as "fi", "ff", and "ffl" with ligatures: "fi", "ff", and "ffl"

- Avoid starting a heading near the bottom of a page

- Insert a standard amount of vertical space around headings, figures, equations, lists, etc.

These are operations word processing rarely takes into account; but such details make documents look polished and professional.

Summary

- Typesetting automatically does more than word processing to enhance the appearance of a document.

- LaTeX does typesetting, not word processing.

1.3 LaTeX Input and Output Files

1.3.1 ASCII Files

In order for LaTeX to typeset your words, it needs to know what the words are, and how you want the words formatted. This information is provided to LaTeX in an "ASCII" file. ASCII—the American Standard Code for Information Interchange—describes a set of characters that are interpreted the same way by all computers. LaTeX uses the following subset of ASCII characters:

```
A B C D E F G H I J K L M N O P Q R S T U V W X Y Z
a b c d e f g h i j k l m n o p q r s t u v w x y z
0 1 2 3 4 5 6 7 8 9
' ~ ! @ # $ % ^ & * ( ) - _ = +
[ ] { } \ / | ; : ' " , . < > ?
```

These are all the characters you ever have to type to create a LATEX document.

1.3.2 Input Files

We have seen that LATEX likes to receive input in an ASCII file. It's not hard to see how plain text can be typed using the ASCII characters above, but how do you describe equations? What about bold and italic fonts? What about other formatting items such as margins, tabs, etc.?

You give LATEX commands to do these things. Most commands are English-like words preceded by a backslash ("\"). These commands are placed right in with your text, but rather than printing out in the output, they cause LATEX to do what you want it to do with your text.

1.3.3 Output Files

LATEX *could* read your input, process it, and send it straight to a printer without ever writing anything to disk, but it has a more efficient way of doing things. The product of a LATEX run is an output file, *not* a printed document. This output file, called a DeVice Independent file, (or DVI file), can then be used by a number of other programs to produce a number of different kinds of output, such as an image on a computer terminal or hard copy on a laser printer or dot matrix printer. This way there can be *one* version of LATEX that produces output suitable for *many* output devices.

Besides the main DVI output file, LATEX produces several "auxiliary" output files with each run. There is a main auxiliary file produced by each LATEX run, as well as other auxiliary files that may or may not be produced, depending on the input. See Sections 3.5.3, 7.2.3, and 7.3.3 for more information on auxiliary files.

1.3.4   File Names

To make things simpler, LaTeX has a naming convention for all of its input and output files. For example, in DOS, (a common operating system for PCs), all file names consist of a first name of eight characters or less, followed by a period, followed by an extension of three characters or less; e.g., `filename.ext`. LaTeX lets you pick the first name for your input file, but it requires that you give it ".`tex`" for an extension; e.g., `first.tex`.

Once you have chosen the first name for your input file, that name will be used on all files associated with this document. LaTeX appends three-letter extensions of its own to the output and auxiliary files. The table below illustrates how this is done:

Type of File	First Name	Extension	Full Name
Input file	`myfile`	`tex`	`myfile.tex`
DVI output file	`myfile`	`dvi`	`myfile.dvi`
Main auxiliary output file	`myfile`	`aux`	`myfile.aux`

Summary

- A LaTeX input file is an ASCII file containing text and LaTeX commands.

- The typical LaTeX command is an English-like word preceded by a "\".

- LaTeX produces output files—not hardcopy—as output.

- A separate program is required to read the DeVice Independent file (DVI file) and print the document.

- You pick the first name of the input file and give it the extension `.tex`; LaTeX picks the extensions to use on all output files, and keeps your first name.

1.4   Printing a LATEX Document

The basic process for obtaining a printed document using LATEX requires three steps:

1. Create an ASCII file containing text and LATEX commands.

2. Run LATEX on the ASCII file to create a DVI file.

3. Run a printer processor program on the LATEX DVI output file to get printed copy.

This book assumes that you have an ASCII editor and know how to use it. It also must assume that you have installed a printer processor, and know how to invoke it. Let's say you type "**prnt** *filename*" to invoke your printer processor. (*filename* is the first name you chose for your input file.) Here is what you would do from beginning to end to produce your document:

1. Using your editor, create an ASCII file named **myfile.tex** containing text. and LATEX commands

2. Type "**latex myfile**" to run LATEX on the file and produce a DVI file.

3. Type "**prnt myfile**" to print the output.

Hang on! You are almost ready to try it! You just need to know a tiny bit more before you can create a LATEX document. Starting with the next chapter you will be able to try out everything you learn.

1.5   What LATEX Does for You

LATEX makes it possible for you to input your documents without worrying about page formatting *at all.* All you need to do is type in the text, and a minimal set of commands, and LATEX will format your pages according to an internal standard called the *document style.* The document style defines the margins; type style; numbering styles for pages, chapters, equations, etc.; the paragraph indentation; and all other formatting parameters needed to produce your document.

Since page formatting is done for you, you have the advantage of

- being free to concentrate on the text;

- knowing your documents will have a standard look and quality;

- being able to create professional-looking documents without having a lot of expertise about formatting style.

Since there is obviously a need for more than one style, LaTeX does provide different document styles that can be used for reports, letters, articles, and other types of documents.

Summary

- Using an internal "document style," LaTeX automatically sets up a high quality formatting standard for all of your documents.

1.6   Customization

Suppose you are an expert in page formatting, and suppose you would like your page format to be different from the internal document styles provided by LaTeX? Well, then the news is even better, because LaTeX is programmable to do whatever you ask it to do. You can even write your own document style if you want to, once you gain enough expertise.

This will take more patience and effort than just accepting the default formatting style, but it can be very rewarding.

If you are ready to try using LaTeX, read on!

Chapter 2

The Very Beginning

2.1 Basic Ingredients

We are now ready to create a simple LaTeX document. The one thing you *must* have in every LaTeX input file is the following structure:

\documentstyle command
\begin{document} command

body of document

\end{document} command

Study this structure and get used to it. It never changes or goes away. Where it says "body of document," you put your text.

Ok! Let's create an actual document and try this out. We'll talk about it afterwards.

9

Exercise 2.1

1. Using your text editor, create an ASCII file named `first.tex`
   containing the following lines:

   ```
   \documentstyle{article}
   \begin{document}

   This is the text of my first document in \LaTeX!

   \end{document}
   ```

2. Notice that the `\documentstyle` command has an "argument"
   enclosed in braces.

3. Now type the following line at your system prompt:

   ```
   latex first
   ```

   Notice that some messages print out on your screen while LaTeX
   is running.

   NOTE: If LaTeX comes across an error and stops with a "?",
   don't panic. Even if it prints all sorts of weird messages before it
   stops, stay cool. It is probably caused by a simple typo in your
   input file. To get back to the DOS prompt, just type "**x**" and a
   carriage return. Check your file carefully for mistyped commands
   and correct any that you find. Then try

   ```
   latex first
   ```

   again. If that doesn't help, refer to Appendix E for help.

4. Type the following line at your DOS prompt:

   ```
   prnt first
   ```

(Remember, we assumed before that this is the way you invoke your printer processor. If not, then, whenever this book says "`prnt filename`," just type the proper commands for your printer processor.)

5. Pick up the page from your printer and admire it!

6. Notice that we just did the three steps described in Chapter 1:

    (a) Create an ASCII file containing text and LATEX commands.

    (b) Run LATEX on the ASCII file to create a DVI file.

    (c) Run a printer processor program on the LATEX DVI output file to get printed copy.

Study these three steps and get to know them.

You should have gotten a page with the sentence you typed, including the handsome LATEX logo, and a page number at the bottom. If something went wrong and you didn't, then you either have a typo in `first.tex`, or you need to consult with whomever installed your LATEX software on your computer. Good news: if it did work (or once you get it to work), you should have an easy time doing the rest of the exercises in this book!

Summary

- Every LATEX file must contain the following three commands:

    - \documentstyle (with arguments)
    - \begin{document}
    - \end{document}

2.2 LATEX Commands

Now, let's talk about the file we created.

```
\documentstyle{article}
\begin{document}

This is the text of my first document in \LaTeX!

\end{document}
```

You can see that the three lines excluding the sentence are commands. What do they have in common? Answer: They all begin with "\", the backslash character. This is a rule that is true of *almost all* LaTeX commands. The "\" tells LaTeX to interpret what follows as a command, not as text. For example, the last word of the sentence, "\LaTeX", is a command that produces the LaTeX logo.

The other three commands are all followed immediately by an element enclosed in curly braces, "{}". This is true of *some* LaTeX commands, but not all. The element enclosed in curly braces is called an *argument*.

One way to think of commands and their arguments is that the commands tell LaTeX what to do, and the arguments tell LaTeX how to do it, or what to do it to.

Study the following rules concerning LaTeX commands:

- Almost all commands start with "\".

- Besides the "\", they can contain only letters a–z and A–Z—no numerals or other symbols.

- Commands are case sensitive; i.e., \dothis is *not* the same command as \DOTHIS.

- They must be followed by a space (which will be ignored, or dropped from the output) or some other character besides a–z and A–Z to signal the end of the command.

- They may take arguments enclosed in curly braces—if so, they cannot be used without these arguments.

- They may also take *optional arguments* enclosed in square braces ("[]")—these arguments are not required.

- Arguments must be contiguous; i.e., there should not be spaces, <CR>s or other characters between them.

2.3 The Document Style

When we typed \documentstyle{article} we selected the "article" *style guide*, one of several available styles. The specifics of different style guides are discussed in Section 3.1, but for now, a simple definition of a style guide will suffice.

The style guide is a set of rules governing page format. It sets up the margins, numbering styles, typestyle and typesize, paragraph indentation and vertical spacing, heading styles, and much more.

Let's go on.

2.4 Sentences

How does LaTeX handle sentences? Add some more sentences to the file first.tex, and find out.

Exercise 2.2

1. Edit your file first.tex, so that the body looks like this:

```
This is the text of my first document in \LaTeX!
A      second      sentence.
It's much more fun to do \LaTeX\ than to
just read about it.
```

2. Notice that this time, the second LaTeX logo seems to have a backslash before *and* after it. The \ following the command is actually part of a "backslash-space" ("\⎵") command, which produces a space. This is needed because, if you recall from Section 2.2, LaTeX commands must be followed by a space (or another character besides a–z or A–Z), but the space will be ignored. Without the "\⎵" command, the logo would run right into the following word. You don't need the "\⎵" if the logo is followed by a comma, or a period, or anything besides a space.

3. Type the following lines at your system prompt:

```
latex first
prnt first
```

4. Notice the following:

    (a) The page now has three sentences on it.

    (b) You do not need to double-space between sentences—LaTeX automatically leaves a bigger space between sentences than between words.

    (c) The line break on the page is not necessarily the same as the one in the input file.

    (d) The extra spaces in the second sentence did not show up in the output.

LaTeX interprets a lowercase character followed by a period to be the end of a sentence, and it introduces a sentence space after the period. (See Section 2.4.1 for exception rules.) It does not matter whether you double-space between sentences in your input or not.

In fact, LaTeX interprets two or more spaces in a row exactly the same as one space. You will learn to use LaTeX commands, instead of your space bar, to do horizontal spacing. But that comes later—for now, try to erase the concept of controlling spacing with the space bar from your mind.

2.4.1   Special Cases

It is possible to have a lowercase letter followed by a period in the middle of a sentence. Abbreviations such as "etc.", "i.e.", and "e.g." must be treated carefully, so that LaTeX does not put extra space after them, thinking that they are the end of a sentence. LaTeX's word-space command—"\⊔"—helps with these cases. If you use "\⊔" immediately after a sentence-ending period, LaTeX will insert a word space *instead of* a sentence space.

Therefore you should type "etc.\⊔", and "i.e.\⊔", and "e.g.\⊔" to produce the correct spacing following these abbreviations.

Similarly, an uppercase letter followed by a period may come at the end of a sentence. This requires special treatment, since it does not look like the end of a sentence to LaTeX, which looks for a lowercase letter followed by a period.

To fix this problem, precede the period with "\@". For example, instead of typing

```
The code is written in FORTRAN. It is a good code.
```

type

```
The code is written in FORTRAN\@. It is a good code.
```

2.4.2 Adjusting Margins and Line Spacing

Although LaTeX automatically sets up appropriate margins and line spacing, these style parameters may be changed by the user, if desired. Appendix C explains what style parameters are and how to change them. See Section C.6, under the heading "Page Formatting" on page 227 for more information on changing the margins and line spacing.

Summary

- Extra spaces between sentences, or between words within a sentence do not come out in the output.

- LaTeX automatically puts extra space between sentences.

- The space bar on the keyboard can't be used to create extra horizontal space in the output.

- Sentences that end with an uppercase letter followed by a period must be treated specially.

- A lowercase letter followed by a period in the middle of a sentence must also be treated specially.

- Margins and line spacing may be adjusted if desired.

2.5   Paragraphs

LaTeX starts a new paragraph whenever it sees a blank line followed by text.

Exercise 2.3

1. Add the following lines to `first.tex` just before the `\end{document}`:

   ```
   <CR>
   Here begins the second paragraph. It follows
   a blank line. I don't have to indent;
   \LaTeX\ does that automatically.
   ```

   Note: throughout this book, `<CR>` denotes the Carriage Return, Return, or Enter key on your keyboard.

2. Type the following lines at your system prompt

   ```
   latex first
   prnt first
   ```

3. Notice the following:

   - The blank line triggered a new paragraph
   - Both paragraphs are automatically indented
   - In the "article" style, no vertical space appears between paragraphs.

The paragraph is too short to show two important LaTeX features—paragraphs are right justified; and text is automatically hyphenated. Note also that just as the space bar is powerless to create horizontal space in LaTeX, so the `<CR>` key is powerless to create vertical space. (Again, you will learn commands to create vertical space.) Here is how LaTeX interprets the `<CR>` key:

One <CR>	— equal to one word space
Two <CR>s	— signals a new paragraph
Three or more <CR>s	— the same as two <CR>s

2.5.1 Avoiding Paragraph Indentation

Sometimes you may wish to "turn off" paragraph indentation for one paragraph. The \noindent command, placed at the beginning of the paragraph does this.

Exercise 2.4

1. Add a third paragraph to first.tex just before the \end{document} as follows:

```
<CR>
\noindent This paragraph won't be indented, since
it starts with a special command for stopping
paragraph indentation.
```

2. Type the following two lines at your system prompt:

```
latex first
prnt first
```

3. Notice that the new paragraph is not indented.

2.5.2 Adjusting Paragraph Indentation

If you wish to specify a certain paragraph indentation, or the amount of vertical space between paragraphs, you may. See Section C.6 under the heading "Page Formatting" on page 227 for more information.

Summary

- A blank line signals a new paragraph.

- Paragraph indentation is automatic.

- LaTeX right justifies text.

- Text is automatically hyphenated.

- The <CR> key on the keyboard can't be used to create extra vertical space.

- The \noindent command may be used at the beginning of a paragraph to suppress indentation on that paragraph.

2.6   Punctuation

Certain punctuation marks need special attention in a LaTeX file.

2.6.1   Quotes

You are probably accustomed to using the double quote mark (") to begin and end quotes. In LaTeX, you must begin a quote with two single left quote marks ("‘ ‘"), and end a quote with two single right quote marks ("’ ’"). As you can see by reading this paragraph, in typeset text there is a difference between open and close quote marks, so the " is not an adequate symbol.

Can you guess how to do a quote within a quote?

Exercise 2.5

1. Start a new paragraph in your file `first.tex` as follows:

```
Yesterday Sally asked, ''Is this how to do quotes?''
She recalled, ''The book says: 'there is a difference
between open and close quote marks'\,''.
```

2. Notice the use of left and right single quote marks to denote a quote within a quote.

3. **latex** and **prnt** the file to find out what the "\," does

As you can see, "\," is a LaTeX command that introduces a very small horizontal space.

2.6.2 Dashes

LaTeX allows you to specify three different kinds of dashes—the hyphen, the inter-number dash, or "en" dash, and the punctuation dash, or "em" dash.

Type of Dash	Appearance	Command
Hyphen dash	-	-
Inter-number dash	–	--
Punctuation dash	—	---

Exercise 2.6

1. Add the following lines to **first.tex**, just before \end{document}:

   ```
   Inter-word dashes, or hyphens, are made with one dash.
   Dashes for number ranges, like 6--12, are made with
   two dashes, and punctuation dashes are made with
   three dashes---like this!!!
   ```

2. **latex** and **prnt** the file.

3. Notice the different lengths of the dashes.

Summary

- Quotes are produced not with double quote marks, but with pairs of single left and right quote marks: (' ') and (' ').

- There are three different dashes—the hyphen, the "en" dash, and the "em" dash. They are produced by "-", "--", and "---", respectively.

2.7   Special Symbols

Certain symbols have a special meaning to LaTeX, and therefore they must be treated carefully in LaTeX files. Since simply typing them into the input file would cause LaTeX to interpret them with their "special meanings," you must use commands to produce them as output. The table below shows these symbols along with the LaTeX commands that produce them as output:

Symbol	Command
#	\#
$	\$
%	\%
&	\&
~	\~
-	_
^	\^
{ and }	\{ and \}
< and >	$<$ and $>$
\	$\backslash$

Exercise 2.7

1. Try adding a line to `first.tex` to produce the following sentence:
   Let's see what's behind door #1—and it is—$10,000!

2. *After* you try it yourself, compare your input with this:

```
Let's see what's behind
door \#1---and it is---\$10,000!
```

3. Now `latex` and `prnt` and see how it looks.

4. Note that these commands are exceptions to the rule that says commands can only contain the letters a–z and A–Z.

5. Also note that these commands do not need to be followed by a space, since LATEX knows they are one character long.

Summary

- Certain symbols are interpreted in a "special" way by LATEX when typed straight.

- These special symbols may be produced as output by using simple commands.

2.8   Footnotes

You're going to love doing footnotes with LATEX! To enter a footnote in your document all you need to do is type \footnote{*some text*}. LATEX puts a footnote marker in the text at the point where the \footnote command occurs, and places the text in the braces at the bottom of the page. Since LATEX does page breaking for you, you don't have to worry at all about leaving room for the footnote on the page.

But to really see how it works, you have to try it.

Exercise 2.8

1. Add the following to the end of your file `first.tex`, just before the \end{document} command:

```
Cats\footnote{Warm, soft, furry animals.} are very
intelligent.
```

2. Try to picture what will happen when LaTeX processes this file.

3. Now `latex` and `prnt` the file and look at the results.

4. Notice that LaTeX automatically assigned the number "1" to the footnote, and placed the footnote at the bottom of the page.

5. NOTE: Do not put a space between the footnoted word and the `\footnote` command. (See what happens to the footnote marker [1] if you do?)

You can control the numbering, or marking, of footnotes in several different ways, if you need to. For example, if you want to specify the number of the footnote instead of letting LaTeX calculate the next logical number for you, you can do it by using an optional argument to the `\footnote` command.

Say you want to insert footnote #5 into your document. Then you would type

```
Cats\footnote[5]{Warm, soft, furry animals.} are very
intelligent.
```

IMPORTANT NOTE:

- Not all commands have optional arguments. Unless specified in this book, don't assume that they do.

- The placement of the optional argument must be just as shown in the example—right after the `\footnote` command and before the braces.

- The optional argument to the `\footnote` command must be an integer—`\footnote[*]{text}` won't produce a footnote marked by an asterisk.

It is possible to use symbols or other numbering styles as well as integers for footnote markers. For more customized usage of footnotes see Section B.4.1 on page 221.

---

[1] Notice the space before the footnote marker in the text above.

2.8.1 Adjusting Spacing Between Footnotes

Spacing between footnotes at the bottom of the page is adjustable. See Section C.6 under the heading "Footnotes" on page 230 for more information.

Summary

- A footnote is produced by placing a \footnote command immediately after the word to be footnoted.

- The text of the footnote is given as an argument to the \footnote command.

- An optional argument allows you to control the number of the footnote, otherwise, LATEX automatically numbers footnotes consecutively.

- Spacing between footnotes is adjustable.

2.9 Marginal Notes

LATEX has the ability to do marginal notes, as long as the number of marginal notes is small—less than five on any one page. To make a marginal note, use the \marginpar command, giving the text of the note in an argument. For example,

```
This is some text in a paragraph. It
will have a marginal note\marginpar{this is
a pretty marginal note} which will be placed
next to the paragraph.
```

would produce

This is some text in a paragraph. It will have a marginal note which will be placed next to the paragraph.

this is a pretty marginal note

By default, marginal notes appear in the right margin when LATEX is typesetting a document for single-sided printing, otherwise they will appear in the left margin for even-numbered pages and in the right margin for odd-numbered pages. (See Section 3.1.1 on page 32 for more information on single-sided versus two-sided printing of documents.)

The `\reversemarginpar` command causes subsequent marginal notes to come out in the opposite margin from the defaults described above. `\normalmarginpar` causes them to come out in the default margins again.

Additionally, an optional argument may be used to specify text for the marginal note when it is placed in the left margin. For example,

`\marginpar[Put this in the left margin]{Put this in the right margin}`

would cause LaTeX to determine which margin is the default margin for marginal notes on the current page (left for an even page, right for odd, if two-sided formatting), and select the appropriate note to place in the margin. This may be useful if the note contains a directional symbol, such as an arrow, pointing to the text.

Normally, marginal notes are positioned vertically so that the top line is even with the text being noted. If this is not possible, because of other marginal notes being in the way, for example, then the note is placed as close to the noted text as possible. See Section C.6, under the heading "Marginal Notes" on page 231 for information on changing the width, separation, and distance from the main text of marginal notes.

Summary

- The `\marginpar` command creates a marginal note; the text of the note is given in a single mandatory argument.

- LaTeX cannot handle large numbers of marginal notes—more than five on a page is too many.

- By default, marginal notes appear in the right margin, except on even-numbered pages in documents formatted for two-sided printing, where they come out on the left margin.

- The `\reversemarginpar` command switches the default margin for marginal notes to the opposite side.

- The `\normalmarginpar` command restores the original default margin.

- The top line of a marginal note is placed even with the text being noted, unless another marginal note is in the way, in which case the marginal note is placed as close as possible to the noted text.

- The width, separation, and distance from the main text are adjustable.

2.10 Simple Formulas

Formulas can be entered in line with the text, or displayed on a line alone. Displayed formulas have the option of being numbered. To enter any formula you must get out of *paragraph mode*, the normal mode for processing text, and get into *math mode*, the mode for handling formulas and equations, since LATEX handles formulas very differently from text.

For in-line formulas, the "$" symbol is used to switch LATEX from paragraph mode into math mode. It also switches LATEX back out of math mode. (In other words, the "$" acts as a toggle.) For example, the formula $x = y + z$ would be entered into the text as **\$x=y+z\$**.

For a discussion of displayed equations, see Section 3.11 on page 70. There are many, many commands for building formulas in math mode, but for now let's stick to a few simple ones: "^", caret, signals a superscript; "_", underscore, signals a subscript; and "'", apostrophe, creates a prime. If the expression in a sub- or superscript is more than one character long, it must be enclosed in braces.

Exercise 2.9

1. Enter the following lines in `first.tex`:

   ```
   Here comes an in-line formula: $x^2 + y^2=z^2$.
   If $x=1$ and $y=2$ then $z=3$!
   Also, $x' + y' = z_{21}$.
   ```

2. **latex** and **prnt** the file.

3. Notice that the formulas are typeset in italics, which sets them off nicely from the text.

4. Notice also that the spacing in the formulas is not dependent on the spacing in the input.

When using in-line formulas, it is important to logically differentiate between text and formulas, and use the "$" toggle as often as necessary. Text does not get typeset correctly in math mode, and formulas do not get typeset correctly in paragraph mode.

Summary

- Use "$" to toggle LaTeX in and out of math mode for in-line formulas.

- "^" signals a superscript; "_" signals a subscript; "'" creates a prime.

- Sub- and superscripts must be enclosed in braces if they are more than one character long.

- Formulas may be displayed on a separate line and numbered if desired.

2.11   The Comment Character

Sometimes it is useful to make a comment or note to yourself at a certain point in the file, without having anything show in the output. The "%" symbol provides this capability in LaTeX. Anything between the "%" and the end of the input line in your file is ignored completely by LaTeX.

Exercise 2.10

1. Add the following lines to `first.tex`:

```
This is real text. % This comment won't print.
% This whole line is a comment and will be ignored.
This is more real text.
```

2. Try to imagine what LaTeX will do with these lines.

3. `latex` and `prnt` the file

4. Notice that everything between a "%" and the end of the line was left out of the output.

5. Notice that you can use "%" at the beginning of a line or in the middle of a line.

6. Were you surprised that the two non-comment sentences came out on the same line? That is because there is no paragraph break (blank line) between them.

2.12 Moving Arguments

Certain LaTeX commands take arguments that are used in more than one place in the document, or else they are moved to a different place in the document from where they occur. They are called *moving* arguments. The \footnote command is a good example, since LaTeX moves its argument from where it appears in the text to the bottom of the page where the footnote belongs.

Other examples of commands with moving arguments are:

- Sectioning commands, (see Section 3.5) whose arguments are put into the Table of Contents.

- The \caption command, (see Sections 7.2.1 and 7.3.1) whose argument is put into the List of Figures or List of Tables.

- The \addcontentsline command, (see Sections 3.5.5, 7.2.5, and 7.3.5) whose argument is put into the Table of Contents, List of Figures, or List of Tables.

- The \markright and \markboth commands, (see Section 3.14) whose arguments are used to produce page headers.

- The letter environment, (see Section 3.2), whose argument is used in the letter header.

- The @-expression, (see Section 5.2.7), whose argument is used repeatedly within a table.

2.12.1   Fragile Commands

Certain other commands are called *fragile* commands and they must be treated specially in the rare cases when they are used in a moving argument. Fragile commands are listed below:

- \footnote (see Section 2.8)

- \begin and \end

- \\ and * (see Section 6.2)

- All commands with a *-form

- \item (see Section 3.10)

- \[and \] (see Section 3.11)

- All commands with optional arguments

2.12.2   The \protect Command

To prevent errors, any fragile command that appears in a moving argument must be preceded by a \protect command. Again, the \protect command is very rarely needed. In fact, it is probably best not to worry about it, especially if you are a new LaTeX user. If you omit a \protect command where it is needed, LaTeX will give an error message, and then you can refer to this section and correct the problem. Here is an example:

```
Here is some text\footnote{And here is a
\protect\\ footnote with a protected line break
in it.} And the next sentence goes on.
```

This information is provided for your reference only. You don't have to understand it all or remember it all right now.

2.13   Verbatim Text

Sometimes it is useful to have a section of text that comes out character for character exactly the same in the output as it is in the input. This can be done in LaTeX by putting some text between a \begin{verbatim} command and an \end{verbatim} command. LaTeX will copy this text straight into the output in a typewriter-like font without interpreting it at all. It can even contain characters such as \, $, %, or others that normally signal LaTeX to do something special.

This method may be used, for example, to simulate computer input and output, or to give examples of LaTeX commands.

To include a very short section of verbatim text within a paragraph, the \verb command may be used, as follows:

```
Here is some text which describes
the \verb+\footnote+ command.
```

Notice that there is a plus sign immediately following the \verb command, and another one at the end of the text to be treated verbatim. Any character may be used in place of the plus sign. For instance, if your verbatim text contains a plus sign, you could type it like this:

```
How do I do an equation?
Like this: \verb!x = y + z!
```

Exercise 2.11

1. Add the following lines to first.tex:

```
Here is a \verb+$%\+ short example.

\begin{verbatim}
I want all this text
to come out verbatim!!
Here is a \LaTeX\ command: \footnote{It won't work}
And here is a formula: $ x = y/z $.
% This line will not be a comment

\end{verbatim}
```

   2. **latex** and **prnt** the file

   3. Notice that everything between **\begin{verbatim}** and
      \end{verbatim} appears exactly as in the input file.

   4. Notice also that even the line breaks are copied from the input.

   You are probably beginning to get a feeling for how LaTeX works.
The main thing to get used to is using *commands* to produce anything
other than straight text. Many simple LaTeX commands do an awfully
large amount of work for you.
   You will be best off, especially in the beginning, if you accept the
work LaTeX does for you, as it is. Later on you can worry about customizing the way things look, *if*, after having time to get used to LaTeX's
way, you still prefer another way.

Chapter 3

Matters of Style

Most of the commands and concepts described up until now have been fairly simple: a blank line starts a new paragraph; two left quote marks make an opening quote; $ toggles you in and out of math mode, etc. There aren't a lot of surprises so far.

As we move on into more intermediate aspects of LaTeX, the user will have more options, and more power, with each command. Naturally, that means more to remember and keep track of. Many people start feeling bogged down by all the information they are learning.

A few words of encouragement: 1) as you use LaTeX day by day, many things will become second nature to you; 2) this manual is here for your reference, for things you can't recall off hand; 3) if you're reading this paragraph, you are probably learning LaTeX for the first time, and you are digesting a lot of new material, so be easy on yourself!

3.1   The Document Style Command

As we have seen in Section 2.3, the \documentstyle command allows the user to pick from a set of style guides that determine page formatting. Following is a short description of the standard LaTeX styles available:

Style	Command	Usage
article	\documentstyle{article}	Generally used for short simple documents
report	\documentstyle{report}	Meant for longer documents that will be broken into chapters and sections
book	\documentstyle{book}	Meant for typesetting actual books. (Used for this book.)
letter	\documentstyle{letter}	(Guess).

Comparing the article, report, and book styles, there are many noticeable differences in the output. Margins, paragraph indentation, paragraph spacing, headers and footers, and section heading styles are all dependent on the style. For information on how to customize these formatting parameters, see Section 6.8; also see Appendix C.

The report and book styles are very similar in usage. A document that is formatted for report style can easily be converted to book style by changing the \documentstyle command, and not much else would have to be changed. The appearance of the document would change drastically, however.

The usage of the letter style is quite different from the others and will be discussed in Section 3.2.

3.1.1   Document Style Options

The \documentstyle command may be given an optional argument (in square braces). The optional argument goes *before* the mandatory argument, and is called a *document style option*.

Document style options allow the user to control the following style parameters:

- overall type size of the document

- the number of columns (1 or 2) on a page

- one-sided versus two-sided printing

- placement of equations and equation numbers

- treatment of the title page.

Table 3.1 describes the defaults for these options and alternate options and their effects. The defaults will be used if no options are specified in an optional argument.

In any document you may omit document style options and accept the defaults, or you may specify one option, or ask for a combination of options. To use a combination of options, simply separate the options with commas. Table 3.2 gives examples of the usage of some document style options.

Exercise 3.1

Question: What document style command would you use to format a report, with 11pt type size, and left justified equations? (Hint: Refer to Tables 3.1 and 3.2.)

ANSWER: \documentstyle[11pt,fleqn]{report}

Summary

- Document style options are specified with an optional argument to the \documentstyle command.

- Options are available for type size, # of columns on a page, one or two sided printing, placement of equations and equation numbers, and title page placement.

- Defaults are used if no options are specified.

- Two or more options may be specified. Options are separated by commas.

Table 3.1: Document style Options

Option	Alternate Options	Effect
Type size (default: 10pt)	`11pt` `12pt`	11 point type 12 point type
# Columns (default: one)	`twocolumn`	Two columns (newspaper style) of text
One/Two-sided (default: one-sided, except in **book** style)	`twoside`	Intended for two-sided copying: binding margin on left side for odd numbered pages, right side for even numbered pages; headers may differ for odd and even numbered pages, depending on document style.
Equation Placement (default: centered)	`fleqn`	Left-align displayed equations
Equation Numbers (default: right justified)	`leqno`	Align equation numbers with the left margin.
Title Page (default: \maketitle places the title page at the top of the first page in **article** style, and on a separate page in other styles.)	`titlepage`	\maketitle places the title page on a separate page. (For use with **article** style.)

Table 3.2: Examples of usage of some document style options

Document style Command	Result
\documentstyle{article}	article style with all default options (10pt type, one column format, one-sided printing, centered equations, right justified equation numbers, title page at top of first page)
\documentstyle[fleqn]{report}	report style with equations left aligned, and defaults for all other options
\documentstyle[twoside]{report}	report style with defaults, except formatted for two-sided copying
\documentstyle[12pt,twoside]{article}	article style with 12pt type and formatted for two-sided copying

3.2   Letter Style

The `letter` style allows you to produce a letter in a standard letter format by using commands to specify the following letter elements:

- address

- return address

- salutation

- date

- signature

- closing

- carbon copy

- enclosures

- P.S.

Exercise 3.2

1. Create a new ASCII file called `myletr.tex` containing the following lines:

```
\documentstyle{letter}
\begin{document}
\begin{letter}{Mrs. Fields\\
              Mrs. Fields Cookie Co.\\
              100 Chocchip Ave.\\
              Sweetville, Nebraska 12345}

\opening{Dear Mrs. Fields,}

I just love your cookies.  Your shop just opened in
our town, and I want to tell you how much I enjoy
shopping there. When are you going to come up with
```

```
a ''low-fat'' cookie?

\signature{Jane Pecan}
\closing{With appreciation,}

\cc{Aunt Jemima\\Betty Crocker}
\encl{Two cookies}

\ps{P.S. My husband loves the cookies, too!}
\end{letter}
\end{document}
```

2. latex and prnt the file by typing

```
latex myletr
prnt myletr
```

NOTE: If LaTeX comes across an error and stops with a "?", remember—don't panic. It is probably caused by a simple typo in your input file. Type "x" and a carriage return to get back to the DOS prompt. Then check your file carefully for mistyped commands. If that doesn't help, refer to Appendix E for help.

3. Notice the following:

- The letter is vertically centered on the page.
- Today's date is printed at the top right.
- The rest of the letter is printed in standard blocked format.
- There is a space for your signature between the closing and the signature.
- Double backslashes ("\\") are used to separate lines in the address (and in other multi-line elements as well).
- The \ps command is the only way to put text after the closing of a letter. (You have to type "P.S." yourself.)

LATEX gets the date from your computer's battery-maintained memory. If your computer does not have the correct date, then neither will LATEX. If you want to specify the date manually, you may do so by using a \date command before the \opening. Example:

```
. . . .
\begin{letter}{Mrs. Fields\\
              Mrs. Fields Cookie Co.\\
              100 Chocchip Ave.\\
              Sweetville, Nebraska 12345}
\date{January 1, 2001}
\opening{Dear Mrs. Fields,}
. . . . .
```

Notice that this letter does not contain a return address, and would probably be used with letterhead stationery. If you want the letter to contain a return address, you can use an \address command before the \opening. Example:

```
. . . .
\begin{letter}{Mrs. Fields\\
              Mrs. Fields Cookie Co.\\
              100 Chocchip Ave.\\
              Sweetville, Nebraska 12345}
\address{Jane Pecan\\
        100 Appetite Way\\
        Dietville, Wyoming 54321}
\opening{Dear Mrs. Fields,}
. . . . .
```

Note the use of \\ to separate lines in the return address.

Exercise 3.3

1. Try altering the letter to include your own return address, and a date of your choice.

NOTE: The \date and \address commands, if used, must come *before* the \opening command. That's because the \opening command uses the information provided by these commands to actually print the whole header; it does not simply print the opening statement. Similarly, the \signature command must come before the \closing command because the \closing command puts out the closing and signature with a space in between for your signature.

This is important to know if you are thinking about trying to change the heading or the closing of the letter. For example, LaTeX won't allow you to insert something between the elements of the header; you have to create the header using *only* the commands provided.

Caution: The argument to \begin{letter} that specifies the addressee's address cannot be left off. If you don't want the address to be printed, leave empty curly braces, e.g. \begin{letter}{}.

Summary

- The letter style guide is provided for letters.

- Letter elements—address, return address, date, opening, signature, closing, cc, enclosure, and P.S.—are created with commands if they are desired.

- The \opening command prints out the whole header using information provided in the \address and \date commands.

- The \closing command prints out the closing and the signature line.

3.3 Title Page

LaTeX provides simple commands for creating a standard title page in **book**, **report** and **article** styles. Remember, Section 3.1 mentioned that the title page is on a separate page for the **book** and **report** styles, but *not* for the **article** style.

Title page commands allow you to specify title, author(s), and date. Lines within each element are separated by \\.

Exercise 3.4

1. Edit `first.tex` and insert the following lines right after the `\begin{document}` command:

   ```
   \title{My First Document}
   \author{Your Name\\Mrs. Fields}
   \date{January 1, 2001}
   \maketitle
   ```

2. `latex` and `prnt` the file

3. Notice that the title, author(s), and date you entered are placed at the top of the first page of your document.

If the `\date` command is omitted, the current date is used. Another way to get today's date, is to use the `\today` command, e.g., `\date{\today}`. (The `\today` command may be used anywhere in your text as well.)

If a footnote to the title, author, or date is needed, the `\thanks` command may be used (for title page only). It is similar to the `\footnote` command used in regular text. It takes the footnote text as an argument, and it uses an asterisk as the footnote marker. One more feature: authors may be separated by the `\and` command, or by `\\`.

Exercise 3.5

1. Change the `\author` command in your file `first.tex` to look like this:

   ```
   \author{Your Name \and
           Mrs. Fields\thanks{Without whose help,
           this endeavor would be fruitless} }
   ```

2. Note the nested braces (the inner set for the `\thanks` command, and the outer set for the `\author` command).

3. `latex` and `prnt` the file

4. Notice how the `\thanks` command produced a footnote on the title page.

Summary

- Title page commands allow you to specify title, author(s), and date.

- The \maketitle command uses information provided by the other commands to actually print out the title page.

3.4 Typestyles

The typestyle you are reading right now is called Computer Modern Roman, and is the default style used by LaTeX. In other words, Roman is what you get unless you ask for something different. For emphasis or variety, or just for fun, you can choose from a variety of styles besides Roman by inserting a simple command in your file. The following table gives examples of the typestyles available in LaTeX, along with the commands to produce them:

Example	Command
This is a bold typestyle	\bf
This is a sans serif typestyle	\sf
This is a slanted typestyle	\sl
THIS IS A SMALL CAPS TYPESTYLE	\sc
`This is a typewriter typestyle`	\tt
This is an italic typestyle	\it
This is the Roman typestyle	\rm

The commands listed in the second column above perform a simple function: they change the typestyle from the point where they occur, until another typestyle-changing command occurs. Typestyle-changing commands take no arguments. Consider the following sentence:

```
Typestyle-changing commands give one
a \bf powerful \rm feeling.
```

This sentence employs the \bf command to change to bold, and then it employs the \rm command to switch back to Roman. The result looks like this:

Typestyle-changing commands give one a **powerful** feeling.

Exercise 3.6

1. Add the following lines to the end of **first.tex**, just before the \end{document}:

   ```
   The \bf rain \rm in \it Spain \rm falls \sl mainly
   \rm on the \sf plain! \rm
   ```

2. Can you visualize what the resulting sentence will look like after processing?

3. **latex** and **prnt** the file to see the result.

4. What would happen if you didn't put \rm at the end of the sentence? (If you don't know, leave it off, then type a few words after the sentence and process it again, and see what happens.)

3.4.1   Type Sizes

LaTeX also allows you to change the size of the type. The following commands select varying sizes of the Roman style:

Example	Command
This is tiny	\tiny
This is script size	\scriptsize
This is footnote size	\footnotesize
This is small	\small
This is normal size	\normalsize
This is large	\large
This is larger	\Large
This is very large	\LARGE
This is huge	\huge
This is very huge	\Huge

Notice that the characters for \LARGE, \huge and \Huge are the same size, and that LaTeX has just spaced the letters further apart as the commands request larger type. This is not a function of LaTeX, but it is a function of the printer driver.

The size-changing commands above are used in the same way as the typestyle-changing commands. They simply change the size until another size-changing command is encountered. They may also be used in combination with the typestyle-changing commands, but not all combinations will work. The best way to find out what works is by experimentation. NOTE: Put the typestyle-changing command *after* the size-changing command, otherwise you will always get Roman.

Exercise 3.7

- Add a line before \end{document} in first.tex that will produce the following sentence, using the \tiny, \normalsize and \Large commands and the \it command:

    The frightened kitten raised its fur and *hissed* at the big
    German Shepherd.

- `latex` and `prnt` your file and see how you did.

- Compare your input with the following

```
The \tiny frightened kitten \normalsize raised its
fur and \it hissed \rm at the \Large big German
Shepherd.
\normalsize
```

- Did you remember to put `\normalsize` at the end?

3.4.2 Using Braces to Form Groups

In the preceding exercises and examples, we used commands to change
the typestyle (and size), and then we used other commands to return
to the normal style. It is possible to change the typestyle or size for a
portion of the text, and then to return to normal automatically. This
is done using *grouping*.

A portion of text may be enclosed in braces, and then it is considered by LaTeX to be a group. (Recall that the { and } symbols are
special symbols to LaTeX and they only print out when you type \{ and
\}.) Certain commands entered inside the group—such as typestyle-
changing commands—will not have an effect after the end of the group
is reached. For example, the following two input lines will have exactly
the same effect:

- `Typestyle-changing commands give one a \bf powerful`
  `\rm feeling.`

- `Typestyle-changing commands give one a {\bf powerful}`
  `feeling.`

Notice that the `\bf` command in the second item was entered *inside*
the group. This must be so for the end of the group to take away its
effect.

Exercise 3.8

1. Look at the previous exercise:

   ```
   The \tiny frightened kitten \normalsize raised its fur
   and \it hissed \rm at the \Large big
   German Shepherd. \rm
   ```

2. How can you get the same effect without using \normalsize or \rm? Try it in your first.tex file.

3. Compare your attempt with the following:

   ```
   The {\tiny frightened kitten} raised its fur and
   {\it hissed} at the {\Large big German Shepherd.}
   ```

4. Now try to typeset the following without using \rm:

   ```
   The \bf rain \rm in \it Spain \rm falls \sl mainly
   \rm on the \sf plain! \rm
   ```

5. **CLUE:** There should be a closing brace in your version everywhere there is a \rm command in the version above.

6. Compare your try with the following:

   ```
   The {\bf rain} in {\it Spain} falls {\sl mainly}
   on the {\sf plain!}
   ```

Caution: It is important to remember that the typestyle-changing command must go *inside the braces* in order to apply to that group only. A common mistake is to type something like the following:

```
The \bf{rain} in ...
```

In this example, the closing brace has no effect on the change to bold font. Only another typestyle-changing command can change the font now.

Summary

- Available typestyles are: **bold, sans serif,** *slanted,* SMALL CAPS, `typewriter,` and Roman.

- Available sizes are: tiny, scriptsize, footnotesize, small, normalsize, large, Large, huge, and Huge.

- Each size and style has a command that produces it.

- A portion of text (and commands) enclosed in braces is considered by LaTeX to be a group.

- Typestyle-changing commands entered inside a group are not in effect after the "}" that ends that group.

3.5   Sectioning Commands

LaTeX makes it very easy for you to start a new chapter or section in your document. One simple command performs all of the following steps:

- Assigns an appropriate number

- Selects a bold or large font

- Puts white space above and below the heading

- Creates the heading (on a new page if appropriate)

- Makes an entry in the Table of Contents, if Table of Contents requested

And all you have to do is type a sectioning command with your heading as an argument! The sectioning commands are:

```
\chapter               \subsubsection
\section               \paragraph
\subsection            \subparagraph
```

All six sectioning commands are available for the book and report styles. In the article style, only five apply—\chapter is not legal in article style.

3.5.1 Appendices

When one or more appendices are to be added to a report, the \appendix command may be used. All \chapter commands encountered after an \appendix command produce appendices rather than chapters. This means that they are given letters instead of numbers, and labelled as appendices instead of chapters. Appendices may contain other sectioning commands, such as \section and \subsection, and these are given appropriate labels as well.

Exercise 3.9

1. Just for fun, let's see how first.tex looks in report style. Edit the \documentstyle command to look like this:

   \documentstyle[12pt]{report}

2. Now let's add some sectioning commands. Put the following line in first.tex before the first sentence, which reads, "This is the text of my ...":

   \chapter{HERE I GO!}

   and put the following \section command before the math exercise that begins with "Here comes an in-line formula":

   \section{My First Math Formula}

3. Now go to the end of the file, just before \end{document}, and add the following lines:

```
\appendix
\chapter{THIS IS AN APPENDIX}
This is the text of the Appendix.
\section{Subheading In An Appendix}
How does this look?
```

4. `latex` and `prnt` the file. Notice the following:

   - The title, author, etc., come out on a separate page since you are now using `report` style.

   - Margins, paragraph indentation and spacing, and other overall document formatting parameters are slightly different.

   - You have a Chapter 1 and a Section 1.1, with nice, big, bold headings

   - There is an Appendix A following Chapter 1.

You can experiment with the other sectioning commands to see how they look.

NOTE: LaTeX does not punctuate the headings automatically. Also, you control whether the headings are upper- or lowercase.

3.5.2   Unnumbered Sections

Sometimes you may want a bold heading that is set off from the rest of the text but does not have a number associated with it. Each of the sectioning commands discussed above has a special "asterisk" form for producing this effect. You simply add an asterisk to the end of the command name, and give the heading as an argument as usual.

For example, to get a heading that looks like a section heading, but with no number, you would type `\section*{My First Math Formula}`. This is a convenient way to get a bold, slightly larger than normal, flush-left line of text that is vertically set off from surrounding text.

Exercise 3.10

1. Put the following asterisk command in `first.tex` just before the exercises about font-changing commands:

`\section*{Font Changes}`

2. Put in some other sectioning commands of your own choice, starred or unstarred and then `latex` and `prnt` the file to see the results.

3.5.3 The Table of Contents

Let's see how these sectioning commands make entries in the Table of Contents. To produce a Table of Contents, a file must have a `\tableofcontents` command and some sectioning commands, and then it must be `latex`ed *twice*.

Each time you `latex` a file with a `\tableofcontents` command in it, LaTeX writes the latest information for the Table of Contents into a special auxiliary file called the `.toc` file. It gets the information for the Table of Contents from the sectioning commands in your file. Each time it sees a `\chapter` command, for example, it writes the chapter heading and the current page number to the `.toc` file. The same thing happens for `\section`, `\subsection`, etc.

The `.toc` file has the same first name as the `.tex` file, but it has `.toc` for an extension. For example, when we request a Table of Contents in `first.tex` we will get a file called `first.toc` after running LaTeX.

Whenever LaTeX sees a `\tableofcontents` command, it reads information from the `.toc` file and uses it to typeset the Table of Contents. The catch is that LaTeX has already typeset the Table of Contents by the time it starts to see `\chapter` and `\section` commands (which provide the headings and page numbers for the Table of Contents). The Table of Contents comes before the first chapter, right? Therefore, it always uses the information written to the `.toc` file during the previous run. That is why you must `latex` twice, without changing your file, to get a correct Table of Contents.

If all that is too confusing, just remember to `latex` twice for a Table of Contents that is completely up to date.

3.5.4 Changing an Entry in the Table of Contents

LaTeX allows you to put an entry into the Table of Contents that is different from the section heading. Each sectioning command takes an

optional argument, before the mandatory argument, which is the entry
for the Table of Contents. For example,

`\section[Entry for the T.O.C.]{Section Heading In The Text}`

would start a section entitled "Section Heading In The Text," but it
would make an entry in the Table of Contents that would be "Entry
for the T.O.C."

3.5.5   Adding a Line to the Table of Contents

Sometimes you may want an entry in the Table of Contents when you
don't have a numbered section heading. For example, an unnumbered
heading like

Here Is My Heading

produced by

`\section*{Here Is My Heading}`

would not make an entry in the Table of Contents, since the `\section`
command has an asterisk on it. The `\addcontentsline` command
forces an entry in the Table of Contents. It takes three arguments.
The first argument tells LaTeX whether to add the entry to the Table
of Contents, the List of Figures, or the List of Tables. For making
an entry to the Table of Contents, this argument should be `toc`. (See
Section 7.2.4 on page 173 for making an entry to the List of Figures,
or Section 7.3.4 on page 179 for an entry to the List of Tables.)

The second argument to `\addcontentsline` is the name of a sectional unit, such as `chapter`, `section`, etc. It controls the formatting
of the Table of Contents entry. LaTeX makes entries for chapters bolder
than entries for sections, for instance.

The third argument to `\addcontentsline` is the text of the entry.
Therefore, to create an unnumbered section with an entry in the Table
of Contents, you could use the following two commands:

`\section*{This Is The Heading}`
`\addcontentsline{toc}{section}{This Is The Heading}`

Note that the \addcontentsline command must fall on the same page with the heading in order for the correct page number to appear in the Table of Contents.

3.5.6 Extra Control over Sectional Numbering

By default, LaTeX numbers all sectional units, down to the paragraph level. By adjusting a special parameter, you can control how many levels actually receive numbers. Also, not all section levels automatically go into the Table of Contents, but another user-definable parameter controls the number of levels that do go in. See Section C.6 under the heading "Section Levels" on page 230 for more information.

Appendix B explains how to change the style of section numbers. If you want them printed as roman numerals, for example, this can be done.

Exercise 3.11

1. Edit the file `first.tex` and place the cursor where you would want the Table of Contents to appear. To get the Table of Contents immediately after the title page, for example, add the following lines after the \maketitle command:

   ```
   \tableofcontents
   \clearpage
   ```

   The \clearpage command causes LaTeX to start the following text on a new page.

2. Add the following sections just before the \appendix command:

   ```
   \section[Heading For TOC]{Heading For Text}
   This is a section whose TOC entry is
   different from its heading in the text!
   ```

3. Add an \addcontentsline command to make an entry in the Table of Contents for the "Font Changes" section. The commands to make the "Font Changes" heading should now look like this:

```
\section*{Font Changes}
\addcontentsline{toc}{section}{Font Changes}
```

4. `latex` the file once.

5. Notice that there is a `first.toc` in the directory now. Also note that if you **prnt** the file now, there will be a blank page with the heading "Contents" written at the top, but no entries.

6. `latex` the file again and **prnt** it.

7. Notice that the Table of Contents comes out with an entry for each unstarred sectioning command, and it is right after the title page.

8. Notice the entry that says "Heading For TOC" and recall that you used the optional argument to the `\section` command to produce it. The heading in the text should read "Heading For Text."

9. Notice the entry for "Font Changes" that was produced by an `\addcontentsline` command.

Summary

- The sectioning commands are: `\chapter` (not available in `article` style), `\section`, `\subsection`, `\subsubsection`, `\paragraph`, and `\subparagraph`.

- The heading is given as the argument to the sectioning command.

- Sectioning commands calculate the number for the sectional unit, print the heading in an appropriate font, leave vertical space above and below the new section, and make an entry in the Table of Contents.

- An optional argument to a sectioning command produces an alternate entry for the Table of Contents.

- Asterisk forms of the sectioning commands do all of the above except they don't assign a number, and they don't put an entry in the Table of Contents.

- An `\addcontentsline` command with `toc` as the first argument makes an entry in the Table of Contents. It can be used with the asterisk forms of sectioning commands. The second argument to `\addcontentsline` is the sectional level, and the third argument is the text of the entry.

- A `\tableofcontents` command produces a Table of Contents at the point in the document where the command falls.

- You must `latex` twice without changing the file between runs to get a Table of Contents that is current and correct.

3.6 Symbolic Referencing

It is common practice in many documents to have references in the text to figures and tables, chapters and sections, pages, equations, etc. These references are usually made in terms of the number of the object being mentioned. For example, a writer might say, "Figure 1 shows the relationship between employee productivity and the number of 15 minute breaks allowed each day." In fact, anything in the document that has a number assigned to it can be referred to in this way.

The only problem with this practice is that, in a subsequent version of the document, the number assigned to a given figure or equation may change, because another figure or equation was inserted before it, or simply because the overall order of things was changed. It could create a lot of tedious work, not to mention errors, if, say, a new figure were inserted between Figures 1 and 2 in a document containing 50 figures! Right?

No, it's not right—not if you are using LaTeX. LaTeX allows you to assign a unique *key* to any numbered object, and to refer to the object by that key. If the key, made up by you, is chosen well, it never needs to change (just as the caption of a figure doesn't change), no matter what number or position the object eventually receives.

The command used to assign the key is the \label command, which takes the key as an argument. A reference is made with a \ref command, which also takes the key as an argument. The \label command attaches the appropriate number to the key, and the \ref command retrieves that number. The key itself can be any word that reminds you of the object you are labelling. It can contain upper- or lowercase characters, and any punctuation characters except those special characters mentioned in Section 2.7.

To label a sectional unit, put the \label command right after the sectioning command. Let's try it.

Exercise 3.12

1. Locate the \chapter{Here I Go!} command in your file first.tex.

2. Place the following \label command on the line after the \chapter command:

   (\chapter{Here I Go!})
   \label{I_Go}

3. Now put the following reference to this chapter at the end of first.tex (before the \end{document}):

   Chapter \ref{I_Go} contains some of my very
   first \LaTeX\ commands!

4. What is the key? ANSWER: "I_Go"

5. Notice that you had to type the word "Chapter." The \ref command produces a number *only*.

6. Now latex and prnt the file.

7. You will see that the sentence you added containing the \ref command produces something like:

> Chapter ?? contains some of my very first LaTeX commands!

8. `latex` and `prnt` the file again.

9. This time the sentence should read:

> Chapter 1 contains some of my very first LaTeX commands!

So, we have seen that it takes two LaTeX runs to resolve references correctly. As with the `\tableofcontents` command, the `\ref` commands pick up information from the *previous* LaTeX run. The first time you run LaTeX after adding the `\ref`, you will see "??" instead of a number. If you run LaTeX twice without changing your input file in between, and you still get "??", it means there is no matching `\label` command for the `\ref` command. Check to see that the key in the `\label` command is the same as the key in the `\ref` command. If you get the incorrect number from the `\ref` command, then the number has changed since the last LaTeX run, and you must simply run LaTeX again.

3.6.1 Labelling and Referencing Pages

To make a reference to a page, use the `\pageref` command. It works exactly like `\ref`, taking the key as its argument, only it gives you the page number that the `\label` with the matching key is on. Only one `\label` command is required to save the section, equation, figure or table number *and* the page number it falls on. Look at the following example:

```
See Chapter~\ref{moreinfo} on page~\pageref{moreinfo}
for more information.
...
...
\chapter{More Information Is Here}
\label{moreinfo}

Here is the information.
```

Note the label after the \chapter command. Now you can see that the \ref and \pageref commands have the same key: moreinfo. The \ref command will give the chapter number, and the \pageref command will give the page number.

Exercise 3.13

1. Edit first.tex once more. Change the sentence that used to read:

   ```
   Chapter \ref{I_Go} contains some of my very
   first \LaTeX\ commands!
   ```

   so that it now reads:

   ```
   Chapter \ref{I_Go} on page \pageref{I_go}
   contains some of my very first \LaTeX\ commands!
   ```

2. Note that the \label command didn't have to be altered.

3. latex first.tex two times and then prnt it. Remember, references need to be latexed twice to be resolved correctly.

4. Verify that the page number came out where you put the \pageref command.

Summary

- Labels are assigned with the \label command, with the key as the argument.

- References are made with the \ref command, with the key as the argument.

- The key is made up by the user, and may contain upper- and lowercase characters and any punctuation characters except "special symbols."

- You must `latex` twice without changing the input file in between to get references resolved correctly, since LaTeX picks up labelling information from the previous run.

- To label a sectional unit, place the `\label` command right after the sectioning command.

- To reference a page, use the `\pageref` command, with the key as its argument.

3.7 User-Specified Hyphenation

As we learned in Chapter 2, LaTeX automatically hyphenates text from its own internal hyphenation dictionary. Rarely, a writer may use a word or a long acronym that is not contained in the dictionary. It is possible to "teach" LaTeX how to hyphenate such a word, or to change the hyphenation on a word contained in the dictionary.

For a word that occurs once in the text, it is sufficient to insert one or more `\-` commands within the word at the point(s) where you would like a hyphen to be allowed. This does not force a hyphen, it simply allows one. Say your text contained the word "soliloquy," for example, which is not in LaTeX's dictionary. You should really type "`so\-lil\-o\-quy`", so that LaTeX can hyphenate it in case it falls very close to the right margin. If a word that is not in LaTeX's dictionary is going to be used many times throughout a document, it would be very inconvenient to always type it with the discretionary hyphens (`\-`) inserted. In this case you may use the `\hyphenation` command once at the beginning of your file to supply the discretionary hyphens for a particular word throughout the entire document. The word, with hyphens inserted where they should be allowed, is the mandatory argument to the `\hyphenation` command, e.g. `\hyphenation{so-lil-o-quy}`. Place this command between the `\documentstyle` command and the `\begin{document}` command in your input file.

Exercise 3.14

This feature is hard to demonstrate because LaTeX is so clever at breaking lines into paragraphs, so please indulge the unusual example.

1. Place the following lines at the end of `first.tex`:

   ```
   Herearesomesillywordsthatfillupthelinesothatmyspecialword,
   xxxxyyyyzzzz, will wind up at the right margin.
   And here are some normal words that will fill
   up the next few lines so that I can see where
   the right margin ought to be.
   ```

2. `latex` and `prnt` the file

3. Notice that "xxxxyyyyzzzz" sticks way out into the right margin. This happens because LaTeX can't hyphenate it.

4. At this point you have a choice about how to fix this problem. Either

   (a) change "xxxxyyyyzzzz" to "xxxx\-yyyy\-zzzz" in the paragraph, or

   (b) put the command \hyphenation{xxxx-yyyy-zzzz} before the \begin{document} command.

5. `latex` and `prnt` the file with the correction

6. Notice that xxxxyyyyzzzz is hyphenated to make the right margin as smooth as possible

Summary

- LaTeX automatically hyphenates words using an internal hyphenation dictionary.

- Discretionary hyphens (\-) may be added to a word if LaTeX's dictionary does not contain it, or if you wish to allow a different hyphenation from LaTeX's.

- A \hyphenation command at the beginning of the file "teaches" LATEX how to hyphenate a word for the entire document.

3.8 LATEX Environments

Sometimes it is convenient to set off a portion of text and treat it slightly differently from the rest of the text. To give two examples, a quote is often set with left and right margins indented; and a list needs to be treated specially, with its own margins, line spacing, and with special labels. LATEX provides *environments* for many of these special structures that need to be treated with different rules than the rest of the text.

A LATEX environment is marked by a \begin command at the beginning and \end command at the end. Each environment has a name, which is used as an argument to the \begin and \end commands. The following is an example of the quote environment:

```
\begin{quote}
Contents of quote go here.
\end{quote}
```

Exercise 3.15

1. Look at the file first.tex.

2. What environment have you been using all along? (Hint: If it begins with \begin and ends with \end, it's an environment.)

3. ANSWER: The document environment.

Summary

- A LATEX environment starts with a \begin command that takes the name of the environment as an argument, and ends with an \end command taking the same argument.

- Text within an environment is treated using special rules.

3.9 Quotations

We saw in Section 2.6.1 that quotation marks are made with pairs of left and right single quote marks, rather than the double quote mark. For a displayed quote, LaTeX provides two environments: `quote` and `quotation`. The `quote` environment is suitable for short (about 1 line) quotes, and the `quotation` environment is intended for quotations of a paragraph or more.

The `quote` and `quotation` environments are both indented on the left and right margins. The difference between them is that the `quotation` environment has a paragraph indentation in it, and the `quote` environment does not.

Exercise 3.16

1. Add the following lines to the end of `first.tex`, before the `\end{document}`:

   ```
   For a short quotation, or a series of one liners:

   \begin{quote}
   ''Is this how to do quotes?'', asked Sally.

   ''Very good, Sally!'', said Jane.

   ''The book says 'there is a difference between
   open and close quote marks'\,'', said Sally.

   ''That is true.'', said Jane.
   \end{quote}

   For a quote of a paragraph or more:

   \begin{quotation}
   Singing is perhaps the most personal of the
   performing arts. When performing, a good singer
   makes each member of the audience feel as if
   ```

```
he or she is receiving a generous and loving gift.
Only in singing is there a direct, unhindered
path between the music in the performer's heart
and the listener's senses.
\end{quotation}
```

2. `latex` and `prnt` the file

3. Can you tell the difference between the two environments?

If you prefer one of these environments over the other, for any length of quote, the choice is up to you. LATEX is not going to know or care if you use `quote` for a long quotation.

3.10 Lists

Section 3.8 mentioned lists as a good candidate for a special environment. In fact, LATEX has environments for three styles of lists: a bulleted list; a numbered list; and a word-labelled list. There is also an environment for a customized list, which will be discussed in Section A.5.

3.10.1 Itemized List

The first list type is the *itemized* list. The `\begin{itemize}` command initializes the list; each item in the list is marked with an `\item` command; and the list is ended with an `\end{itemize}` command.

Each item—entered with an `\item` command—will be given a *label* by LATEX. In a simple list, for example, each item is marked with a bullet. The `\item` command takes an optional argument that specifies a customized label. In other words, if you wanted your list items to be marked with "o", instead of "•", you would say `\item[o]` for each item.

Exercise 3.17

1. Let's open a fresh new file called `new.tex`. (Remember: All LATEX input files must have the extension `.tex`!)

2. Enter the three essential commands for any LaTeX input file. Do you remember what they are?
(ANSWER: \documentstyle, \begin{document}, and \end{document}).
Use the **report** document style, so that your file starts out as follows:

```
\documentstyle{report}
\begin{document}

\end{document}
```

Remember, all your text will be entered between the \begin- and \end{document} commands. Anything entered after the \end{document} will be ignored, and *most* things entered before the \begin{document} will be illegal. (More on that later.)

3. Now enter the following simple list:

```
Here comes a beautiful list:
\begin{itemize}
\item This is the first list item! Let's make it a
   long one, so that we can demonstrate how nicely
   \LaTeX\ indents list items.
\item groceries
\item laundry
\end{itemize}
```

4. Notice that the list has three items. Now latex and prnt the file. (Remember, the file name is new.tex, so you say latex new and prnt new.)

5. See how the items are set off by bullets?

6. Now, suppose you wanted to enter a sublist of things under groceries. You can simply make a whole new list *within* that item.

7. Enter the sublist lines under the \item groceries, as follows:

```
\item groceries
      \begin{itemize}
      \item potatoes
      \item celery
      \item frying chicken
      \item milk
      \end{itemize}
```

8. If you indent your entries as they are indented here, you will be able to visualize the logical structure of the list—the sublist that you just entered is a complete list in itself, and it is a part of the "groceries" item.

9. `latex` and `prnt` the file `new.tex`.

10. Notice that the sublist is set off by dashes, and is further indented than the outer bulleted list.

    NOTE: Altogether, there are four levels available: the outer, bulleted list, plus three sublevels that are set off by dashes, asterisks, and dots, respectively.

11. Let us say that you wish to change the labels on the sublist from dashes to hearts. Edit your sublist to look like the following:

```
\begin{itemize}
\item [$\heartsuit$] potatoes
\item [$\heartsuit$] celery
\item [$\heartsuit$] frying chicken
\item [$\heartsuit$] milk
\end{itemize}
```

12. `latex` and `prnt new.tex`.

13. Notice that the items in the sublist are now set off by little hearts. (See Tables 4.2–4.6 in Section 4.6 on page 95 for more on available symbols.)

14. Enter the following lines in `new.tex`

```
This is a new list:

\begin{itemize}
\item This is the first level

   \begin{itemize}
   \item This is the second level

      \begin{itemize}
      \item This is the third level

         \begin{itemize}
         \item This is the fourth level
         \item Another item in the fourth level
         \end{itemize}
      \item Another item in the third level
      \end{itemize}
   \item Another item in the second level
   \end{itemize}

\item Another item in the first level
\end{itemize}
```

15. `latex` and `prnt` the file

16. Now look at the results, and at the same time take a look at your input file.

17. Notice that a `\begin{itemize}` command was used each time to get to the next sublevel; and an `\end{itemize}` command was used to end each sublevel.

   IMPORTANT NOTE: Each `\begin{itemize}` *must* have an `\end{itemize}` to match. The list levels are said to be nested— that is, if you draw a bracket to join each `\begin` with its matching `\end`, the brackets fit into each other like stacked cups. NOTE: I strongly suggest that you use indentation, as in this example, to mark the different list levels—it is a good tool to help in understanding the logic, and to help in remembering all the matching \end commands.

3.10.2 Enumerated List

To get a numbered list, use the **enumerate** environment. The rules about levels, nesting, and matching \begin and \end commands are all the same as with the itemized list. The labels for the different levels, instead of being symbols, are numbers of varying styles.

Exercise 3.18

1. Make a second copy of the last list you entered, only replace all occurrences of "itemize" with "enumerate". It should look like this:

```
This is a new list:

\begin{enumerate}
\item This is the first level

   \begin{enumerate}
   \item This is the second level

      \begin{enumerate}
      \item This is the third level
         \begin{enumerate}
         \item This is the fourth level
         \item Another item in the fourth level
         \end{enumerate}
      \item Another item in the third level
      \end{enumerate}

   \item Another item in the second level
   \end{enumerate}
```

```
\item Another item in the first level
\end{enumerate}
```

2. `latex` and `prnt` the file with this addition.

3. Notice that items are labelled with numbers and letters.

4. NOTE: A sublist does not have to be the same type of list as the higher level list. In other words, the fourth `\begin{enumerate}` in this exercise could have been a `\begin{itemize}`. Then the innermost list would have been bulleted instead of lettered. Four is still the maximum number of list levels allowed, even if list types are mixed.

3.10.3   References to List Items

Recall that in Section 3.6 it was said that a symbolic reference can be made to any numbered entity. You can refer to items in an enumerated list using the `\label` and `\ref` commands as follows. Put the `\label` command right after the `\item` command in the list. Then use the `\ref` anywhere in your text where you wish to refer to that item. For example, take the following list:

```
\begin{enumerate}
\item \label{list:one} This is list item number one.
\item \label{list:two} Here is number two.
\item \label{list:three} And here is number three.
\end{enumerate}
```

It looks like this after `latex`ing:

1. This is list item number one.

2. Here is number two.

3. And here is number three.

We could refer to any one of the items above with a \ref command. Say, for instance, that we want to mention the second item. We could say:

```
See Item~\ref{list:two} in the list above
for a description of number two.
```

After latexing twice, this would come out:

See Item 2 in the list above for a description of number two.

Exercise 3.19

1. The enumerated list may be used to enter a list of references or footnotes in a document. Enter the following short bibliography at the end of **new.tex**, before the \end{document}:

```
\section*{BIBLIOGRAPHY}
\begin{enumerate}
\item \label{bib:milne} Milne, A. A., {\it Winnie
      The Pooh}, E.P. Dutton \& Co., Inc.,
      New York,  1926.
\item \label{bib:carroll} Carroll, Lewis,
      {\it Alice In Wonderland}, A. L. Burt
      Company, New York.
\end{enumerate}
```

2. Now put this paragraph before the bibliography:

```
To refer to a bibliography item in the style
of a footnote, use the math superscript command,
as in Carroll$^{\ref{bib:carroll}}$.  Or you
can just do it like this: see
Reference~\ref{bib:milne} for a great story
about a boy and a bear.
```

3. Notice the placement of the dollar signs in the reference to Carroll. You must be in math mode to invoke the superscript. Also, the entire superscript itself must be enclosed in braces.

4. Notice the tilde "~" between the word "Reference" and
   \ref{bib:milne}. This tilde prints out as a space, and prevents a
   line break from occurring there. The tilde may be used anywhere
   in text where you wish to have a word space without allowing a
   line break.

5. *latex* the file *twice* (remember, correctly resolved references require two LaTeX runs) and *prnt* it.

6. See that the \ref commands produced the correct number of the
   books from the bibliography list.

3.10.4   Descriptive List

The third list type takes a little more thought, since the labels are
specified by you, the user. That means on each \item command, you
must enter an optional argument (in brackets) that is the word you
want for the label. This list style is called a "descriptive list" because
it may be used to describe a list of items.

Exercise 3.20

1. We will describe various types of household pets. Enter the following lines at the bottom of **new.tex**:

```
This is a descriptive list

\begin{description}
\item [Dogs] Dogs, with their friendly, obedient
  nature, make excellent pets. There are many
  different sizes of dogs, ranging from a bundle
  you can hold in one hand to a 50--60 pound animal
  that begins to resemble a horse.

\item [Cats] Cats make ideal pets for people who
  are on-the-go. Independent and intelligent in
  nature, they do not require a great deal of
  attention. While being well able to entertain
```

```
and take care of themselves, cats also offer
warmth and affection to their owners.

\item [Birds] Birds add a splash of color and a
pleasant background music to the household. The
patient bird owner can train his pet to talk and
sit on his finger, and even ride around town on
his shoulder.
\end{description}
```

2. The blank lines between items are only included for clarity in the example; LaTeX doesn't need them. Similarly, the blank spaces between the \item commands and the optional arguments are not needed. Since it does not hurt LaTeX, however, it is a very useful way to make a file readable—and easy to debug.

3. latex and prnt the file.

4. Notice that each label is bolded and set off from the description part of the item.

   The descriptive list may be used as a sublist to another style of list, or its items may contain sublists of other styles.

3.10.5 Spacing Between Items

To a certain degree, the spacing in itemized, enumerated and descriptive lists is adjustable. See Section C.6 under the heading "Lists" on page 232 for more information on list formatting parameters.

Summary

- There are three styles of lists: itemized, for bullets and other symbols as labels; enumerated, for numbers as labels; descriptive, for words as labels.

- Each list must have a \begin and an \end command, taking the name of the list as an argument.

- Items in a list are set off by the \item command.

- Up to four levels of sublists are allowed.

- A \begin{itemize}, \begin{enumerate} or
  \begin{description} command begins a new level of list; a
  matching \end command ends a level.

3.11 Displayed Formulas

Section 2.10 noted that equations may be entered in-line with the text
or displayed on a line alone. We will now see how to display a formula.
This section describes how to enter a displayed formula that fits onto
one line in the output. Sections 5.3 and 5.4 explain how to typeset
multi-line formulas.

A numbered, displayed formula is produced with the equation environment; an unnumbered, displayed formula is produced with the
displaymath environment.

A shorthand notation is available for the displaymath environment:

```
\[
x = y + z
\]
```

means exactly the same thing as

```
\begin{displaymath}
x = y + z
\end{displaymath}
```

Exercise 3.21

1. Taking a very simple formula, $x = y + z$, let's practice. Enter the
   following lines at the end of new.tex. (Before the
   \end{document}):

> Here is a paragraph of text. It leads up to a
> brilliant (numbered) equation:
> \begin{equation}
> x = y + z
> \end{equation}
>
> And another paragraph may follow the equation.
> To produce the same equation without a number,
> type the following:
>
> \begin{displaymath}
> x = y + z
> \end{displaymath}
>
> Using the shorthand notation, \[x = y + z \]
> let us see what \LaTeX\ will do with a displayed
> equation entered in the middle of the paragraph.

2. Notice that there are no blank lines within the **equation** and **displaymath** environments. Blank lines within the displayed math environments, as in

   \begin{equation}
   x = y + z

   \end{equation}

   are illegal.

3. **latex** and **prnt** the file.

4. Looking at the page you printed, you will notice that the first equation, made with the **equation** environment, has a number at the right margin, while the others, made with the **displaymath** environment, don't have numbers. Also, using the "\[, \]" notation makes it convenient to place a displayed equation in the middle of a paragraph. (The following text is not indented.)

3.11.1   Referring to Numbered Equations

The \label and \ref commands may be used to refer to numbered
equations in a document. The \label command should be placed just
before the \end{equation} command.

Exercise 3.22

1. Put the following \label command in your first displayed equation of the previous exercise:

   ```
   \label{eq:first}
   (\end{equation})
   ```

   (Don't enter the line in parentheses.)

2. Now put the following sentence after the displayed equation:

   ```
   That was Equation~\ref{eq:first}.
   ```

3. latex the file twice and prnt.

4. Notice that the equation number shows up where you put your
   \ref command.

3.11.2   Integrals and Summations

LaTeX provides many, many commands for producing mathematical
symbols. Tables 4.1 through 4.9 list these symbols and the commands
to produce them. Two special symbols, the integral (\int) and the
summation (\sum), can be given lower and upper limits by entering the
limits as sub- and superscripts.

Exercise 3.23

1. Enter the following lines at the end of new.tex:

```
\begin{equation}
\int_{0}^{1} f(x) = g(x)
\end{equation}

\[
\sum_{1}^{5} x = 15
\]
```

2. `latex` and `prnt` the file and see how these symbols with their limits are typeset. NOTE: Any formula may be put into the sub- or superscript to produce limits for the integral and summation functions.

3.11.3   Text Mode versus Display Mode

Looking at the formulas in the previous exercise, you will notice that the integrals and summations with their limits are tall. LaTeX will typeset them slightly differently if they are entered in-line with the text to take away some of the height. There may be times when the writer wants the taller style of symbol in an in-line formula, or wants the shorter style in a displayed formula. These effects can be made with the `\displaystyle` and `\textstyle` commands in math mode. These commands work much like the typestyle and typesize-changing commands of Section 3.4 to change the way formulas are typeset within the scope of the command.

Exercise 3.24

1. Enter the same formulas as in the previous exercise as in-line formulas as follows:

   ```
   Here is an in-line integral: $\int_{0}^{1} f(x) =
   g(x)$, and here is an in-line summation:
   $\sum_{1}^{5} x = 15$. They look different from
   the displayed forms.
   ```

2. Now, suppose you want a tall formula in with the text, and a shorter formula in a displayed equation. Enter these lines:

```
Here is a {\it tall} in-line integral:
$\displaystyle \int_{0}^{1} f(x) =g(x)$.   And here is
a {\it short} displayed summation:

\[
\textstyle \sum_{1}^{5} x = 15
\]
```

3. latex and prnt the file new.tex.

4. Notice that in Item 1. the in-line examples use smaller integral
   and summation signs, and different placement of the limits. This
   way the formulas are not too tall, therefore they do not introduce
   too much white space between text lines.

5. Now compare the formulas in Item 2. containing \displaystyle
   and \textstyle commands with the formulas having the natural
   height for in-line and displayed equations.

6. Note that the dollar signs create a group, as do the \[and \]
   commands that begin and end the displayed equation.

3.11.4   Other Math Typestyles

Besides \displaystyle and \textstyle, there are two more commands for controlling the size of type in math mode.   They are
\scriptstyle and \scriptscriptstyle. The following table describes
all four size-controlling commands of math mode:

Command	Effect
\displaystyle	Use default size for displayed formula.
\textstyle	Use default size for in-text formula.
\scriptstyle	Use default size for a first-level sub- or superscript
\scriptscriptstyle	Use default size for a second-level sub- or superscript.

To set only a portion of a formula in a particular size, enclose that
portion of the formula and the command in curly braces.

3.11.5 Left-Justified Equation Numbers

Section 3.1.1 mentioned that the `leqno` document style option causes equation numbers to be aligned along the left margin, instead of the default placement along the right margin. Let us try an exercise using this option.

Exercise 3.25

1. Change the \documentstyle command in `new.tex` to look like the following:

   \documentstyle[leqno]{report}

2. `latex` and `prnt` the file `new.tex`.

3. Notice that the equation numbers are now along the left margin.

3.11.6 Left-Justified Equations

Section 3.1.1 also described the `fleqn` document style option, which causes displayed equations themselves to be aligned along the left margin, instead of being centered. Let us see what effect this option has on `new.tex`.

Exercise 3.26

1. Change the \documentstyle command in `new.tex` to look like this:

   \documentstyle[fleqn]{report}

2. `latex` and `prnt` the file `new.tex`.

3. Notice the alignment of the displayed equations.

4. Change the \documentstyle command in `new.tex` back to

   \documentstyle{report}

3.11.7   Customization of Displayed Equations

It is possible to adjust the amount of vertical space left above and below displayed equations by changing style parameters that control this. Also, when equations are left justified, they may be indented a certain amount. See Section C.6 under the heading "Math" on page 234 for more information on this topic.

Summary

- Numbered, displayed equations are made with the `equation` environment.

- Unnumbered, displayed equations are made with the `displaymath` environment. It has a shorthand notation: `\[ ... \]`.

- Some symbols are typeset larger in display mode than in in-text mode.

- The `\displaystyle`, `\textstyle`, `\scriptstyle`, and `\scriptscriptstyle` commands can be used to control the size of symbols within their scope.

- The contents of any complete formula are considered by LaTeX to be a group.

- The `\sum` and `\int` commands make summation and integral symbols. Their limits are entered as sub- and superscripts.

- The `leqno` document style option causes equation numbers to be aligned on the left margin.

- The `fleqn` document style option causes displayed equations to be aligned on the left margin.

- The vertical space left above and below displayed equations, and the indentation of left-justified equations may be adjusted.

3.12 Foreign Symbols and Accents

You can make a wide variety of foreign symbols, accents and other special symbols using LaTeX. Table 3.3 provides a complete list of these

Foreign Accents

ò	\`{o}	õ	\~{o}	ǒ	\v{o}	ǫ	\c{o}
ó	\'{o}	ō	\={o}	ő	\H{o}	ọ	\d{o}
ô	\^{o}	ȯ	\.{o}	oͦo	\t{oo}	o̲	\b{o}
ö	\"{o}	ŏ	\u{o}				

Foreign Symbols

œ	\oe	å	\aa	ł	\l	¿	?`
Œ	\OE	Å	\AA	Ł	\L	¡	!`
æ	\ae	ø	\o	ß	\ss		
Æ	\AE	Ø	\O				

Special Symbols

†	\dag	§	\S	©	\copyright
‡	\ddag	¶	\P	£	\pounds

Table 3.3: Foreign Symbols and Accents

symbols, with the commands to produce them. Note that these are different from the mathematical symbols mentioned in Section 3.11.2 in that they are not to be used in math mode, but in paragraph mode. To give you an idea of how they work, here are a few examples.

Generally, accents that go over a letter take that letter as an argument. Other symbols, which stand by themselves, are simple commands without arguments.

Exercise 3.27

1. Add the following lines to `new.tex`:

```
?'Como est\'{a} usted?
Notre amour est chose l\'{e}g\'{e}re.
Ein V\"{o}gelein fliegt \"{u}ber den Rhein.
Here are some foreign symbols:
\oe, \AE, \AA, and \o.
```

2. Now that you're totally confused, `latex` and `prnt` the file, and see how the commands you typed produce accents and symbols.

3. Note that the ? produces an upside-down question mark. A question mark followed by a space produces a regular question mark. One followed by anything other than a space produces this special symbol.

3.13   Page-Numbering Style

Normally, LaTeX numbers the pages of your document sequentially with arabic numbers centered at the bottom of the page. With a simple command, you can select one of five numbering styles for your page-numbering. The command is the `\pagenumbering` command, and its argument is the style you choose.

A `\pagenumbering` command affects all pages from the present one forward until another `\pagenumbering` command is encountered. The following table illustrates the use of this command:

Command	Effect
\pagenumbering{arabic}	Page numbers are arabic
\pagenumbering{roman}	Page numbers are lowercase roman numerals.
\pagenumbering{Roman}	Page numbers are uppercase roman numerals.
\pagenumbering{alph}	Page numbers are lowercase letters.
\pagenumbering{Alph}	Page numbers are uppercase letters.

As well as changing the page-numbering style, the **\pagenumbering** command also resets the page number to one.

NOTE: To produce a document with no page numbers, see the **\pagestyle{empty}** command described in Section 3.14.

Exercise 3.28

We have already seen the arabic numbering style, so let's experiment with the others.

1. First add a \clearpage command in **new.tex** just after the last list and before the sentence that starts "To refer to a bibliography item. . . ."

2. Add another \clearpage just before the paragraph that starts with "Here is an in-line integral:".

3. Now **new.tex** will produce four pages. To make the first page have lowercase roman numerals place a **\pagenumbering** command right after the **\begin{document}** command as follows:

   ```
   (\begin{document})
   \pagenumbering{roman}
   ```

4. Now add the following lines before the first **\clearpage** command.

   ```
   This is the end of page 2. There is still time
   to change the numbering command as long as we
   are on page 2.
   \pagenumbering{Roman}
   ```

5. Put the following \pagenumbering command right after the first \clearpage command:

   \pagenumbering{alph}

6. And put this command right after the second and last \clearpage:

   \pagenumbering{Alph}

7. Now latex and prnt the file and look at the page numbers. Notice that the \pagenumbering command sets the page number to 1 (or A) and then begins sequentially numbering the pages with the requested style.

Summary

- The \pagenumbering command, with the style as its argument, begins numbering pages in the requested style.

- The \pagenumbering command also sets the page number to 1.

3.14   Headers and Footers

By default, LaTeX leaves the *header* of each page blank, and puts the page number centered in the *footer* of the page. All other text on the page (including footnotes) is the *body* of the page. The *page style* is what determines the contents of the header and footer of the page.

If you wish to specify a page header or footer that is different from the default page style (called the plain page style), you may use the \pagestyle command, giving the style you desire as the argument. The four page styles available are: plain, empty, headings, and myheadings.

A \pagestyle{empty} command causes the header and the footer to be empty. LaTeX still calculates a number for each page, but does not print it on the page. A \pagestyle{headings} command places the page number and other information in the header, and leaves the footer blank. The "other information" is dependent on the document style, and is generally something like the chapter or section heading.

The `\pagestyle{myheadings}` command is used for customizing the page header. It works like a `\pagestyle{headings}` command, except that you supply the "other information." This is discussed in more detail in Section 3.14.1.

Exercise 3.29

1. Edit `new.tex` and remove all the `\pagenumbering` commands, except for the first one. For this `\pagenumbering` command (which we placed right after the `\chapter` command), pick your favorite numbering style (besides arabic) and place it in the argument; e.g., `\pagenumbering{Alph}`, if you like capital letters.

2. Now put a `\pagestyle{headings}` command right after the `\pagenumbering` command.

3. `latex` and `prnt` the file.

4. Pretty boring, eh? Notice that in the `report` document style, the page number is there in the header, but nothing else. Let's try changing the document style to `book`.
   Your `\documentstyle` command should look like this:

   `\documentstyle{book}`

5. Now, enter the following `\section` command right after the `\chapter` command:

   `\section{Lists, Etc.}`

6. `latex` and `prnt` the file.

7. Recall from Section 3.1 that two-sided printing is the default in the `book` document style. Therefore we can expect the headers and/or footers to be different on odd and even pages!

8. Notice that the page number, as well as the chapter heading (on even pages) and the section heading (on odd pages), is in the header. The one exception is the first page of the chapter, which is completely different! The page number is centered in the footer, and the header is empty. That's the way the **headings** page style works in **book** document style.

3.14.1   Myheadings Page Style

The **myheadings** page style allows the user to input information that will be displayed in the page header. The headers are handled differently depending on whether or not the **twoside** document style option is in effect. (See Section 3.1.1.)

If the document is being processed for one-sided printing, the **\markright** command is used to specify the header for all pages. It takes the text desired for the header as an argument; e.g., **\markright{Text of Header}**.

If the document is being processed for two-sided printing, the **\markboth** command is used to specify headers for left- and right-hand pages. It takes two arguments—the first is the header for left-hand (even) pages; the second is the header for right-hand (odd) pages; e.g.,

\markboth{Header for even pages}{Header for odd pages}

The **\markright** and **\markboth** commands may be used as often as the user wishes to change the headers.

Exercise 3.30

1. Edit **new.tex** and change the **\pagestyle{headings}** command to **\pagestyle{myheadings}**. Now the **\markboth** command can be used to set the headers for left- and right-hand pages.

2. Enter the following line right after the **\pagestyle{myheadings}** command:

   \markboth{Left-hand (even) page header}{Right-hand (odd) page header}

(If you want to replace the headers given above for something more original, please feel free to make up your own!)

3. `latex` and `prnt` the file.

4. You will see that the headers come out as specified in the `\markboth` command, with the first argument being used on even pages and the second argument being used on odd pages. The one exception is the first page of the chapter, which always has a pre-defined page style.

3.14.2 Adjusting the Height of Headers and Footers

The amount of vertical space reserved for the header and footer on each page may be adjusted by the user, if desired. See Section C.6 under the heading "Page Formatting" on page 227 for more information on this topic.

Summary

- Four page styles are available.

- `\pagestyle{plain}` (the default for all styles except book), puts the page number in the footer and leaves the header blank.

- `\pagestyle{empty}` leaves the header and the footer blank. (Page numbers are calculated, just not printed.)

- `\pagestyle{headings}` puts the page number and other information (which depends on the document style) in the header, and leaves the footer blank.

- `\pagestyle{myheadings}` puts the page number in the header, as well as other information supplied by the user.

- The `\markright` command is used in `myheadings` to specify the header for right-hand pages. Its argument is the text desired for the header.

- The \markboth command is used in **myheadings** to specify the header for left- and right-hand pages. It takes two arguments: the first is the desired header for left-hand pages; the second is the desired header for right-hand pages.

Chapter 4

Typesetting Mathematics

LaTeX's ability to typeset mathematics is probably its most useful feature. Entering mathematics is as easy as reading a formula out loud. In other words, most of LaTeX's math commands and structures are designed to be very similar to the English words used to describe them. For example, as we have seen, the integral, from 0 to infinity, of $f(x)$ is produced by `$\int_0^{\infty} f(x)$`. The commands are entered in the same order as the English.

In addition to being easy to learn and use, the mathematics capability of LaTeX is full and complete, so that only very rarely will a formula or symbol be needed that is not available in a simple command. No special menus, alternate keyboards, or downloadable font sets are needed, so the typist's fingers never need to leave the keyboard for any reason.

Enough with the sales pitch—when you try mathematics for yourself, it will sell itself. Most of the commands in this chapter will be math commands. It is important to remember that math commands are only legal in math mode—that is between dollar signs, or within a math environment such as `equation` or `displaymath`. Using math commands in paragraph mode causes an error.

4.1   Superscripts and Subscripts

We have seen in Section 2.10 that a superscript is signalled by a caret, "^", and a subscript is signalled by an underscore, "_". The super- or subscript itself must be enclosed in braces if it is more than one character long. Using braces properly, you can create superscripts to superscripts, superscripts to subscripts, subscripts to . . ., well, you can imagine that there are endless possibilities. In fact there is no limitation on the number of levels of scripts. If you really wanted to, you could typeset a formula like:

$$y = x^{a^{b^{c^{d^{e^{f^{g^{h^i}}}}}}}}$$ (4.1)

by using braces correctly.

The input for equation 4.1 looks like this:

```
\begin{equation}
y = x^{a^{b^{c^{d^{e^{f^{g^{h^i}}}}}}}}
\label{eq:sclots}
\end{equation}
```

Let's present the expression on the right side of the equals sign a different way:

```
  1  2  3  4  5  6  7  8    87654321
x^{a^{b^{c^{d^{e^{f^{g^{h^i}}}}}}}}
```

Notice that the outermost set of braces, labelled 1, encloses the entire superscript to variable x. Set 2 encloses the superscript to the a, set 3 encloses the superscript to the b, etc. All of the superscripts in this formula are more than one character long, except for i, the superscript to the h. Therefore the i is the only superscript not enclosed in braces.

Exercise 4.1

1. Open a new file called `math.tex` and put in the following commands:

```
\documentstyle[12pt]{report}
\begin{document}
\chapter{Math}
\section{Super and Subscripts}

\end{document}
```

2. Now let's experiment with some common structures for super- and subscripts. Using the following as an example, enter a formula containing a variable with a two-character superscript: `$x^{-1}$` (Make up your own!)

3. Now enter the following displayed equation:

`\[y = x^{a^b}\]`

Question: Why doesn't the *b* need braces around it? ANSWER: It is only one character long.

4. How would you produce $y = x^{a^{-b}}$? Try it, then compare your try with this: `y = x^{a^{-b}}` .

5. What would be the result of `$x^a_b$`? How is it different from `$x^{a_b}$`. Enter these two formulas into your file.

6. One more experiment: Sometimes a subscript is an English word, instead of a variable or formula. Let's see how that looks. Enter the following formula: `\[I_{ground} = VR\]`

7. Now `latex` and `prnt` the file.

NOTE: Remember—if LaTeX comes across an error and stops with a "?," don't panic. It is probably caused by a simple typo in your input file. Type "x" and a carriage return to get back to the DOS prompt. Then check your file carefully for mistyped commands. If that doesn't help, refer to Appendix E for help.

8. Notice the difference between the two formulas in item 5. In the first one the subscript goes to the *x*, and in the second one the braces make it go to the *a*.

9. Look at the result of item 6. See how the word "ground" is in italics? It is probably better to set it in roman type, especially since the italic font used in math mode is not meant to set text, as is the normal italic font. Edit this formula to look like this:

   `\[I_{\rm ground} = VR\]`

10. `latex` and `prnt` the file again and notice the difference. Now the word "ground" can't be mistaken for a bunch of math variables— g,r,o,u,n, and d.

Summary

- A caret, "^", signals a superscript.

- An underscore, "_", signals a subscript.

- Super- and subscripts must be enclosed in braces if more than one character long.

- Any number of levels of scripts is allowed, as long as braces are nested correctly.

- A variable cannot have more than one super- or subscript. In other words, `x^1^2` is illegal—it must be either `x^{12}` or `x^{1^2}`, two entirely different formulas.

- A super- or subscript that is an English word should be set in roman type, e.g., `$I_{\rm ground}$`.

4.2   Fractions

A fraction is produced with the `\frac` command. `\frac` takes two arguments: the first is the numerator, (top of the fraction), and the second is the denominator (bottom of the fraction). In other words, `$\frac{\rm top}{\rm bottom}$` would produce $\frac{\rm top}{\rm bottom}$.

Any formula can be put into the numerator or denominator of a fraction. Just enclose the entire formula in braces. If the fraction is in a displayed formula, LaTeX will set the numerator and denominator with the \textstyle font. The numerator and denominator of an in-text fraction will be set with the \scriptstyle font. These defaults can be overridden by including a \displaystyle, \textstyle, \scriptstyle, or \scriptscriptstyle command in the braces enclosing the argument.

LaTeX automatically centers the numerator and denominator above and below the bar. It also vertically aligns the bar on center with the rest of the formula.

Exercise 4.2

1. Edit the file math.tex and add the following lines before the \end{document}:

```
\section{Fractions}
<CR>
Now, let's try some formulas with fractions.

\begin{equation}
x = \frac{y}{z} + \frac{y^2}{z^2}
\label{eq:frac1}
\end{equation}

How about a fraction in the numerator
of a fraction?

\begin{equation}
x = \frac{ \frac{1}{y} }{z}
\label{eq:frac2}
\end{equation}

Now, try an integral in the denominator.

\begin{equation}
y = \frac{p^2}{ \int_0^1 f(x) }
\label{eq:frac3}
```

```
\end{equation}
```

2. Notice that these numbered equations are labelled so that they can be referred to later.

3. You don't have to leave extra spaces in the input when the numerator or denominator gets complicated, but it can help to make the formula more readable, and easier to debug later.

4. Save the file, and then `latex` and `prnt` it.

5. Notice that even though these are displayed equations, some of the characters—notably, a fraction within a fraction—are quite small. Some authors may prefer to have them set in larger type. Edit the second fraction to look like this:

```
\begin{equation}
x = \frac{ \displaystyle \frac{1}{y} }{z}
\label{eq:frac2}
\end{equation}
```

6. `latex` and `prnt` the file again, and notice the difference that the `\displaystyle` command makes.

Summary

- Fractions are produced with the `\frac` command. Its first argument is the numerator, and its second argument is the denominator.

- The numerator and denominator of the fraction are set in the `\textstyle` font, but this can be overridden with the `\displaystyle`, etc., commands.

- The numerator and denominator are centered above and below the bar of the fraction.

- The bar of the fraction is vertically centered with the rest of the equation.

4.3 Roots

The \sqrt command produces a square root. It takes one argument that is the contents of the square root. The radical symbol will automatically stretch, vertically as well as horizontally, to fit around the argument.

Exercise 4.3

1. Try the following experiment with the \sqrt command. Edit math.tex and add these lines before the \end{document} command:

```
<CR>
\subsection{Square Roots}

Here is a formula with roots in it:

\[
x = \sqrt{y} + \sqrt{ \frac{1}{y} } +
                \sqrt{ y^{a^{b^{c^d}}} }
\]
```

2. latex and prnt math.tex.

3. Note that the size of the radical symbol changes to accommodate the argument.

4.3.1 Cube Roots, Etc.

For a cube root or an nth root—that is, not a plain square root—the \sqrt command takes an optional argument, before the mandatory argument. For instance, the cube root of x would be $\sqrt[3]{x}$, which looks like $\sqrt[3]{x}$.

Summary

- The \sqrt command produces a square root.

- \sqrt takes one mandatory argument, which goes under the radical sign. The argument can be any formula.

- The radical sign stretches in the horizontal and vertical directions to accommodate an argument of any size.

- For roots other than square roots, \sqrt takes an optional argument (before the mandatory argument) that specifies the type of root.

4.4   Ellipses

An ellipsis is a group of three dots indicating the continuation of a pattern. Its meaning could be expressed with the phrase "and so on." In mathematical formulas, four types of ellipses are useful:

1. Low horizontal (\ldots)—for use between commas in a series

2. Centered horizontal (\cdots)—for use between plus signs or other vertically centered operators in a series

3. Diagonal (\ddots)—for use in arrays and matrices

4. Vertical (\vdots)—for use in arrays and matrices

Exercise 4.4

1. To emphasize the difference between the usage of \ldots and \cdots, enter the following lines into math.tex before the \end{document}:

```
\subsection{Ellipses}
<CR>
Correct:
\[ x = a_1 + a_2 + a_3 + \cdots + a_n \]
```

Incorrect:
```
\[ x = a_1 + a_2 + a_3 + \ldots + a_n \]
```

2. latex and prnt the file and note the difference.

3. Study the following example of usage of \ddots, \vdots, and \cdots in a matrix:

$$
\begin{array}{ccccc}
x_1 & 0 & 0 & \cdots & 0 \\
0 & x_2 & 0 & \cdots & \vdots \\
0 & 0 & \ddots & 0 & \vdots \\
\vdots & \vdots & 0 & \ddots & 0 \\
0 & \cdots & \cdots & 0 & x_n
\end{array}
$$

Here are the commands to create this array:

```
\[
\begin{array}{ccccc}
x_1    & 0      & 0      & \cdots & 0      \\
0      & x_2    & 0      & \cdots & \vdots \\
0      & 0      & \ddots & 0      & \vdots \\
\vdots & \vdots & 0      & \ddots & 0      \\
0      & \cdots & \cdots & 0      & x_n    \\
\end{array}
\]
```

Summary

- Four kinds of ellipses are available: \cdots for centered horizontal; \ldots for low horizontal; \ddots for diagonal; and \vdots for vertical.

- \cdots go between centered operators; \ldots go between low operators.

- \ddots and \vdots are useful in typesetting matrices and arrays.

4.5   Greek and Calligraphic Letters

4.5.1   Greek Letters

Greek letters are created with commands that are like the names of the letters. For example, `$\alpha$` produces α. All of the lowercase Greek letters plus a subset of uppercase letters are available. Some Greek letters have two different forms. Table 4.1 shows the Greek letters and the commands to produce them.

Lowercase

α	\alpha	θ	\theta	o	o	τ	\tau
β	\beta	ϑ	\vartheta	π	\pi	υ	\upsilon
γ	\gamma	ι	\iota	ϖ	\varpi	ϕ	\phi
δ	\delta	κ	\kappa	ρ	\rho	φ	\varphi
ϵ	\epsilon	λ	\lambda	ϱ	\varrho	χ	\chi
ε	\varepsilon	μ	\mu	σ	\sigma	ψ	\psi
ζ	\zeta	ν	\nu	ς	\varsigma	ω	\omega
η	\eta	ξ	\xi				

Uppercase

Γ	\Gamma	Λ	\Lambda	Σ	\Sigma	Ψ	\Psi
Δ	\Delta	Ξ	\Xi	Υ	\Upsilon	Ω	\Omega
Θ	\Theta	Π	\Pi	Φ	\Phi		

Table 4.1: Greek Letters

4.5.2   Calligraphic Letters

The twenty-six uppercase letters in the English alphabet may be printed as calligraphic letters in math mode using the `\cal` typestyle command. The `\cal` command works like other typestyle-changing commands (`\it`, `\sl`, etc.) in that it stays in effect until another typestyle-changing command is encountered, or until the group that contains it ends. Usually, \cal should be used with braces to form a group.

Exercise 4.5

1. Add the following lines to `math.tex`:

   ```
   Here is an example using $\alpha$ and $\beta$.
   $\cal G$ is also used.
   \begin{equation}
   {\cal G} = \frac{\alpha + \beta}{\alpha - \beta}
   \end{equation}
   ```

2. `latex` and `prnt` the file.

3. Note that dollar signs are needed to use these math commands in text.

4. Also note that the dollar signs around the `$\cal F$` form a group.

Summary

- Greek letters are created with commands like the names of the letters.

- They must be entered between dollar signs if mentioned in text.

- All uppercase letters in the English alphabet can be printed in calligraphic style with the \cal command. It works like other typestyle-changing commands.

4.6 Math Symbols

LaTeX has a rich vocabulary of mathematical symbols. Tables 4.2 through 4.6 list these symbols with the commands to produce them. The symbols in Table 4.6 have the added feature of appearing in a larger size in displayed equations than in in-text equations. The two different sizes are shown. (See Section 3.11.2 for details on producing different sized symbols.)

±	\pm	∩	\cap	◇	\diamond	⊕	\oplus
∓	\mp	∪	\cup	△	\bigtriangleup	⊖	\ominus
×	\times	⊎	\uplus	▽	\bigtriangledown	⊗	\otimes
÷	\div	⊓	\sqcap	◁	\triangleleft	⊘	\oslash
*	\ast	⊔	\sqcup	▷	\triangleright	⊙	\odot
⋆	\star	∨	\vee	◁	\lhd	○	\bigcirc
∘	\circ	∧	\wedge	▷	\rhd	†	\dagger
•	\bullet	\	\setminus	⊴	\unlhd	‡	\ddagger
·	\cdot	≀	\wr	⊵	\unrhd	II	\amalg

Table 4.2: Binary Operation Symbols

≤	\leq	≥	\geq	≡	\equiv	⊨	\models
≺	\prec	≻	\succ	∼	\sim	⊥	\perp
⪯	\preceq	⪰	\succeq	≃	\simeq	|	\mid
≪	\ll	≫	\gg	≍	\asymp	‖	\parallel
⊂	\subset	⊃	\supset	≈	\approx	⋈	\bowtie
⊆	\subseteq	⊇	\supseteq	≅	\cong	⋈	\Join
⊏	\sqsubset	⊐	\sqsupset	≠	\neq	⌣	\smile
⊑	\sqsubseteq	⊒	\sqsupseteq	≐	\doteq	⌢	\frown
⊢	\vdash	⊣	\dashv				

Table 4.3: Relation Symbols

←	\leftarrow	⟵	\longleftarrow	↑	\uparrow
⇐	\Leftarrow	⟸	\Longleftarrow	⇑	\Uparrow
→	\rightarrow	⟶	\longrightarrow	↓	\downarrow
⇒	\Rightarrow	⟹	\Longrightarrow	⇓	\Downarrow
↔	\leftrightarrow	⟷	\longleftrightarrow	↕	\updownarrow
⇔	\Leftrightarrow	⟺	\Longleftrightarrow	⇕	\Updownarrow
↦	\mapsto	⟼	\longmapsto	↗	\nearrrow
↩	\hookleftarrow	↪	\hookrightarrow	↘	\searrow
↼	\leftharpoonup	⇀	\rightharpoonup	↙	\swarrow
↽	\leftharpoondown	⇁	\rightharpoondown	↖	\nwarrow

Table 4.4: Arrow Symbols

ℵ	\aleph	′	\prime	∀	\forall	∞	\infty
ℏ	\hbar	∅	\emptyset	∃	\exists	□	\Box
ı	\imath	∇	\nabla	¬	\neg	◇	\Diamond
ȷ	\jmath	√	\surd	♭	\flat	△	\triangle
ℓ	\ell	⊤	\top	♮	\natural	♣	\clubsuit
℘	\wp	⊥	\bot	♯	\sharp	♢	\diamondsuit
ℜ	\Re	‖	|	\	\backslash	♡	\heartsuit
ℑ	\Im	∠	\angle	∂	\partial	♠	\spadesuit

Table 4.5: Miscellaneous Symbols

Σ	∑	\sum	∩	⋂	\bigcap	⊙	⨀	\bigodot
Π	∏	\prod	∪	⋃	\bigcup	⊗	⨂	\bigotimes
∐	∐	\coprod	⊔	⨆	\bigsqcup	⊕	⨁	\bigoplus
∫	∫	\int	∨	⋁	\bigvee	⊎	⨄	\biguplus
∮	∮	\oint	∧	⋀	\bigwedge			

Table 4.6: Variable-sized Symbols

4.6.1   Special Functions

Certain functions, such as the trigonometric functions for cosine, sine, tangent, etc., traditionally appear in roman type, as opposed to the default italic type of math mode. To make this simple, LaTeX provides commands for producing such functions. These commands are listed in Table 4.7.

arccos	\arccos	cos	\cos	csc	\csc	exp	\exp
ker	\ker	lim sup	\limsup	min	\min	sinh	\sinh
arcsin	\arcsin	cosh	\cosh	deg	\deg	gcd	\gcd
lg	\lg	ln	\ln	Pr	\Pr	sup	\sup
arctan	\arctan	cot	\cot	det	\det	hom	\hom
lim	\lim	log	\log	sec	\sec	tan	\tan
arg	\arg	coth	\coth	dim	\dim	inf	\inf
lim inf	\liminf	max	\max	sin	\sin	tanh	\tanh

Table 4.7: Trigonometric Functions, Etc.

4.6.2   Delimiters

Table 4.8 lists several delimiter symbols available in LaTeX along with

(	(	)	)	[	[	]	]
{	\{	}	\}	⌊	\lfloor	⌋	\rfloor
⌈	\lceil	⌉	\rceil	⟨	\langle	⟩	\rangle
/	/	\	\backslash	|	|	‖	\\|
↑	\uparrow	↓	\downarrow	⇑	\Uparrow	⇓	\Downarrow
↕	\updownarrow	⇕	\Updownarrow				

Table 4.8: Delimiters

the commands to produce them. Each of these delimiters may also be stretched vertically to properly surround a tall formula. This is done by preceding the *delimiter commands* with "\left" and "\right"; e.g.,

\left(and \right), for parentheses and other delimiter commands that don't require a backslash, and \left\{ and \right\} for braces and other delimiter commands that do require a backslash. Here is an example:

$$x = \left\{ \frac{(a+b)}{(a-b)} \right\}$$

which is produced by

```
\[
x = \left\{ \frac{(a + b)}{(a - b)} \right\}
\]
```

Every \left command must have a matching \right command. Perhaps the reader will anticipate the problem with this rule—that is, sometimes you want a tall left brace without a matching tall right brace in a formula. Example:

$$f(x) = \left\{ \begin{array}{cc} a & \text{for } x < 0 \\ b & \text{for } x \geq 0 \end{array} \right. \tag{4.2}$$

In cases like this, you must put an "invisible" right delimiter on the other side of the tall formula. Adding a period to the \left and \right commands—i.e., \left. or \right.—will make an invisible delimiter on the appropriate side of the expression. The formula above was produced with the following commands:

```
\begin{equation}
f(x) = \left\{ \begin{array}{cc}
             a & \mbox{for $x<0$} \\
             b & \mbox{for $x\geq 0$}
             \end{array}
      \right.
\end{equation}
```

Even though you don't know the **array** environment yet, you can see that everything between the \left\{ and the \right. is what creates the right hand side of the equation, which is the tall part.

LATEX looks at whatever is *in between* the left and right delimiter
commands and sees how tall it is, and then creates delimiter symbols
that are the right height. This means that even if one delimiter is invisible, you must put the `\left.` or `\right.` command on the opposite
side of the tall portion of the formula to make the delimiter the right
size—not, for instance, right next to the visible delimiter.

Exercise 4.6

1. Enter the following lines in `math.tex`:

   ```
   \section{Symbol-Mania!}

   Here are some examples of math symbols:

   \[ a \leq x \div y \]

   \[ x = y \longleftrightarrow y = x \]

   Some symbols are almost silly---like
   $\clubsuit$, $\flat$, and $\heartsuit$!

   \[x = \left\{
     \frac{\int_0^\infty y}{2} \right\} + z \]
   ```

2. `latex` and `prnt` the file to see the results.

Summary

- Many symbols are available through simple commands.

- Some symbols are printed in a larger size in displayed equations.

- Many functions that are traditionally set in roman type may be
  produced with commands.

- Delimiters may be made to fit around a tall sub-formula by using
  the `\left` and `\right` commands combined with the delimiter
  commands.

- Every \left command must have a matching \right command; \left. or \right. is used to make an invisible delimiter.

4.7 Words as Part of a Formula

Sometimes a formula has an English word or phrase in it; e.g.,

$$f(x) = a \text{ for negative values of } x \qquad (4.3)$$

The \mbox command, with the word or phrase as an argument, can be used to produce roman type, and to preserve word spaces. Remember—normally, all characters in math mode are italic, and the spacing you input is ignored by LaTeX. The argument of an \mbox command is processed in paragraph mode, *not* in math mode. Therefore any non-math portions of a formula should be entered with an \mbox command. Equation 4.3 was input as follows:

```
\begin{equation}
f(x) = a \mbox{ for negative values of } x
\end{equation}
```

Without the \mbox command, the results would be much different. If you typed

```
\[ f(x) = a  for all negative values of x \]
```

you would get

$$f(x) = a for all negative values of x$$

See?

Exercise 4.7

1. Try entering the following formula into `math.tex`:

$$x = y \text{ as long as } y \leq 0$$

2. `latex` and `prnt` the file and see how you did.

3. Compare your try with this:

```
\[ x = y \mbox{ as long as } y \leq 0 \]
```

Did you remember the spaces at the outer ends of the phrase?

Summary

- When a formula has an English word or phrase in it, the word or phrase should be set with an \mbox command.

4.8   Fancy Details

4.8.1   Math Mode Accents

Table 4.9 lists the accents available in math mode. The examples show the accents used with the letter "p," but they work with any letter or symbol.

$\hat{p}$	\hat{p}	$\acute{p}$	\acute{p}	$\bar{p}$	\bar{p}	$\dot{p}$	\dot{p}
$\check{p}$	\check{p}	$\grave{p}$	\grave{p}	$\vec{p}$	\vec{p}	$\ddot{p}$	\ddot{p}
$\breve{p}$	\breve{p}	$\tilde{p}$	\tilde{p}				

Table 4.9: Math Mode Accents

Some kinds of accents may be stretched over more than one letter. The \hat and \tilde commands have analogous \widehat and \widetilde commands that try to stretch the hat or tilde over the span of the arguments they are given. The size of these wide accents is limited, however.

4.8.2   Horizontal Braces and Bars

To put a horizontal bar over a portion of a formula, use the \overline command with the portion of the formula to be overlined as an argument. Similarly, \underline puts a horizontal line under its argument. For example:

```
\[
x = \overline{a+b} + \underline{c+d}
\]
```

produces

$$x = \overline{a+b} + \underline{c+d}$$

The \overbrace and \underbrace commands work the same way as \overline and \underline except they produce horizontal braces instead of lines, e.g.

```
\[
x = \overbrace{a+b} + \underbrace{c+d}
\]
```

produces

$$x = \overbrace{a+b} + \underbrace{c+d}$$

Additionally, the braces can be labelled by using super- or subscripts as in the following example:

```
\[
x = \overbrace{a+b}^6 + \underbrace{c+d}_{24}
\]
```

to get

$$x = \overbrace{a+b}^6 + \underbrace{c+d}_{24}$$

Horizontal lines and braces stretch to any length. They may also be nested. For example, to get

$$\overbrace{\overbrace{a}+b} + \underbrace{\underbrace{c}+d}$$

you would type

```
\[
\overbrace{\overbrace{a} + b} +
  \underbrace{\underbrace{c} + d}
\]
```

4.8.3   Dotless i and j

The two dotted letters in the English alphabet, i and j, should not be dotted when they are accented, since the dots would only get in the way. LaTeX provides the \imath and \jmath commands to produce these letters without dots in math mode. In other words, you should type \vec{\jmath} and \hat{\imath} instead of \vec{j} and \hat{i}, etc. The result will look like $\vec{\jmath}$ and $\hat{\imath}$.

4.8.4   Stacking Two Symbols

The \stackrel command allows you to stack one symbol above another. It takes two arguments: the first argument is printed in small type over the second argument. Example:

```
\[
X \stackrel{a}{\rightarrow} Y
 \stackrel{b}{\rightarrow} Z
\]
```

produces

$$X \stackrel{a}{\rightarrow} Y \stackrel{b}{\rightarrow} Z$$

In this, as in all math mode commands, the default sizes of the symbols may be overridden with the math typestyle-changing commands \textstyle, \displaystyle, etc., described in Sections 3.11.3 and 3.11.4. For example, to get the top symbol in the same font as the bottom symbol, you would enter

```
\[
X \stackrel{\textstyle a}{\rightarrow} Y
\stackrel{\textstyle b}{\rightarrow} Z
\]
```

and the result would be

$$X \stackrel{a}{\rightarrow} Y \stackrel{b}{\rightarrow} Z.$$

4.8.5 Customizing Spacing in Math Mode

One of the first rules to learn about math mode is that LaTeX controls the spacing—you don't. Most of the time LaTeX knows the proper spacing for mathematics, which is the reason for that rule. There may be situations, however, when you want to override LaTeX's spacing.

Four little spacing commands are provided that can be inserted into a formula to add more space, or to take some out:

\, thin space (| |)	\: medium space (| |)
\! negative thin space (||)	\; thick space (| |)

These commands add (or subtract) the amount of space shown between the bars. For example: $\int f(x)dx$ looks better like this: $\int f(x)\,dx$, which is produced by `$\int f(x) \, dx$`.

For information about how to change the vertical spaces above and below a displayed equation, see Section C.6 under the heading "Math" on page 234.

4.8.6 Bolding in Math Mode

The typestyle-changing commands \bf, \sl, etc., described in Section 3.4, work in math mode, but they only affect the letters and numbers; the symbols will not be bolded. (NOTE: Uppercase Greek letters are considered letters; lowercase Greek letters are considered symbols.) For example, `$\bf x - y = z $` would produce $\mathbf{x} - \mathbf{y} = \mathbf{z}$. Notice that the minus sign and the equals sign are not bold.

The \boldmath command is provided to make symbols as well as letters and numbers bold. *However, it can't be used in math mode.* Therefore, the \boldmath command must be placed outside of the math environment, and braces must be used to restrict its scope. Example:

```
{ \boldmath $ x - y = z $ }
```

This is one way to get the entire formula bolded: $\boldsymbol{x - y = z}$. Note that if the braces were left out of this example, all formulas from then on would come out bold, unless an \unboldmath command were used to switch back to the regular math italic font.

To get *some* of the symbols in a formula to come out bold is complicated, but possible because \boldmath only works outside of math mode. The \mbox command is the key. For example, in

```
\[
 x \mbox{\boldmath $- y$ } = z.
\]
```

the \mbox command puts you out of math mode, so you can use the \boldmath command, and the dollar signs put you back into math mode, where the bolding takes effect. Here the \boldmath command is only effective within the argument of the \mbox command. The resulting formula is:

$$x - y = z.$$

Whew!!

Exercise 4.8

1. Enter the following formulas into math.tex:

```
\[ \vec{\jmath} \stackrel{\mbox{def}}{=}
                          (j_1,\ldots,j_n) \]

\[ x = \overbrace{a + \overbrace{b+c}^2 + d}^1 \]

\[\int_0^\infty g(x) \, dx
 \mbox{ looks better than }
 \int_0^\infty g(x) dx\]
```

2. latex and prnt the file to see the results

Summary

- The accents in Table 4.9 are available in math mode.

- The \widehat and \widetilde accents can be stretched over more than one character, but not too far.

- Horizontal bars and braces, created with the \overline, \underline, \overbrace and \underbrace stretch as far as needed to span their arguments.

- Horizontal bars and braces may be nested, and they may be labelled by using sub- and superscripts.

- \imath and \jmath should be used to produce dotless i and j when these letters have accents.

- The \stackrel command stacks two symbols, the first symbol being placed on top of the second in smaller type.

- The \textstyle command may be used in the first argument to the \stackrel command to make the top symbol larger.

- The \,, \:, and \; commands may be used to add a small, medium, or thick space within a formula, and \! removes a thin space, or adds a "negative" thin space.

- The \boldmath command, which may only be used outside of math mode, causes all letters, numbers, and symbols in math formulas to be bolded within its scope.

Chapter 5

Rows and Columns

Setting up tables is often the most tedious task in preparing a report. With LaTeX you may find that it is exciting and fun. Once you learn to see a table in a logical way, LaTeX provides commands that eliminate the unpleasant jobs of calculating the width of columns and manually justifying columns.

Tables may be anchored to a certain point in the text and allowed to migrate or "float" to the best possible position in the document. For information on how to get floating tables, see Chapter 7.

5.1 Tabbing Environment

For simple alignment jobs of two or three lines, the `tabbing` environment, which works like the tabs on a typewriter, is sufficient. \= sets a tab stop, \> goes to a tab stop, and \\ must be at the end of each line except the last. Here is a simple example:

This is a line of text with a tab stop here
Second line: go to tab   see?
Now set new tabs one and two and three
Go to   one   two   three

can be produced with the following commands:

```
\begin{tabbing}
This is a line of text with a tab stop \= here \\
Second line: go to tab \> see? \\
Now set new tabs: \= one and \=two and \=three \\
Go to \>one \>two \>three
\end{tabbing}
```

The first \= entered on a line (or since the last \\) is always tab #1, the second is always #2, et cetera. When you use \> commands to go to tab stops, you always go to tab stops in *numerical order*, not necessarily to the next tab stop to the right. Some interesting results can be obtained this way. For example, if the text flows past a tab stop, then a \> command is given to go to that tab stop, you will get overlapping text. Also, if tabs are previously set, it is possible to set a new tab stop #1 that is to the right of subsequent tab stops.

Sometimes it is useful to set the tabs with a dummy line, but not to have that line printed. This is accomplished with the \kill command. Any line that ends with \kill instead of \\ will not be printed.

Exercise 5.1

1. Open a new file called table.tex and enter the required \documentstyle, \begin{document}, and \end{document} commands.

2. Now enter the following lines between the **\begin{document}** and \end{document}:

```
\begin{tabbing}
This is a dummy line \= to set up
                the \= tab stops \= \kill
Go to tab \>one;  go to \>two; go to \>three \\
Now I will reset tab stop one to be way out to
the right of the others like \= this.\\
Now go to tab \>one, go to \>two, go to \>three
\end{tabbing}
```

3. `latex` and `prnt` the file.

   NOTE: If LaTeX comes across an error and stops with a "?", remember—don't panic. It is probably caused by a simple typo in your input file. Type "x" and a carriage return to get back to the DOS prompt. Then check your file carefully for mistyped commands. If that doesn't help, refer to Appendix E for help.

4. Notice that the dummy line was not printed.

5. Note that after tab #1 is reset, it is way to the right of tab #2.

Summary

- The `tabbing` environment simulates the tab stops on a typewriter.

- `\=` sets a tab; `\>` goes to a tab.

- Every line but the last must end with `\\`.

- `\=` and `\>` commands always apply to tabs in numerical order, starting with #1 on each line.

- A line ending with `\kill` instead of `\\` will not be printed.

5.2 Tabular Environment

The `tabular` environment should be used for creating columns of text. It allows you to specify the number of columns needed, and the justification of each column. You can insert vertical and/or horizontal bars in the table. Headings may span more than one column.

The first step is to decide how many columns the table has and the justification of each column. Let us suppose that you have a table with four columns, one left-justified, one right-justified, one centered, and another right-justified, as in the table below:

Left-justified	Right-justified	Centered	Right-justified
one	two	three	four
1	2	3	4
i	ii	iii	iv

You would set this up by typing \begin{tabular}{lrcr}. As you can see below, \begin{tabular} takes a special argument that specifies the columns. There is one letter for each column, and the letter indicates the justification—l for left, r for right, and c for centered.

Once the columns have been defined as shown above, the basic rule is to separate columns with &, and end all rows, *except the last*, with \\. Therefore the table above would be typeset with the following commands:

```
\begin{tabular}{lrcr}
Left-justified & Right-justified
      & Centered & Right-justified \\
one        & two        & three    & four \\
1          & 2          & 3        & 4 \\
i          & ii         & iii      & iv
\end{tabular}
```

The ampersands are aligned here for clarity. It makes no difference whether or not they are lined up in the input.

Once the table has been typeset by LaTeX, it is considered as a solid box. In fact, it is treated exactly the same as a single letter. Therefore, unless the tabular environment is surrounded by blank lines it will be embedded into an adjacent paragraph, with sometimes alarming results.

5.2.1   Normal Tabular Spacing

LaTeX places a little horizontal space between tabular columns to prevent adjacent columns from running into each other. Likewise, it puts enough space between rows to prevent them from running together. Normally, this spacing should be just right. For cases where the spacing needs to be increased or decreased for a certain table, it is possible to alter the parameters that control `tabular` spacing. For more information, see Section C.6 under the heading "Tabular and Array" on page 237.

5.2.2 Added Vertical Space

To add a little vertical space after a row, you can specify a length in square brackets after the \\. In other words, the double backslash command, \\, can take an optional argument that is the amount of vertical space to add after the line ended by the \\. For example, to add a quarter of an inch after the first line, you would input

```
Left-justified & Right-justified & Centered
                      & Right-justified \\ [.25in]
```

(For other units of measure, see Section 6.6 on page 148.)
NOTE: If the first character on a line is "[", you need to put "{}[" to keep LaTeX from thinking the [is part of an optional argument to the \\ of the previous line.

5.2.3 Horizontal Lines

The \hline command inserts a horizontal bar between two lines. To put a horizontal bar after the first line, you would type

```
Left-justified & Right-justified & Centered
                      & Right-justified \\ \hline
```

You can also put a double horizontal bar with \hline\hline. The \hline command always follows the \\.

Sometimes you may want a horizontal line between two rows, but not all the way across the table. The \cline command lets you do this. You tell it the beginning column and the ending column in its argument. For example, if we wanted to put a horizontal line across columns 2 through 4 on the second row, we would type

```
one       & two      & three    & four \\ \cline{2-4}
```

and the table would look like this:

Left-justified	Right-justified	Centered	Right-justified
one		two	three	four
1		2	3	4
i		ii	iii	iv

and to make that a double line you would simply type
`\cline{2-4}\cline{2-4}`.
The `\cline` command also follows the `\\`.

5.2.4   Vertical Lines

Vertical bars are inserted by putting the vertical bar character, "|"
in the appropriate place in the argument to `\begin{tabular}` that
specifies the columns. For example, to get vertical lines on either side
of the first column, you would type

`\begin{tabular}{|l|rcr}`

Then the table would look like this:

Left-justified	Right-justified	Centered	Right-justified
one		two	three	four
1		2	3	4
i		ii	iii	iv

5.2.5   Headings over More than One Column

The `\multicolumn` command is used to enter a heading that spans more
than one column. It takes three arguments: the first is the number of
columns to span; the second is the justification of the heading; and the
third is the heading itself. Suppose we want a heading centered over
all four columns of the table we have been working with:

Overall Heading of Table

Left-justified	Right-justified	Centered	Right-justified
one		two	three		four

Overall Heading of Table

Left-justified	Right-justified	Centered	Right-justified
one		two	three		four
1		2	3		4
i		ii	iii		iv

We would add a line before the first row as follows:

```
\multicolumn{4}{c}{\bf Overall Heading of Table} \\
```

The "{4}" says to span 4 columns; the "{c}" says to center the heading, and the rest is obvious. We may also want a subheading spanning columns 1 and 2, and another one over columns 3 and 4. Then we would add the following line:

```
\multicolumn{2}{c}{\bf Columns 1 \& 2} &
          \multicolumn{2}{c}{\bf Columns 3 \& 4} \\
```

and the result would be

Overall Heading of Table

Columns 1 & 2		**Columns 3 & 4**	
Left-justified	Right-justified	Centered	Right-justified
one	two	three	four
1	2	3	4
i	ii	iii	iv

\multicolumn commands must be separated from each other, and from other column entries, with ampersands.

The \multicolumn command may also be used to override the justification of a column by making the first argument 1, and the second argument the desired justification. For instance, to make all the entries centered on the last line of the table, you could type

```
\multicolumn{1}{c}{i} & \multicolumn{1}{c}{ii} & iii &
    \multicolumn{1}{c}{iv} \\
```

This technique is useful for centering a heading over a non-centered column.

For another example, this is one way that this table would look nice:

Overall Heading of Table			
Left-justified	Right-justified	Centered	Right-justified
one	two	three	four
1	2	3	4
i	ii	iii	iv

And the LaTeX commands are:

```
\begin{tabular}{|l|r|c|r|} \hline
\multicolumn{4}{|c|}{\bf Overall Heading
                      of Table}\\ \hline
\multicolumn{1}{|c|}{Left-justified} &
 \multicolumn{1}{c|}{Right-justified} & Centered &
 \multicolumn{1}{c|}{Right-justified} \\ \hline\hline
one      & two     & three    & four \\ \cline{2-4}
1        & 2       & 3        & 4 \\
i        & ii      & iii      & iv \\ \hline
\end{tabular}
```

Note two things: First, the vertical bars have to be specified again in the second argument of the **\multicolumn** commands, otherwise they will be lost in that row. Second, the one time you need to put the \\ on the last line of the **tabular** environment is when you have an **\hline** after that row.

5.2.6 Paragraph Columns

There is one more type of column besides left-justified, right-justified, and centered, and that is a paragraph column. You specify a column of a certain width, and text entries in that column are formatted into paragraphs of that width. Paragraph columns are specified with a p, plus an argument that is the width desired. For example, p{3.in} would give a paragraph column three inches wide. p-columns can be combined with other types of columns in a table. We could replace the fourth column in our sample table with a p-column like this:

```
\begin{tabular}{|l|r|c|p{2.in}|} \hline
\multicolumn{4}{|c|}{\bf Overall Heading
    of Table}\\ \hline
\multicolumn{1}{|c|}{Left-justified} &
    \multicolumn{1}{c|}{Right-justified} &
    Centered &
    \multicolumn{1}{c|}{Paragraph}
    \\ \hline\hline
one & two & three & This is a paragraph on
row 1 of the table. \\ \cline{2-4}
1   & 2   & 3      & Here we are now on row 2
 and still going strong! \\
i   & ii & iii   & Row three is beginning
 to get boring, but the method is getting
 across. \\ \hline
\end{tabular}
```

and the result would be:

Overall Heading of Table			
Left-justified	Right-justified	Centered	Paragraph
one	two	three	This is a paragraph on row 1 of the table.
1	2	3	Here we are now on row 2 and still going strong!
i	ii	iii	Row three is beginning to get boring, but the method is getting across.

(NOTE: The spacing in the input file has no effect on the output. This example is lined up for clarity only.)

p-columns are very useful, but they have to be used with some discrimination. If you make a p-column very narrow, say less than an

inch and a half, it becomes very difficult for LaTeX to set text within
the column, since it tries to right justify. As a result, you may get large
gaps between words. So, it is best to use p-columns of two inches or
wider.

5.2.7   Inserting an Expression into Each Row

Sometimes it is useful to be able to insert an expression into every row.
For example, consider the following table:

Household Budget	
Item	% of Budget
Housing	50.0
Food	25.0
Toys	10.5
Pet Supplies	7.5
Clothes	5.25
Charity	1.75

It looks like a two-column table, but the second column is not
exactly right- or left-justified, and it's not centered, and it's not a
p-column. Oh no! What is it?! The second column can be seen itself as three columns: one column of right-justified numbers; one column of periods; and one column of left-justified numbers. If you used
`\begin{tabular}{|lrcl|}` and put each number in as three entries—
the portion left of the decimal point, the decimal point, and the portion
right of the decimal point—it would be close, but it would not be right.
It would look like this:

Household Budget		
Item	**% of** **Budget**	
Housing	50	. 0
Food	25	. 0
Toys	10	. 5
Pet Supplies	7	. 5
Clothes	5	. 25
Charity	1	. 75

There's too much space around the decimal point, right? Since you normally don't want columns running into each other, LaTeX inserts space around each column.

What you need is a way to insert the decimal point into each row without any space around it, and LaTeX provides the @-expression to allow you to do just that. Its argument is the expression to be inserted, and it goes in the argument to `\begin{tabular}`. The LaTeX commands that typeset this table properly are as follows:

```
\begin{tabular}{|l|r@{.}l|}\hline
\multicolumn{3}{|c|}{\bf Household
                    Budget} \\ \hline\hline
  & \multicolumn{2}{c|}{\bf \% of} \\
\bf Item & \multicolumn{2}{c|}{\bf Budget} \\ \hline
Housing & 50 & 0 \\
Food & 25 & 0 \\
Toys & 10 & 5\\
Pet Supplies & 7 & 5 \\
Clothes & 5 & 25 \\
Charity & 1 & 75 \\ \hline
\end{tabular}
```

Notice that you *don't* have to type the decimal point in each row; the @-expression does that for you, as well as removing the normal spacing between columns where it appears. The result is

Household Budget	
Item	% of Budget
Housing	50.0
Food	25.0
Toys	10.5
Pet Supplies	7.5
Clothes	5.25
Charity	1.75

5.2.8   Tables as Paragraphs

One more word about `tabular` environments. Once LaTeX has typeset the table, it has a rectangular block that is all one piece. It thinks of the table *just as if it were a word in a paragraph.* This means that a table set with `tabular` can very easily be stuck in the middle of a paragraph, with very strange results! The sure way to avoid this is to be certain to have blank lines above and below every `tabular` environment. Then the `tabular` will be its own paragraph. Now, paragraph indentation will apply to this paragraph, like all others, so if you want a tabular to appear on the left margin, you must precede it with a `\noindent` command. For example,

`\noindent\begin{tabular}`.....

See Section 2.5.1 for a description of the `\noindent` command.

5.2.9   Aligning Tables with Surrounding Text

It was suggested above that `tabular` environments be surrounded by blank lines to avoid having them typeset as part of another paragraph. Well, sometimes you may actually want a `tabular` within a sentence or paragraph, or you may want more than one `tabular` on one line. This can be done by omitting the blank lines. For example,

```
This is a line of text with a
\begin{tabular}{cc}
a & b \\
c & d
\end{tabular}
table in the middle of it.
```

would produce

This is a line of text with a $\begin{matrix} a & b \\ c & d \end{matrix}$ table in the middle of it. Notice that the table is vertically centered with the rest of the line. You may use an optional argument to **\begin{tabular}** to align the top or bottom of the table with the line also. Example:

```
A top-aligned table:
\begin{tabular}[t]{cc}
a & b \\
c & d
\end{tabular}
and a bottom aligned table:
\begin{tabular}[b]{cc}
a & b \\
c & d
\end{tabular}
```

would produce

A top-aligned table: a b and a bottom aligned table: $\begin{matrix} a & b \\ c & d \end{matrix}$

  c d

Exercise 5.2

1. Look at the following table:

PORTABLE HOOK-ON CHAIRS		
BRAND	Graco	Strolee
MODEL	Tot Loc Chair	Meal Mate
PRICE	$23	$31
OVERALL JUDGEMENT	Satisfactory	Satisfactory
WEIGHT	7 lb. 9 oz.	6 lb. 8 oz.

2. How many columns does it have, and what justifications? (AN-SWER: Three columns: left-justified, centered, and right-justified.)

3. Taking this into consideration, and noting the positions of the vertical bars, open `table.tex` and add a `\begin{tabular}` command, (with the proper argument), to set up this table.

4. Now, forgetting for the moment the heading line "**PORTABLE HOOK-ON CHAIRS**," begin making entries into the table. Remember, column entries should be separated by **&**, and each line should end with \\. Don't forget the `\hline` commands to insert horizontal lines.

5. After you have filled in the table, put an `\end{tabular}` at the end.

6. `latex` and `prnt` to see how you did. Make adjustments if necessary.

7. Now look at the heading row. How many columns does it span, and what is its justification? (ANSWER: Three columns, centered.)

8. Now get back into `table.tex` and enter a `\multicolumn` command right after the `\begin{tabular}` command, and remember that the first argument is the number of columns spanned, the second argument is the justification, and the third argument is the text itself.

9. `latex` and `prnt` now and see the results. Did you remember to reenter the vertical bars in the `\multicolumn` command?

10. Compare your input with this:

```
\begin{tabular}{|l|cr|}\hline
\multicolumn{3}{|c|}{\bf PORTABLE
                     HOOK-ON CHAIRS} \\ \hline\hline
\bf BRAND & \bf Graco & \bf Strolee \\ \hline
\bf MODEL & Tot Loc Chair & Meal Mate \\ \hline
\bf PRICE & \$23 & \$31 \\ \hline
\bf OVERALL JUDGEMENT & Satisfactory &
                       Satisfactory \\ \hline
\bf WEIGHT & 7 lb. 9 oz. & 6 lb. 8 oz. \\ \hline
\end{tabular}
```

11. Notice that the \bf commands only apply to the entry they are in. This brings out the fact that each column entry is treated as a complete group by LaTeX.

12. Study the table below:

THE CATECHISM
Q. What are we by nature?
A. We are part of God's creation, made in the image of God.
Q. What does it mean to be created in the image of God?
A. It means that we are free to make choices: to love; to create, to reason, and to live in harmony with creation and with God.
Q. Why then do we live apart from God and out of harmony with creation?
A. From the beginning, human beings have misused their freedom and made wrong choices.

13. How many columns are there in this table, and what justifications? (ANSWER: Two columns, left-justified and p-column.)

14. Get into **table.tex** again, and input a **\begin{tabular}** command to create this table. (You have a choice of estimating the width of the second column or measuring it.) Then try your hand at filling out the table, ending it with **\end{tabular}**.

15. **latex** and **prnt** the file and see how you did, making adjustments, and rerunning if necessary.

16. Compare your input with this:

```
\begin{tabular}{|lp{3.in}|}\hline
\multicolumn{2}{|c|}{\bf THE CATECHISM} \\ \hline
Q. & What are we by nature? \\
A. & We are part of God's creation, made in the
      image of God. \\ [3mm]
Q. & What does it mean to be created in the image
      of God? \\
A. & It means that we are free to make choices:
      to love; to create, to reason, and to live in
      harmony with creation and with God. \\ [3mm]
Q. & Why then do we live apart from God and out
      of harmony with creation? \\
A. & From the beginning, human beings have
      misused their freedom and made
      wrong choices. \\ \hline
\end{tabular}
```

17. One more example to study:

Chapter Summary

Title	Pages	First Sentence
1. Becoming Parents	3–20	Pregnancy is a state of becoming: an unborn baby is becoming a person capable of life outside the safe, protective, and totally sufficient environment of the mother's body, and a man and woman are becoming parents.
2. Pregnancy	21–40	The normal and healthy process of pregnancy brings profound physical and emotional growth for the expectant mother and similar psychological changes for the expectant father.
3. Prenatal Care	41–50	Thorough prenatal care helps assure the birth of a healthy baby.

18. What character appears in the same position in every row, and could be put into an @-expression? (ANSWER: The "–" in the PAGES column.)

19. Now, not counting the "–", but counting the numbers on either side of it separately, how many columns are in the table, and what justifications? (ANSWER: Four columns—left, right, left, and p.)

20. So, using an @-expression, make up a \begin{tabular} for this table.

21. Enter the first heading line, using one \multicolumn command.

22. Enter the second heading line, using three \multicolumn commands. Remember, the information under "**PAGES**" is really two columns. \multicolumn commands should be separated by ampersands if they are on the same row.

23. Now fill out the rest of the table.

24. **latex** and **prnt** the file, making corrections if needed. Compare your input with this:

```
\begin{tabular}{lr@{--}lp{2.in}}
\multicolumn{4}{c}{\bf Chapter
          Summary}\\ \hline\hline
\multicolumn{1}{c}{\bf Title} &
   \multicolumn{2}{c}{\bf Pages} &
       \multicolumn{1}{c}{\bf First
          Sentence} \\ \hline
\bf 1. Becoming Parents & 3 & 20 & Pregnancy
     is a state of becoming: an unborn baby
     is becoming a person capable of life
     outside the safe, protective, and
     totally sufficient environment of the
     mother's body, and a man and woman are
     becoming parents. \\
\bf 2. Pregnancy & 21 & 40 & The normal and
     healthy process of pregnancy brings
     profound physical and emotional growth
     for the expectant mother and similar
     psychological changes for the expectant
     father. \\
\bf 3. Prenatal Care & 41 & 50 & Thorough prenatal
     care helps assure the birth of a healthy
     baby. \\ \hline
\end{tabular}
```

Summary

- The **tabular** environment is for formatting tables, or vertically aligning text.

- A completed **tabular** is considered by LaTeX to be one piece, like a letter or word in a paragraph.

- The \begin{tabular} command takes a mandatory argument in which the number and justification of columns is specified.

- Columns are specified as follows:

  l   left justified
  r   right justified
  c   centered
  p{*length*}   paragraph column

- The \begin{tabular} command takes an optional argument that specifies the vertical alignment of the table with surrounding text: t for top-alignment, b for bottom.

- Column entries are separated with &; all rows but the last are ended with \\. (When there is a horizontal line at the very bottom of a **tabular**, the last line must end with \\ \hline.)

- The \hline command following a \\ adds a horizontal line spanning the entire table after a row.

- Adding a length in square braces after the \\, such as \\ [.25in], adds vertical space after a row. (If the first character on a new row is "[", input it as "{}[" to avoid confusing LATEX.)

- To place vertical bars in the table, use the | character in the appropriate positions around column-specifying letters in the argument to \begin{tabular} command.

- The \cline command following a \\ places a horizontal line across a subset of columns in a table. Its argument gives the range of columns to be spanned.

- The \multicolumn command allows an entry to span multiple columns. It is useful for headings in tables. It takes three arguments: the first is the number of columns to be spanned, the second is the justification, and the third is the text.

- \multicolumn turns off vertical bars, so they must be re-specified in the second argument to the \multicolumn command with |.

- Row and column spacing as well as line thickness may be adjusted by changing formatting parameters.

5.3   Array Environment

The array environment works exactly the same as the tabular environment, except that the entries are processed in math mode. Therefore, it should be used for vertically aligning mathematical formulas or expressions. The array environment may only be used in math mode.

In the array environment, as in tabular, you specify the number of columns needed, and the justification of each column in an argument to \begin{array}. In this argument there is one letter for each column, and the letter indicates the justification—l for left, r for right, and c for centered.

You can insert vertical bars in the table by placing the | character in the appropriate positions around the letters in the argument to \begin{array}. Horizontal bars are created using an \hline or \cline command following a \\. Entries may span more than one column.

Once the columns have been defined as described above, the basic rule is to separate columns with &, and end all rows, *except the last*, with \\. Consider the following array:

$$
\begin{array}{rcl}
a+b+c & a+b+c & a+b+c \\
a+b & a+b & a+b \\
a & a & a
\end{array}
\tag{5.1}
$$

It has three columns, one right-justified, one centered, and one left-justified. These are the commands for typesetting this array:

```
\begin{equation}
 \begin{array}{rcl}
    a + b + c & a + b + c & a + b + c \\
    a + b     & a + b     & a + b \\
    a         & a         & a
```

```
\end{array}
\end{equation}
```

Notice that the array is within a math environment. If you try to use it outside of math mode, you will get an error. The equation number, provided by the **equation** environment, is vertically centered with the array. Remember that the spacing in the input does not affect the spacing in the output. The ampersands in this example are lined up for clarity. As in the **tabular** environment, \hline puts a horizontal line across the row, and \cline puts a horizontal line across a range of columns. If you wanted horizontal and vertical bars in the array, like this:

$$
\begin{array}{|r|c|l|}
\hline
a+b+c & a+b+c & a+b+c \\ \hline
a+b & a+b & a+b \\ \hline
a & a & a \\ \hline
\end{array}
\tag{5.2}
$$

you would edit the input to look like

```
\begin{equation}
 \begin{array}{|r|c|l|}\hline
    a + b + c & a + b + c & a + b + c \\ \hline
    a + b     & a + b     & a + b \\ \hline
    a         & a         & a \\ \hline
  \end{array}
\end{equation}
```

You may have more than one **array** environment in a formula. For example,

$$
\begin{array}{c} x \\ y \\ z \end{array} -
\begin{array}{c} x_1 \\ y_1 \\ z_1 \end{array} =
\begin{array}{c} x-x_1 \\ y-y_1 \\ z-z_1 \end{array}
$$

is obtained by typing

```
\[
\begin{array}{c} x \\ y \\ z \end{array}  -
 \begin{array}{c} x_1 \\   y_1 \\ z_1 \end{array} =
  \begin{array}{c} x-x_1 \\ y-y_1 \\ z-z_1 \end{array}
\]
```

in which each array has one centered column.

LaTeX automatically vertically centers the **array** environment with the rest of the formula. An optional argument to
`\begin{array}` may be used to align the top or bottom of the array with the formula. Example:

$$
\begin{array}{c}
x_1 \\
y_1 \quad\quad x - x_1 \\
x \;-\; z_1 \;=\; y - y_1 \\
y \quad\quad\quad z - z_1 \\
z
\end{array}
$$

would result from the following commands:

```
\[
\begin{array}[t]{c} x \\ y \\ z \end{array}  -
  \begin{array}[b]{c} x_1 \\    y_1 \\ z_1 \end{array} =
    \begin{array}{c} x - x_1 \\
                  y - y_1 \\ z - z_1 \end{array}
\].
```

The **array** environment may also be used to typeset a system of equations that has one overall equation number, such as

$$
\begin{array}{rcl}
x & = & y + z + p \\
y - y' & = & x - z \\
z & = & x - y
\end{array}
\tag{5.3}
$$

by inputting

```
\begin{equation}
 \begin{array}{rcl}
  x & = & y + z + p\\
y - y' & = & x - z\\
  z & = & x - y
 \end{array}
\end{equation}
```

Note that the middle column may contain any relation symbol—it does not have to be "=".

Please refer to Section 4.6.2 for information about using large delimiters with arrays.

5.3.1 Adjusting Array Spacing

LaTeX sets up arrays with spacing rules similar the rules used in the `tabular` environment. You may change the spacing between rows or columns, and the default line thickness for horizontal lines created by the `\hline` and `\cline` commands and vertical lines created by | commands in the argument to `\begin{array}`. See Section C.6 under the heading "Tabular and Array" on page 237 for more information.

Exercise 5.3

1. Add the following lines to `math.tex`:

    ```
    This is an example of an array:

    \[
    X = \left\| \begin{array}{ccc}
                \pi & x & y+2 \\
                \mu & y & z \\
                \delta & z & p
                \end{array}
        \right\|
    \]
    ```

2. `latex` and `prnt` to see the resulting array.

Summary

- The `array` environment works like the `tabular` environment.

- The `array` environment is for vertically aligning formulas.

- The `\array` environment may only be used within math mode.

- The \begin{array} command takes a mandatory argument in which the number and justification of columns is specified.

- Columns are specified as follows:

  l   left-justified
  r   right-justified
  c   centered

- The \begin{array} command takes an optional argument that specifies the vertical alignment of the table with surrounding text: t for top-alignment, b for bottom.

- Column entries are separated with &; all rows but the last are ended with \\. (When there is a horizontal line at the very bottom of an array, the last line must end with \\ \hline.)

- Adding a length in square braces after the \\, such as \\ [.25in], adds vertical space after a row. (If the first character on a new row is "[", input it as "{}[" to avoid confusing LATEX.)

- The \hline command following a \\ adds a horizontal line spanning the entire array after a row.

- To place vertical bars in the table, use the | character in the appropriate positions around column-specifying letters in the argument to \begin{array} command.

- The \cline command following a \\ places a horizontal line across a subset of columns in an array. Its argument gives the range of columns to be spanned.

- Column and row spacing, as well as line thickness, are user-adjustable.

5.4 Eqnarray Environment

In fact, systems of equations like Equation 5.3 on page 130 are so common that LaTeX provides a special environment just for them. The **eqnarray** environment is like a specialized **array** environment where there are three predefined columns: one right-justified, one centered, and one left-justified. In fact, **eqnarray** is limited to this arrangement of columns.

Additionally, **eqnarray** automatically puts an equation number on each line of the environment. This is not possible with the **array** environment. The **\nonumber** command allows you to omit the number on selected lines in **eqnarray**. To label an **eqnarray** line for cross-referencing, place the **\label** command just before the \\, or at the end of the final line, which has no \\.

The **\begin{eqnarray}** command, which does not take any argument, puts LaTeX into math mode as well as setting up the environment. So you do not have to be in math mode to use **eqnarray**. Let's set the previous example in **eqnarray** and see how it differs from **array**:

$$x = y + z + p \tag{5.4}$$
$$y - y' = x - z \tag{5.5}$$
$$z = x - y \tag{5.6}$$

This is produced by these commands:

```
\begin{eqnarray}
  x & = & y + z + p \label{line1} \\
y - y' & = & x - z \label{line2} \\
  z & = & x - y \label{line3}
\end{eqnarray}
```

We could eliminate the equation number on the second equation as follows:

$$x = y + z + p \tag{5.7}$$
$$y - y' = x - z$$
$$z = x - y \tag{5.8}$$

by typing

```
\begin{eqnarray}
  x & = & y + z + p \label{line1} \\
y - y' & = & x - z \nonumber \\
  z & = & x - y \label{line3}
\end{eqnarray}
```

Note that the use of \hline and | to produce vertical bars is not appropriate in the **eqnarray** environment.

5.4.1   Eqnarray* Environment

The **eqnarray*** environment is identical to **eqnarray** except that it produces no equation numbers. In other words,

$$
\begin{aligned}
x &= y + z + p \\
y - y' &= x - z \\
z &= x - y
\end{aligned}
$$

would be produced by typing

```
\begin{eqnarray*}
  x & = & y + z + p\\
y - y' & = & x - z \\
  z & = & x - y
\end{eqnarray*}
```

5.4.2   Breaking Lines in Formulas

The **eqnarray** (and **array**) environment(s) may be used to set a formula that doesn't fit on one line. For example,

$$
\begin{aligned}
x &= a + b + c + d + e + f \\
  &\; + g + h + i + \cdots
\end{aligned}
$$

can be set by the following commands:

```
\begin{eqnarray*}
x & = & a + b + c + d + e + f \\
  &   & + g + h + i + \cdots
\end{eqnarray*}
```

5.4.3 Extra Space Between Eqnarray Rows

To add vertical space after a certain row, you may use the optional argument to the \\ command. For example,

```
\begin{eqnarray*}
x & = & a + b + c + d + e + f \\ [.25in]
  &   & + g + h + i + \cdots
\end{eqnarray*}
```

would produce the following result:

$$x \ = \ a+b+c+d+e+f$$

$$+g+h+i+\cdots$$

Additionally, LaTeX allows you to adjust a parameter that adds space after every row in **eqnarray** environments. See Section C.6 under the heading "Math" on page 234 for more information.

Exercise 5.4

1. Add the following lines to `math.tex`:

```
\subsection*{Use of eqnarray
    for multi-line formulas}
Here is a formula containing equations~\ref{eq2}
and~\ref{eq3}.
\begin{eqnarray}
x & = & a + b + c + d + e + \nonumber \\
  &   & f + g + h \label{eq2} \\
y & = & z \label{eq3}
\end{eqnarray}
```

2. Notice that the \\ is left off of the last line. This is important in eqnarray. Also note the placement of the labels.

3. latex *twice* and prnt to see the results.

4. Edit the eqnarray and put \\ after the last line.

5. latex and prnt again an notice what bad thing happens.

Summary

- \begin{eqnarray} puts you into math mode, as well as beginning the environment. Therefore, you may not use eqnarray within math mode.

- \begin{eqnarray} doesn't take an argument, since the columns are pre-defined to be r, c, and l.

- Each line of the environment is automatically numbered.

- The \label command goes before the \\, except on the last line.

- To turn off the number on a line, put \nonumber before the \\.

- The eqnarray* environment works just like eqnarray except it produces no numbers.

Chapter 6

Customization

Up till now you have been learning all the things LaTeX can do for you, LaTeX's way. Now you will see some ways to make LaTeX do things more the way you have in mind.

6.1 Page Breaks

LaTeX is very capable of managing page breaks if you don't want to bother with it. But there may be times when you need some control over where a page stops or starts.

6.1.1 Forcing a Page Break

The simplest thing is to force a page break at a certain place in the text. The `\clearpage` command does exactly that—it forces LaTeX to start a new page immediately.

For example, you may have a paragraph followed by a table, and you may want the table to start at the top of the next page. You would place a `\clearpage` command between the paragraph and the table as follows:

```
. . .  and here is the end of the paragraph.
\clearpage
\begin{tabular}{lll}
. . .
```

The rest of the page after the paragraph would be blank space, and the tabular would start the next page.

6.1.2   Suggesting a Page Break

The \pagebreak and \nopagebreak commands allow you to suggest, strongly, or not so strongly, that a page break should occur or not occur at a given point. They both take an optional argument, which is an integer between 1 and 4, with 1 being a mild suggestion ranging to 4 being a strong suggestion. Used without the optional argument, \pagebreak insists on a page break, and \nopagebreak insists on there not being a page break.

If \pagebreak and \nopagebreak are used between paragraphs, they apply to that point. If they are used within a paragraph, they apply *immediately after the current line*. This way you can force a page break in the middle of a paragraph, and the last line on the current page will still be flush-right, and the first line on the next page will not be indented.

Be warned, however, that sometimes LaTeX will not obey a \nopagebreak command. It will only put so much text on a page, and you can't force more. Therefore, it is best not to try to jam too much text onto a page.

In the following example, \nopagebreak is used to avoid a page break after the first paragraph, and \pagebreak is used to put the page break in the middle of the second paragraph.

```
This is paragraph one. It goes on blah, blah, blah.
It may be near the bottom of the page, but we don't
want a page break immediately after it, so what
can we do?

\nopagebreak
Now this is paragraph two. We want the page break
to occur after this line, \pagebreak so we put the
command in the line somewhere. \LaTeX\ starts the
next line of the paragraph on the next page.
```

6.1.3 Keeping Text Together on a Page

Sometimes you may know that you want a certain portion of text on a page together. The **\samepage** command keeps all text *within its scope* on the same page. You must use braces to define the scope of the **\samepage** command, or you will inhibit all page breaks from the current point on!

LaTeX may need extra coercion to make it obey the **\samepage** command if it thinks a page too full. In this case use **\nopagebreak** between paragraphs (after blank lines) within the scope of the **\samepage**, and use **\pagebreak** commands where you do want the page to break.

Example:

```
{\samepage This is a block of text that should come
all together on one page. It is enclosed in the scope
of the command with braces. \LaTeX\ will obey this
command if this block of text is not at the very end
of a full page.}
```

And here is an example of how to use \samepage, \pagebreak, and \nopagebreak together:

```
...the end of a paragraph before the block of text in
question.
\pagebreak[4]

{\samepage Now here is the block of text to be kept
together. We have already suggested that \LaTeX\ might
break the page before this block.

\nopagebreak
This command will inhibit page breaks between
paragraphs within the block of text. At the
end of the block of text, there will be a
closing brace.}
\pagebreak[2]

And this paragraph may start on a new page....
```

In this example, the user prefers that the page break occur *before* the block of text, so the optional argument of 4 is used with the `\pagebreak` command there. If that is not possible, LATEX may break the page after the block of text.

Exercise 6.1

1. Open a new file called `custom.tex` with the article style, and type in a paragraph. Make the paragraph long enough to fill 3 or 4 lines after LATEX processes it.

2. Now `latex` and `prnt` the file to see how the paragraph is split into lines.

   NOTE: In this or any other exercise, if LATEX comes across an error and stops with a "?", remember—don't panic. It is probably caused by a simple typo in your input file. Type "x" and a carriage return to get back to the DOS prompt. Then check your file carefully for mistyped commands. If that doesn't help, refer to Appendix E for help.

3. Pick a spot in the middle of the paragraph and insert a `\clearpage` command there.

4. `latex` and `prnt` the file. Notice that the paragraph is cut short at the very point where the `\clearpage` was inserted. The next word is indented on the next page. In fact it is as if the `\clearpage` not only starts a new page, but it splits the paragraph into two paragraphs.

5. Now replace the `\clearpage` command with a `\pagebreak` command.

6. `latex` and `prnt` again. Notice that the page break occurs at the end of the line containing the command, and the next line of the paragraph is on the next page, not indented. The paragraph is still one paragraph, but is split over two pages.

Summary

- **\clearpage** forces a page break immediately. If placed within a paragraph, it breaks up the paragraph.

- **\pagebreak** puts a page break at the end of the current line if used within a paragraph. If used between paragraphs, it causes a page break immediately.

- **\nopagebreak** inhibits a page break at the end of the current line if used within a paragraph. If used between paragraphs, it inhibits a page break at that point.

- **\pagebreak** and **\nopagebreak** may be used with an optional argument, an integer between 1 and 4, with 1 meaning a mild suggestion, and 4 meaning a strong suggestion.

- **\nopagebreak** will not work if it tries to make LATEX jam too much text on a page.

- **\samepage** keeps text within its scope on the same page. The command and the text must be enclosed in braces.

- **\samepage** may work better if it is used together with **\pagebreak** commands where breaks are o.k., and **\nopagebreak** commands between paragraphs within the block of text.

6.2 Line Breaks

We have seen that LATEX automatically breaks up a paragraph into lines in a very capable way. What, however, if the user wants to control where the line breaks occur? In fact, there are three different ways of doing this.

The **\linebreak** and **\nolinebreak** commands are analogous to the **\pagebreak** and **\nopagebreak** commands. They cause or inhibit a line break at the point within the paragraph that they occur. They may be used with an optional argument, an integer between 1 and 4, with 1 meaning a mild suggestion, and 4 meaning a strong suggestion.

The text just before the `\linebreak` command will be right-justified, which may result in a lot of extra white space between words.

Two other commands, `\newline`, and `\\`, cause a new line to start, and do not justify the previous text. The `\\` command takes an optional argument that specifies vertical space to be added before the new line. For example, `\\[.25in]` would leave .25 inch of extra space and then start the new line. If the text immediately following a `\\` command starts with "[" then put "{}[" so LaTeX doesn't think an optional argument is coming.

The `\\` command also has a special asterisk form, `\\*` that inhibits a page break before the new line.

6.2.1   Inhibiting Line Breaks: Special Cases

Since it is not good to have a line break in certain places, such as the space between a first initial and a last name, LaTeX provides the ˜ command to produce a space but not allow a line break there. You should get into the habit of typing names as follows:

```
J.~Hahn      A.~Einstein
W.~Mozart    J.~S.~Bach
```

Another instance where ˜ should be used is in a reference to a section, figure, table, or equation in a report, such as `Section~1`, or `Table~15`. Also, it may be used in number ranges: `Verses 1 to~4`.

The `\mbox` command also inhibits line breaks in its argument. Therefore, a word in the argument to an `\mbox` command, such as `\mbox{explorer}`, will not be hyphenated.

Exercise 6.2

1. Get into the file `custom.tex` and take any `\clearpage` and `\pagebreak` commands out of the paragraph that you typed in.

2. Now put a `\linebreak` command after about the fourth word in the paragraph.

3. `latex` and `prnt` the file. Notice that the first line of the paragraph has way too much white space (unless you typed some *very* long words).

4. Now change that `\linebreak` to `\newline`.

5. Add the following paragraph after the first paragraph:

```
Here is an example of the use of the optional argument
to the double-backslash command\\[.5in]
to leave blank space after a line.
```

6. `latex` and `prnt` again, and notice that the first line is shortened, and word spaces are the normal size.

7. Also notice the vertical space created by the optional argument to \\.

Summary

- The `\linebreak` and `\nolinebreak` commands force or inhibit a line break within a paragraph.

- Text before a `\linebreak` command is right-justified.

- `\linebreak` and `\nolinebreak` take an optional argument, an integer from 1 to 4, with 1 meaning a mild suggestion and 4 meaning a strong suggestion.

- The `\newline` command causes a line break within a paragraph. Text before the command is not right-justified.

- The \\ command also causes a line break within a paragraph, and text before the command is not right-justified. \\ takes an optional argument, a length, which cause extra vertical space to appear before the new line.

- The ~ command produces a space where a line break is inhibited.

- The argument of an `\mbox` command will never be broken across lines. It may be used to keep LaTeX from hyphenating a word.

6.3   Centering

To horizontally center one or more lines of text, use the **center** environment. End each line to be centered, except the last one, with \\. Use the optional argument to \\ to insert extra vertical space after a line.

Many environments whose end result is a typeset box of a certain size, such as **minipage**, **tabular** and others, may be centered using the **center** environment.

Exercise 6.3

1. Get into the file **custom.tex**. Enter the following lines right after the \begin{document}:

   ```
   \begin{center}
   A PARAGRAPH \\ [.25in]
   by A. U. Thor
   \end{center}
   ```

2. Now enter the following lines after the first paragraph:

   ```
   \begin{center}
   \begin{tabular}{|cc|}\hline
   a & b \\
   c & d \\ \hline
   \end{tabular}
   \end{center}
   ```

3. **latex** and **prnt** the file. Notice that the lines before the first paragraph are centered, and there is space between them. Notice also that the little table is centered on the page.

Summary

- The **center** environment is used for centering text.

- Each line of the environment, except the last, must end with \\.

- The \\ may be used with an optional argument, a length, to add extra space after the line.

- A `tabular` environment may be centered by placing it within the `center` environment.

6.4 Making Text Flush

For making text flush against the left margin, with a ragged right margin, the `flushleft` environment is provided. The `flushright` environment puts text flush against the right margin, and leaves the left margin ragged. Each line in both of these environments, except the last, must end with \\. The optional argument may be used with the \\.

As with the `center` environment, many environments whose end result is a typeset box of a certain size, such as `minipage`, `tabular` and others, may be placed within the `flushleft` and `flushright` environments.

Exercise 6.4

1. Add the following lines just after the \begin{document} in `custom.tex`:

   ```
   \begin{flushright}
   \today
   \end{flushright}

   \begin{flushleft}
   A few short \\
   lines to be \\
   set against \\ [.1in]
   the left margin
   \end{flushleft}
   ```

2. `latex` and `prnt` the file. Notice the date set against the right margin, and the lines you entered that are against the left margin.

Summary

- The `flushleft` environment places text flush against the left margin.

- The `flushright` environment places text flush against the right margin.

- Each line but the last in both environments must be ended with \\.

- The optional argument to \\ may be used to add extra vertical space after a line.

- `tabular` and some other environments may be placed inside a `flushleft` or `flushright` environment.

6.5   Vertical and Horizontal Space

We have learned that, in most cases, the spacing in LaTeX output is automatically determined. Pressing the space bar a bunch of times does not create any horizontal space, and pressing the return key a bunch of times does not create any vertical space. So how do you create extra horizontal and vertical space where you want it?

We know that the \\ command, used with an optional argument of a length, adds extra space after a line. But \\ can't be used everywhere. Not, for example, between paragraphs, or after a `tabular` or `center` environment.

The `\hspace` command, whose argument is a length, adds horizontal space of that length at the current point. If the `\hspace` is the first thing on a line, it will be ignored. Use `\hspace*`, with the same argument, to add space at the very beginning of a line.

The `\vspace` command, whose argument is also a length, adds vertical space of that length at the current point. If it falls in the middle of a paragraph, the space is added *after the current line*. If the `\vspace` is the first thing on a page it will be ignored. To add vertical space as the first thing on a page use `\vspace*` with the same argument.

Three standard vertical spacing commands are provided as alternatives to using \vspace. The \bigskip command adds a "big" vertical space; \medskip adds a "medium" vertical space; and \smallskip adds a "small" vertical space.

Exercise 6.5

1. Add the following line to custom.tex right after the \begin{document}:

   \vspace*{1.in}

2. Add a \vspace{.25in} command right after the first center environment to separate the heading from the paragraph.

3. Replace the [.1in] in your flushleft environment with \bigskip.

4. Now on that same line, put an \hspace*{.25in} command at the very beginning, so that line now looks like:

   \hspace*{.25in} set against \\ \bigskip

5. latex and prnt the file, and notice the differences from the previous run.

Summary

- The \hspace command, whose argument is a length, such as {.5in}, inserts a horizontal space of that length at the current point on the line.

- If \hspace is the first thing on a line, it will be ignored. Use \hspace* to insert space at the very beginning of a line.

- The \vspace command, whose argument is also a length, inserts a vertical space of that length. If \vspace is used within a paragraph, the space will come after the current line. Otherwise, it comes immediately.

- If \vspace is the very first thing on a page, it will be ignored. Use \vspace* to insert space at the very top of a page.

- The \bigskip, \medskip, and \smallskip commands insert a "big", "medium", or "small" vertical space. If used within a paragraph, the space comes after the current line.

6.6   Lengths

Now that we have touched the subject of creating horizontal and vertical space of a desired length, it would be good to discuss the different ways of expressing length to LaTeX. LaTeX understands the following units of length:

Units	Abbreviation	Example
Inches	in	.25in
Centimeters	cm	1cm
Millimeters	mm	5mm
Points[a]	pt	30pt
Picas[b]	pc	2pc
"Em"s[c]	em	2.5em
"Ex"s[d]	ex	2ex

[a] A point is 1/72 of an inch.
[b] A pica is twelve points.
[c] An "em" about the width of a capital "M" in the current font.
[d] An "ex" is the height of a small "x" in the current font.

Lengths can be positive, like 5cm, or negative, like -.25in. Since LaTeX can understand many different units of length, it is imperative that you remember to put units on all length specifications—even a length of 0. It is a common mistake to forget the units on a 0 length, and it causes LaTeX to stop with an error.

You may also express length in terms of a known length parameter. For example, to create a horizontal space that is two times the paragraph indentation, you could say \hspace{2\parindent}. (See Section C.6 for a definition of \parindent.)

6.6.1 Expandable Lengths

Sometimes it is useful to have a length that acts like a spring, expanding until it hits something that holds it back. Consider, for example, the following line:

This is on the left.   This is on the right.

    To create such a line, you need a command that will insert enough space to push the right-hand sentence all the way to the right margin. It would be very inconvenient to have to measure the space. What if there were a length that would expand like a spring to push the text all the way to the right?

    There is such a length and it is called \fill. In other words, you could produce the line above with the following commands:

```
\noindent This is on the left.\hspace{\fill}This
is on the right.\\
```

The \fill length command may be used any time a length is required. For example, it may be used in the argument to \hspace, or \vspace, or in the optional argument to \\.

6.6.2 Length Commands

You may define your own length variables in LaTeX by using the \newlength command. It takes one argument, which is the name of the new variable. The name should begin with a backslash. For example,

```
\newlength{\mylength}
```

defines a length variable called \mylength.

    The \setlength command allows you to set a length variable to a certain length value. It takes two arguments: the first is the name of the variable; and the second is the length value. For example,

```
\setlength{\mylength}{2.in}
```

sets \mylength equal to 2 inches. Now an \hspace command that has \mylength as an argument, such as

\hspace{\mylength}

would be equivalent to saying \hspace{2in}. The \setlength command may be used to change existing lengths, as well as setting new ones.

To add a certain amount to a length, use the \addtolength command. It too takes two arguments: the name of the length variable, and the amount to add to the variable. For example,

\addtolength{\mylength}{.5in}

would add .5 inch to \mylength, making it equal to 2.5 inches. To add a negative length you would type

\addtolength{\mylength}{-1in}

and that would change \mylength from 2.5 inches to 1.5 inches.

And one more useful command allows you to set a length variable equal to the width of some text. It is the \settowidth command, and it takes two arguments: the first is the name of the length variable; the second is the text whose width the length variable will be set to. For example,

\settowidth{\mylength}{As wide as this phrase}

would set \mylength to be ... as wide as that phrase!

All of the length commands described may be applied to existing lengths, or to new lengths defined with the \newlength command. Some of LaTeX's existing lengths should only be changed in the preamble, so be cautious when using these commands. See Appendix C for information on LaTeX's length parameters, what they are, and when they should and should not be changed.

Exercise 6.6

1. Edit custom.tex and change the \vspace* command right after the \begin{document} to look like the following:

```
\vspace*{2.5cm}
```

2. Add the following lines just before the \end{document} command:

```
Let's set the paragraph indentation to 0.
Don't forget the units!
\setlength{\parindent}{0pt}

\newlength{\playtime}
\setlength{\playtime}{2.in}
Here is some space:\hspace{\playtime}
and here is more text.

\addtolength{\playtime}{72pt}

Three inches!\hspace{\playtime}of blank space.

\setlength{\playtime}{\fill}

Three \hspace{\playtime} little \hspace{\playtime}
words.\\

Now let's set playtime equal to the width of a phrase!
\settowidth{\playtime}{How long is this? }

\hspace*{\playtime}  This long!\\
How long is this?  This long!
```

3. latex and prnt custom.tex. Notice that when \playtime was equal to \fill it pushed the words as far apart as possible.

4. Also notice that setting \playtime equal to the length of a phrase can be used to align text on adjacent lines.

Summary

- LATEX understands the following units of length: inches (`in`), centimeters (`cm`), millimeters (`mm`), points (`pt`), picas (`pc`), ems (`em`), and exs (`ex`).

- Lengths may be positive or negative.

- Lengths must always be expressed in terms of units.

- Lengths may be expressed in terms of other lengths.

- `\fill` is a length that stretches to fill as much space as possible, pushing surrounding text away from itself.

- The `\newlength` command defines a new length variable. It takes one argument: the name of the length variable.

- The `\setlength` command sets a length variable to a specified length. Its first argument is the name of the variable, and its second argument is the length desired.

- The `\addtolength` command adds a specified length to a length variable. Its first argument is the name of the variable, and its second argument is the length to add.

- The `\settowidth` command sets a length variable named in its first argument to the width of some text in its second argument.

6.7 Boxes

A box is an element that LATEX treats just as if it were a single letter. We learned in Section 5.2 that a `tabular` environment creates a box. Certain other environments and commands also create boxes. A box will never be split across lines. And a box may be inserted into a paragraph, or set as a paragraph alone.

6.7.1   One Line of Text Inside a Box

The \mbox command described in Section 4.7 puts its argument into an invisible box. The box is exactly the width of the text in the argument. The \makebox command, which takes text as an argument, allows you to set that text in an invisible box that is any width. It takes two optional arguments: the first is a length specifying the width of the box (which is the length of the text if no optional argument is given); the second is a letter indicating the justification of the text in the box—l for left-justified, or r for right-justified (default is centered). For example:

```
\makebox[2.in][l]{text in a box} text
  following the box
```

would yield

text in a box   text following the box

but

```
\makebox[2.in][c]{text in a box} text
  following the box
```

would yield

        text in a box   text following the box.

Notice that \makebox commands may be used to vertically align text in adjacent lines. Use \makeboxes of the same width on adjacent lines, and the text after the boxes will align. Example:

```
\begin{flushleft}
\makebox[3.in][l]{This is the first line.} It
  has two sentences.\\
\makebox[3.in][l]{Second line.} This text
  lines up.
\end{flushleft}
```

would produce

This is the first line.   It has two sentences.
Second line.   This text lines up.

The \fbox command works like \mbox, except that the box surrounding the text in the argument is visible:

```
\fbox{text in a visible box}
```

gives

text in a visible box .

The \framebox command is analogous to the \makebox command except that the box around the text in its argument is visible. framebox takes two optional arguments: the first is a length specifying the width of the box; and the second is the justification of the text within the box—l for left-justified, and r for right-justified. (Defaults are the same as for \makebox above.) For example:

```
\framebox[2.in][l]{text}
```

gives

text

but

```
\framebox[2.in][r]{text}
```

gives

text .

6.7.2   Adjusting Frame Thickness and Spacing

The thickness of the frame drawn by an \fbox command or a \framebox command may be adjusted by the user. Also, the amount of white space left between the frame and the text may be changed. See Section C.6 under the heading "Boxes" on page 238 for more information on this topic.

6.7.3   Wrapping Text Inside a Box

The \parbox command allows you to specify the width of an invisible box in which some text will be set. It takes two arguments: the first is the width for the box; and the second is the text itself. The resulting box is treated just as a single letter or word. For example,

```
This is a line of text.\hspace{.5in}
\parbox{1.in}{This is some text inside
a narrow parbox.}
```

would give

This is a line of text.
This is some text that is set inside a narrow parbox.

Notice that the resulting box is vertically centered with the surrounding text. An optional argument to the \parbox command allows you to align the top or bottom line of the box with the surrounding text: t for the top line; b for the bottom line. For example,

Now a slightly wider box aligned on its bottom line.
This is a line of text. This is a box AND aligned on its top line.

results from

```
This is a line of text.
\parbox[t]{1.in}{This is a box aligned
on its top line.} AND
\parbox[b]{1.5in}{Now a slightly wider
box aligned on its bottom line.}
```

A \framebox command may be used with the \parbox in its argument to produce a frame around the parbox. For example,

This is a line of text. | This is a box aligned on its top line | AND | Now a slightly wider box aligned on its bottom line.

could be produced by

```
This is a line of text.
\framebox{\parbox[t]{1.in}{This is a box aligned
on its top line.}} AND
\framebox{\parbox[b]{1.5in}{Now a slightly
wider box aligned on its bottom line.}}
```

The \parbox command is intended for relatively short blocks of text. For longer blocks of text, or text containing other commands and arguments, the minipage environment should be used. The arguments to the minipage environment are the same as those for \parbox: one optional argument specifies the vertical alignment of the box; and one mandatory argument specifies the width. The text is between \begin{minipage} and \end{minipage} instead of in braces. In other words, to set the previous example with the minipage environment, you would type

```
This is a line of text.
\begin{minipage}[t]{1.in}
This is a box aligned
on its top line.
\end{minipage} AND
```

```
\begin{minipage}[b]{1.5in}
Now a slightly wider box aligned
on its bottom line.
\end{minipage}
```

and the result looks like this:

Now a slightly wider
box aligned on its bot-
This is a line of text. This is a box AND tom line.
aligned on its
top line.

6.7.4 Boxes Filled In with Ink

The \rule command allows you to create a rectangular shape that is
filled in with ink. You specify its width and height in two mandatory
arguments. The \rule command is most commonly used to create a
very long, thin rectangle, or a rule. It may be used to create an invisible
rule, called a strut, by making the width or height equal to zero.

The lower left corner of the rule is placed on the baseline of the
current line by default. The rule can be raised by placing a length value
in an optional argument. A negative value in the optional argument
lowers the rule. Examples:

Here is a square rule: ∎   \rule{.2in}{.2in}
A horizontal rule: ——————   \rule{1.in}{.02in}
A raised horizontal rule: ————   \rule[.1in]{1.in}{.02in}

A vertical rule: | \rule{.02in}{.25in}
A lowered vertical rule: | \rule[-.25in]{.02in}{.25in}

Now, let's put a rule all the way across the page.

———————————————————————————————————————

Notice that .02 inches makes a line of a nice width.

6.7.5   Raising a Box Full of Text

The \raisebox command allows you to set a line of text in a box and
raise the box above the baseline. The default size of the box is the size
of the text, but two optional arguments allow you to specify any height
above the baseline and depth below the baseline for the box to extend.
For an example of a box that is the default size,

```
Raise the following text:
\raisebox{.25in}{Text in a box.}
```

would give you

                              Text in a box.

Raise the following text:

In the following example, the box will extend above the letters of
the text, and extend below the baseline:

```
Here is a line of text.\\
\raisebox{0.in}[.25in][.25in]{Text in a tall,
   deep box.}\\
Here is another line of text.
```

would look like this:

Here is a line of text.

Text in a tall, deep box.

Here is another line of text.

Notice how much space is left between the lines for the tall box, even
though most of the box is invisible. If the first argument is negative,
the box will be lowered.

6.7.6   Saving a Box of Text for Later Use

You may save some text, such as a company name or logo, in a box
for later use or for repeated use. There are three basic steps to this

operation: 1) pick a name for the box; 2) put the text in the box; and 3) use the box. The box will only be printed on step three.

To accomplish step one, pick a name that is not already a command name or the name of another box. Then use the **\newsavebox** command, with the name as the argument. To initialize a box named **\mybox**, for example, type

\newsavebox{\mybox}

Note that the box's name must begin with a backslash, since it is like a new command.

There are two ways to put text into the box. The **\sbox** command puts text into the box and makes the box the same width as the text. It has two arguments: the first is the name of the box; and the second is the text. For example, we could define **\mybox** as follows:

\sbox{\mybox}{This is some text}

The **\savebox** command allows you to define the box to be any width, and justify the text any way within the box. It works like the **\makebox** command, taking optional arguments for the width of the box and the justification of the text. An example of using **\savebox** to define **\mybox** would be:

\savebox{\mybox}[3.in][c]{Centered Text}

Now whenever **\mybox** is used, a 3-inch space with the centered words "Centered Text" will appear. Now, the easy part is using the box. Simply type **\usebox** with the name of the box as an argument: **\usebox{\mybox}**, for example, will cause the box to be printed.

Exercise 6.7

1. Open the file custom.tex and enter the following lines:

   Let us show how makebox and framebox compare.

   \begin{flushleft}
   A box without a frame:

```
\makebox[3.in][c]{Text in a box.}\\
A box with a frame:
    \framebox[3.in][c]{Text in a box.}\\ [.25in]
Put a \fbox{box} around a word!\\ [.25in]
\end{flushleft}


We will now make a parbox:
\parbox{1.5in}{This is a set of words in a
thin column. I tried to pick small words.}

Let's do something interesting, like a list,
inside a minipage:

\begin{minipage}[t]{2.in}
\begin{itemize}
\item This is the first item in the list
\item Notice how the items wrap around in
a two inch column
\item We can put another list next to this
one, too
\end{itemize}
\end{minipage}
    \hspace{.5in}
\begin{minipage}[t]{2.in}
\begin{enumerate}
\item See? These two lists are side by side,
since there is no blank line between them to
start a new paragraph.
\item So now you know how to put two lists
side by side!
\end{enumerate}
\end{minipage}
Now let's experiment with
\raisebox{.25in}{raising text} above the baseline,
and \raisebox{-.25in}{lowering text}
below the baseline.
```

> I now want to define a box. I name it by saying
> \newbox{\funbox}, which prints nothing. I define
> it by saying, \sbox{\funbox}{This is the text in
> my fun box}, which also prints nada. Now I can
> use the box by typing \usebox{\funbox}, and voila!
> I can also use it again as many times as I want:
> \usebox{\funbox}, \usebox{\funbox}, etc.

2. I know that's a lot of typing, but really, do it!

3. latex and prnt the file, and you will see how the commands work!

Summary

- The contents of a one-line box are never split between two lines.

- Finished boxes are treated just as a single letter or word would be treated.

- The \mbox command puts the text in its argument into an invisible box. The box's width is the width of the text. (\mbox may also be used within math mode to set words or phrases in paragraph mode.)

- The \makebox command puts a line of text in a box. Optional arguments specify the width of the box, and justification of the text. The text goes in a mandatory argument. (If the optional arguments are omitted, the box is the size of the text. If only the first optional argument is given, the text is centered.)

- The \framebox command works just the same as \makebox except it draws a frame around the box.

- The \fbox command works just like \mbox, putting a line of text in a box the width of the text, and it also draws a frame around the box.

- Frame thickness and the spacing between the frame and the text may be user-specified.

- The `\parbox` command is used for setting paragraphs of text in a box. The width of the box and the text itself are given in two mandatory arguments. An optional argument gives the vertical justification of the resulting box, if other than the default— centered.

- The `minipage` environment sets text and other structures in a box. The width of the box is in a mandatory argument. The contents of the box are given within the environment. An optional argument specifies the vertical justification of the resulting box, if other than the default—centered.

- The `\rule` command produces a rectangular box that is filled in with ink. Two mandatory arguments give the width and height of the box. An optional argument gives a distance to raise the rule.

- The `\raisebox` command is for raising text above the baseline. Two mandatory arguments give the distance to raise the box, and the text. Two optional arguments give the height (above the baseline) and the depth (below the baseline) of the box. The default height and depth of the box is that of the text.

- Text may be set in a box and then used repeatedly using the `\newsavebox`, `\sbox`, `\savebox` and `\usebox` commands.

- `\newsavebox` initializes the name of the box. Its argument must be a name that is not already a command or box name. The name must start with a backslash.

- `\sbox` saves the text in its second argument in the box specified in its first argument. The box is the size of the text. It doesn't print anything.

- `\savebox` saves the text in its second mandatory argument in the box specified in its first mandatory argument. The width of the box and the justification of the text are given in two optional arguments. (If the optional arguments are omitted, the box is the size of the text, and if only the first optional argument is given, the text is centered.) It doesn't print anything.

- The \usebox command, with a box name as its argument, causes the contents of the named box to be printed.

6.8 Margins

Each of LaTeX's pages is made up of a header, a body, and a footer. The body is where the text you type will go. The footer may contain the page number and other information. The information in the header depends on the document style, and may be customized by the user. (See Section 3.14 for details on headers and footers.) The default margins are defined by the document style.

To set the left and right margins as you want them, you specify the distance from the left edge of the paper to the left margin, then you specify the width of the text. The space left over on the right side of the paper will be the right margin.

Setting the top and bottom margins is more involved, since space must be left for the header and footer. Starting from the top, first the distance from the top edge of the paper to the top of the header is set. Then the height of the header is set, and the separation between the header and the body. Next is the height of the body, followed by the distance from the bottom of the body to the bottom of the footer. The space left over at the bottom of the page is the bottom margin.

All of the dimensions above may be set with the \setlength command. The first argument to \setlength is the name of a parameter, and the second argument is the desired length of that parameter. The parameter names and their meanings are listed below:

\oddsidemargin- for odd pages if two-sided printing, or for all pages if one-sided printing—the distance from the left edge of the paper to the left margin minus 1 inch. In other words, \setlength{\oddsidemargin}{0in} would make a 1-inch left margin.

\evensidemargin- for even pages if two-sided printing, the distance from the left edge of the paper to the left margin minus 1 inch. In other words, `\setlength{\evensidemargin}{0in}` would make a 1-inch left margin.

\textwidth- the text width. `\setlength{\oddsidemargin}{0in}` and `\setlength{\textwidth}{6.5in}`, for example, would make a 1-inch right margin.

\topmargin- the distance from the top edge of the paper to the header minus 1 inch. In other words,
`\setlength{\topmargin}{0in}` would make a 1-inch top margin. (If space is left for a header, and the header is blank, the top margin will appear larger.)

\headheight- the height of the header.

\headsep- the space between the header and the body.

\textheight- the height of the body of text.

\footskip- the distance from the bottom of the body to the bottom of the footer.

\footheight- the height of the footer. (Within `\footskip`.)

The parameters listed above should be fixed for the duration of a document. They must be set *before* the `\begin{document}` in order to avoid anomalies. Any commands between the `\documentstyle` and the `\begin{document}` are called the *preamble*. All LaTeX commands that produce text are illegal in the preamble, but `\setlength` is a command that is legal.

Please see Section C.6 under the heading "Page Formatting" on page 227 for more examples.

Exercise 6.8

1. Look at the last print out of `custom.tex` and notice that in article style the left margin is about 1.5 inches wide, and the width of

the text is about 5.5 inches. Change the margins by putting the following lines before the \begin{document}:

```
\setlength{\oddsidemargin}{0.in}
\setlength{\textwidth}{6.5in}
```

2. It is difficult to tell what the \headheight and \headsep are set to without looking into the style guide itself. One method of getting the desired top and bottom margins is to set \topmargin to 0 inches, and \textheight to what you want. Then, after seeing what the resulting top margin is, you can adjust \topmargin. So, type the following lines just before \begin{document}:

```
\setlength{\topmargin}{0.in}
\setlength{\textheight}{8.5in}
```

3. latex and prnt the file. Notice that the left and right margins are now 1 inch.

4. If you think the top margin is too large, then set \topmargin to a negative value to move the text up higher. For example, \setlength{\topmargin}{-.5in} would raise it by one half-inch. If it is too small, set \topmargin to a positive value to move the text down. The height of the body of text will not be changed by these changes.

5. After adjusting the \topmargin, latex and prnt again and note the effect.

Summary

- The margins and other aspects of page layout are normally determined by the document style, but they can be customized.

- The page is made up of three elements:

  - The header, its contents set by document style but customizable

- The body, which contains the text

- The footer, which may contain the page number and other information

- Parameters that specify the margins, and the width and height of the text, are set with the `\setlength` command. Its first argument is the name of the parameter, and its second argument is the desired length.

- The left margin is determined by the `\oddsidemargin` parameter for odd pages (all pages if one-sided printing), and `\evensidemargin` for even pages. The length given should be 1 inch less than the desired length, since a value of 0 inches gives a 1-inch margin.

- The page is divided vertically into the following dimensions:

  - `\topmargin`, which is the distance from the top edge of the paper to the header minus 1 inch. (Setting `\topmargin` to 0 inch makes a 1-inch margin.)

  - `\headheight`, the height of the header.

  - `\headsep`, the distance between the header and the body.

  - `\textheight`, the height of the body of text.

  - `\footskip`, the distance between the bottom of the body and the bottom of the footer. `\footheight` is the height of the footer.

6.9   Underlining Text

LaTeX was written with the idea that emphasized text should be italicized, *not* underlined, but if you need to underline text, you may use the `\underline` command to do so. The text to be underlined goes in the argument. For example,

```
This is some \underline{text to be underlined}.
```

would produce

This is some <u>text to be underlined</u>.

NOTE: LaTeX will not perform line-breaks on underlined text. Therefore, you must do line breaks by hand as follows:

```
\underline{Here is some text to be underlined
that extends} \newline
\underline{over more than one line!}
```

and the result is

<u>Here is some text to be underlined that extends</u>
<u>over more than one line!</u>

Chapter 7

Floating Objects

Positioning figures and tables properly in a document can be a difficult job. A figure or table must appear near the place in the text where it is referenced, but since it is a fixed size, it may not always fit on the same page as the reference. And when significant changes are made to the text, the whole puzzle of placing the figures and tables has to be solved over again. Unless, that is, you are using LaTeX.

7.1 What Is a Float?

LaTeX can handle figures and tables as objects that "float" in the document. In other words, they don't have a fixed position. You "tie" the floating object to its reference in the text, and then LaTeX finds the best possible position for it. LaTeX places a floating object (or float) as soon as possible after the text refers to it—if not on the same page, on the following page. This is a very useful feature, since you usually do not know how the text will fall on the page until after you process. If you had to place the floats manually, it would be a long process of trial and error.

A single float may never be split across pages, but more than one float may appear on a page. Floats may appear on the page with text, or on a page of floats only. For floats that are on a page with text, there are three possible positions: top of the page, bottom of the page, or immediately following the reference. You may specify your order of preference for any combination of these four positioning options.

Summary

- Floats are objects, such as figures and tables, that don't have a fixed position in the document.

- LaTeX automatically finds the best position for a float.

- Floats are output as soon after the reference as possible.

- The position of the float may be specified as top of a page, bottom of a page, in the middle of a page immediately following the reference, or on a page of floats.

- Floats are never split across pages.

7.2   Figures

The `figure` environment is provided for inputting floating figures. It may contain vertical space for pasting in a picture, other figure contents, and one or more captions, and is entered right after the reference in the text. Depending on which positioning options you specify, the figure may actually come out at that point, or later on the same page, or on the following page.

The positioning options are given in an optional argument to `\begin{figure}`. They are specified as follows:

t   top of a page of text

b   bottom of a page of text

h   here, where the environment appears in the text

p   on a page of floats (not a text page) .

You may specify any one of these options, or any combination of them. A combination of options gives LaTeX a choice of positions, but the order in which they appear is your order of preference. In other words,

```
\begin{figure}[t]
\vspace{1.in}
\end{figure}
```

would tell LaTeX to start a 1-inch-high figure at the top of a text page, but

```
\begin{figure}[tbh]
\vspace{1.in}
\end{figure}
```

would give LaTeX the option of starting it at the top or bottom of a page, or right at the point where the `figure` environment is entered. LaTeX would pick the best place for the figure, trying first the top of a page, then the bottom, then where the `figure` environment falls in the text. If the optional argument is omitted, the default order of preference is `[bthp]`.

LaTeX will be more efficient at figure placement the more options you give it. In fact there is danger in saying `\begin{figure}[h]`, because, depending on the size of the figure, and the current position on the page, it may be impossible to place the figure at the location of the `figure` environment. If this happens, then this figure, and all other figures and tables after it, will be stuck in LaTeX's memory until a `\clearpage` command, the end of a chapter, or the end of the document is encountered, at which time all unprocessed floats will be flushed out.

7.2.1 Captions and Figure Numbering

The `\caption` command, with the text of the caption as an argument, places a caption on the figure, and also assigns a figure number one greater than the previous figure. For example, to create a 2-inch-high figure with a caption, you would type

```
\begin{figure}[tbh]
\vspace{2.in}
\caption{This is the caption of the figure.}
\end{figure}
```

Figure 7.1: This is the caption of the figure.

The result would be 2 inches of white space, and then the caption above:

Any number of captions may be placed within a figure. Each `\caption` command increments the figure counter. Two figures may be tied together on a page by placing them both within one `figure` environment, such as:

```
\begin{figure}[p]
\vspace{2.in}
\caption{This is one figure.}
\vspace{2.in}
\caption{This is another figure that will always
be on the same page as the one just above.}
\end{figure}
```

The `\vspace{2.in}` commands may be replaced with the contents of the figures.

7.2.2   Labelling and Referencing Figures

A `\label` command *following the* `\caption` *command* may be used to label a figure. The figure may then be referenced in the text with the `\ref` command. Here is an example:

```
This is some text that refers to Figure~\ref{figone}.
...
\begin{figure}[tbh]
\vspace{2.in}
\caption{Figure referenced in the text.}
\label{figone}
\end{figure}
```

7.2.3   The List of Figures

You can automatically create a List of Figures containing all the figure numbers and captions in the document and their page numbers by using the \listoffigures command. It should be placed after the \tableofcontents command, or wherever you want the List of Figures to come out.

During each run, LaTeX writes the information for the List of Figures in a special auxiliary file called the .lof file. The .lof file has the same first name as the .tex file, but it has .lof for an extension.

Now, since LaTeX only looks through the document once for each run, it can't know what page Figure 22 in Chapter 10 is on when it is making the List of Figures, (since it hasn't even gotten to Chapter 1 yet). It simply reads the .lof file that was written on the previous run to produce the List of Figures for this run. Therefore the List of Figures always has the information from the previous run, and you must LaTeX twice without changing your file in between to get the most current information in the List of Figures. If that is too confusing, just remember to LaTeX twice for a List of Figures that is completely up to date.

7.2.4 Alternate Entry to the List of Figures

LaTeX allows you to put an entry into the List of Figures that is different from the caption. The \caption command takes an optional argument, before the mandatory argument, which is the entry for the List of Figures. For example,

```
\begin{figure}
\vspace{2.in}
\caption[Entry for the L.O.F.]{Caption on the figure}
\end{figure}
```

would make a figure with the caption "Caption on the figure", but it would make an entry in the List of Figures that would be "Entry for the L.O.F.".

7.2.5 Adding a Line to the List of Figures

Sometimes you may want an entry in the List of Figures when you don't have a \caption command. For example, an figure may have sub-captions as in the following:

```
\begin{figure}
\vspace{2.in}
\begin{center}
a. Sub-caption number one.
\end{center}
\vspace{2.in}
\begin{center}
b. Sub-caption number two.
\end{center}
\caption{Overall caption for figure}
\end{figure}
```

and those sub-captions would not make an entry in the List of Figures since they aren't produced by \caption commands.

The \addcontentsline command can force an entry in the List of Figures (or the Table of Contents, or the List of Tables). It takes three arguments. The first argument tells LaTeX whether to add the entry to the Table of Contents, the List of Figures, or the List of Tables. For making an entry to the List of Figures, this argument should be lof. (See Section 3.5.4 on page 49 for making an entry to the Table of Contents, or Section 7.3.4 on page 179 for an entry to the List of Tables.)

The second argument to \addcontentsline should be figure when it is being used to make an entry to the List of Figures. The third argument to \addcontentsline is the text of the entry. Therefore, to create entries in the List of Figures for the two sub-captions above, your figure environment should contain two \addcontentsline commands as follows:

```
\begin{figure}
\vspace{2.in}
\begin{center}
a. Sub-caption number one.
\end{center}
\addcontentsline{lof}{figure}{a. Sub-caption number one.}
\vspace{2.in}
\begin{center}
b. Sub-caption number two.
```

```
\end{center}
\addcontentsline{lof}{figure}{a. Sub-caption number two.}
\caption{Overall caption for figure}
\end{figure}
```

Note that the \addcontentsline command must fall on the same page with the sub-captions in order for the correct page numbers to appear in the List of Figures.

Exercise 7.1

1. Open a new file called floats.tex, and enter the following lines:

   ```
   \documentstyle[12pt]{report}
   \begin{document}
   \tableofcontents
   \listoffigures
   \chapter{FIGURES AND TABLES}
   This is an experiment with floating objects.
   ```

2. Now enter the following figure:

   ```
   \begin{figure}[tbh]
   LEAVING BLANK SPACE FOR PASTE-UP
   \vspace{3.in}
   \caption{Make up your own caption.}
   \label{fig:makeup}
   \end{figure}
   ```

3. Now put a sentence of text with a reference to the figure as follows:

   ```
   In Figure~\ref{fig:makeup} we show that
   blank space is very interesting.
   ```

   (Make sure the sentence is not inside the figure environment!)

4. Place an \end{document} command at the end of the file.

5. `latex` the file twice (for the List of Figures) and `prnt` it. NOTE: If LaTeX comes across an error and stops with a "?", remember— don't panic. It is probably caused by a simple typo in your input file. Type "x" and a carriage return to get back to the DOS prompt. Then check your file carefully for mistyped commands. If that doesn't help, refer to Appendix E for help.

6. Notice the entry in the List of Figures, and the figure on the first page of text.

7. Now change the `\caption` command so that it has an optional argument, such as:

```
\caption[Put this in the L.O.F.]{Make up
your own caption.}
```

8. `latex` twice again and `prnt`.

9. Notice how the entry in the List of Figures has changed.

Summary

- Figures are entered using the `figure` environment.

- The `figure` environment takes an optional positioning argument.

- The position specifiers are: t for top of a page of text; b for bottom of a page of text; h for here on a page of text; and p for on a page of floats. (NOTE: p doesn't mean this will be the only float on the page.)

- The position specifiers may be given in any combination and in your order of preference.

- The `\caption` command, with the text of the caption as its mandatory argument, places a figure number and caption on the figure.

- An optional argument to the `\caption` command places an alternate entry into the List of Figures.

- Any number of captions may be put in one **figure** environment. Each \caption command increments the figure counter.

- One **figure** environment will never be split across pages.

- The \label command following the \caption command labels the figure. The figure can then be referenced with a \ref command.

- The \listoffigures command creates a List of Figures containing all figure numbers, captions, and page numbers.

- To get the most current information in the List of Figures, you must LaTeX twice without changing your input file.

7.3 Tables

The **table** environment is provided for inputting tables. It works just as the **figure** environment. The environment, which may contain vertical space for pasting in a table, or tabular data, and a caption, is entered right after the reference in the text. Depending on which positioning options you specify, the table may actually come out at that point, or later on the same page, or on the following page.

The positioning options are given in an optional argument to \begin{table}. They are specified the same way as in figures. See Section 7.2 above. As with figures, the more placement options you give LaTeX the more efficient it will be at table placement.

7.3.1 Captions and Table Numbering

The \caption command, with the text of the caption as an argument, places a caption on the table, and also assigns a table number, which is one greater than the previous table. For example, to create a 4-inch-high table with a caption, you would type

```
\begin{table}[tbh]
\vspace{4.in}
\caption{This is the caption of the table.}
```

```
\end{table}
```

The result would be four inches of white space, and then the following caption:

Table 7.1: This is the caption of the table.

As with figures, any number of captions may be placed within a table. Each \caption command increments the table counter. Two tables may be tied together on a page by placing them both within one table environment, such as

```
\begin{table}[p]
\vspace{2.in}
\caption{This is one table.}
\vspace{2.in}
\caption{This is another table that will always
be on the same page as the one just above.}
\end{table}
```

The \vspace{2.in} commands may be replace with the contents of the tables.

7.3.2   Labelling and Referencing Tables

A \label command following the \caption command may be used to label a table. The table may then be referenced in the text with the \ref command. Here is an example:

```
This is some text that refers to Table~\ref{tabone}.
...
\begin{table}[tbh]
\vspace{2.in}
\caption{Table referenced in the text.}
\label{tabone}
\end{table}
```

7.3.3 The List of Tables

You can automatically create a List of Tables containing all the table numbers and captions in the document and their page numbers by using the \listoftables command. It should be placed after the \listoffigures command, or wherever you want the List of Tables to come out.

During each run, LaTeX writes the information for the List of Tables in a special auxiliary file called the .lot file. The .lot file has the same first name as the .tex file, but it has .lot for an extension.

As with the List of Figures, since LaTeX only looks through the document once for each run, it can't know what page Table 22 in Chapter 10 is on when it is making the List of Tables, (since it hasn't even gotten to Chapter 1 yet). It simply reads the .lot file that was written on the previous run to produce the List of Tables for this run. Therefore the List of Tables always has the information from the previous run, and you must LaTeX twice without changing your file in between to get the most current information in the List of Tables.

If all that is too confusing, just remember to LaTeX twice for a List of Tables that is completely up to date.

7.3.4 Alternate Entry in the List of Tables

LaTeX allows you to put an entry into the List of Tables that is different from the caption. The \caption command takes an optional argument, before the mandatory argument, which is the entry for the List of Tables. For example,

```
\begin{table}
\caption[Entry for the L.O.T.]{Caption on the table itself}
\vspace{2.in}
\end{tables}
```

would make a table with the caption "Caption on the table itself," but it would make an entry in the List of Tables that would be "Entry for the L.O.T.".

7.3.5   Adding a Line to the List of Tables

Sometimes you may want an entry in the List of Tables when you
don't have a \caption command. For example, a table may have sub-
captions, as in the following:

```
\begin{table}
\begin{center}
a. Sub-caption number one.
\end{center}
\vspace{2.in}
\begin{center}
b. Sub-caption number two.
\end{center}
\vspace{2.in}
\caption{Overall caption for table}
\end{table}
```

and those sub-captions would not make an entry in the List of Tables
since they aren't produced by \caption commands.

The \addcontentsline command can force an entry in the List of
Tables (or the Table of Contents, or the List of Figures). It takes three
arguments. The first argument tells LaTeX whether to add the entry
to the Table of Contents, the List of Figures, or the List of Tables.
For making an entry to the List of Tables, this argument should be
lot. (See Section 3.5.4 on page 49 for making an entry to the Table
of Contents, or Section 7.2.4 on page 173 for an entry to the List of
Figures.)

The second argument to \addcontentsline should be table when
it is being used to make an entry to the List of Tables.

The third argument to \addcontentsline is the text of the entry.
Therefore, to create entries in the List of Tables for the two sub-captions
above, your table environment should contain two \addcontentsline
commands as follows:

```
\begin{table}
\begin{center}
a. Sub-caption number one.
```

```
\end{center}
\addcontentsline{lot}{table}{a. Sub-caption number one.}
\vspace{2.in}
\begin{center}
b. Sub-caption number two.
\end{center}
\addcontentsline{lot}{table}{a. Sub-caption number two.}
\vspace{2.in}
\caption{Overall caption for table}
\end{table}
```

Note that the \addcontentsline command must fall on the same page with the subcaptions in order for the correct page numbers to appear in the List of Tables.

Exercise 7.2

1. Open the file **floats.tex** and add the following lines just before the \end{document}:

   ```
   Now let's see what a table looks like, o.k?
   Here comes Table~\ref{tab:veryoff}:
   \begin{table}[tbh]
   \caption{Very official columns of numbers.}
   \label{tab:veryoff}
   \begin{tabular}{cc}
   1.1 & 1.2 \\
   5.4 & 2.6 \\
   0.2 & 4.7 \\
   0.3 & 3.6
   \end{tabular}
   \end{table}
   What happens if we type some more text
   right after the table?
   ```

2. Now place a \listoftables command right after the \listoffigures command.

3. **latex** the file twice and **prnt**.

4. Notice that the **table** environment did not disturb the paragraph. (The two sentences on either side of the **table** environment are one paragraph, since there is no blank line separating them.)

5. Also notice that the caption may be placed before the body of the table, or after it.

6. Go back into **floats.tex** and change the optional arguments on the **figure** and **table** environments to [p].

7. **latex** and **prnt** again.

8. Notice that the figure and table moved to the next page in order to be on a page of floats (no text).

Summary

- Tables are entered using the **table** environment.

- The **table** environment takes an optional positioning argument.

- The position specifiers are: t for top of a page of text; b for bottom of a page of text; h for here on a page of text; and p for page of floats. (NOTE: p doesn't mean this will be the only float on the page.)

- The position specifiers may be given in any combination and in your order of preference.

- The \caption command, with the text of the caption as its argument, places a table number and caption on the table.

- An optional argument to the \caption command places an alternate entry into the List of Tables.

- Any number of captions may be put within one **table** environment. Each \caption command increments the table counter.

- One **table** environment will never be split across pages.

- The \label command, following the \caption command labels the table. The table can then be referenced with a \ref command.

- The \listoftables command creates a List of Tables containing all table numbers, captions, and page numbers.

- To get the most current information in the List of Tables, you must LaTeX twice without changing your input file.

7.4 Floats in Two-Column Format

When the twocolumn document style option is in effect, figures and tables may occupy one column, or they may extend across both columns. The figure and table environments, when used in two-column format, produce floats that occupy one column, and these floats are treated the same way as in one-column format.

To produce figures and tables that extend across both columns in two-column format, use the figure* and table* environments. They are treated like the figure and table environments, except that the optional placement arguments for here ("h") and bottom of the page ("b") are not available.

7.5 Rules for Float Placement

LaTeX has internal rules that determine how many floats may appear on a page, and what percentage of a page may be occupied by floats, and other specifications as well. The rules may be adjusted by the user, if desired. See Section C.6 under the heading "Floats" on page 235 for a complete list of adjustable float placement parameters.

Chapter 8

Preparing Large Documents

8.1 Splitting the Document into Small Files

When working with a large document, it is nice to be able to split the document into several small files. This gives the advantage of easier and faster editing. LaTeX allows you to split your document into many files, and then allows you to process one portion of the document at a time, taking into account the numbering in other portions, plus cross-referencing to other portions.

8.2 The Root File

Each document has only one `\documentstyle` command and one `\begin{document}` and one `\end{document}`. These commands go in what is called the *root* file. Other information that controls how the document will be processed also goes in the root file. The main text of the document goes into other files.

The two important elements that control how the document will be processed are as follows: 1) a list of *all the files* in the document; and 2) a list of the files to be processed *in this run*. The `\includeonly` command, whose argument is the list of files to be processed this run, goes in the preamble (before the `\begin{document}` command). The list of all the files in the document goes after the \begin{document}, and consists of one \include command for each file. The argument of each \include command is the name of a file. Each \include command causes LaTeX to start a new page.

The \include and \includeonly commands assume that the extension for each file name is .tex; so, unless the extension is something other than .tex, you may give the first names only.

For example, if you have a report with three chapters and two appendices, you may want to put each chapter into a separate file and name the files ch1.tex, ch2.tex, ch3.tex, ap1.tex and ap2.tex. Then your root file (say it's called root.tex) might look like this:

```
\documentstyle{report}
\includeonly{ch2,ch3}
\begin{document}
\include{ch1}
\include{ch2}
\include{ch3}
\appendix
\include{ap1}
\include{ap2}
\end{document}
```

This run will only process chapters two and three, because they are the only ones in the argument to \includeonly. Notice that all the files are still listed in \include commands. Assuming that you have already processed the other chapters at an earlier time, and therefore the auxiliary files for them (ch1.aux, ap1.aux and ap2.aux) exist, LaTeX will do two things for you:

- First it will number pages, sections, figures, tables, and equations as if the other files are being processed. In other words, it will know that this is chapter two, because ch1.tex has chapter one. It will not just start with page one, but the page number will be one greater than the last page in chapter one. Similarly, the number for the first figure, table and equation, in chapter two will be one greater than the last figure, table and equation number in chapter one.

- Secondly, any cross references to pages, figures, sections, etc., in other chapters and appendices will come out correctly.

To process this document, assuming the root file is named `root.tex`, you would say `latex root` and `prnt root`.

WARNING: You may be tempted to make the mistake of saying `latex ch1` after you have edited `ch1.tex` and want to process it, but this is incorrect and will not work. To process only chapter one, you must edit the `\includeonly` command in `root.tex` to say

`\includeonly{ch1}`

and then you must say `latex root`.

If the `\includeonly` command is omitted altogether, LaTeX will process all files in the list of `\include` commands.

Besides the commands mentioned so far, any commands that pertain to, or affect the entire document should be placed in the root file. In this way, by looking at the root file you can get a good idea of how the document will look. Here is a more complete example of how your root file might look:

```
\documentstyle{report}
\includeonly{ch2,ch3}
\oddsidemargin 0.in
\textwidth 6.5in
\hoffset 0.in
\begin{document}
\pagenumbering{roman}
\tableofcontents
\listoffigures
\listoftables
\pagenumbering{arabic}
\include{ch1}
\include{ch2}
\include{ch3}
\appendix
\include{ap1}
\include{ap2}
\end{document}
```

8.2.1   The Input Command

We have seen that the \includeonly and \include commands work together to make LaTeX process certain files while taking into account the numbering in certain other files, even if they aren't being processed in this run. Sometimes you may want to put a portion of a document whose numbering doesn't relate to the rest of the document (such as a preface or abstract) into a separate file and process that file along with the document. The \input command, which takes the name of a file as its argument, causes LaTeX to read and process the contents of the file just as if they were present in the document.

Let's say a preface to your document is in a file called pref.tex. If you want the preface to be processed, the root file must contain an \input command. It would look something like this:

```
\documentstyle{report}
\includeonly{ch1}
\begin{document}
\tableofcontents

\input{pref}

\include{ch1}
\include{ch2}
\end{document}
```

If you don't want the preface processed for a run, leave out the \input command; LaTeX will then ignore the preface.

Remember, each document may contain only *one* \documentstyle, \begin{document} and \end{document} command.   Therefore, pref.tex should not contain either command; nor should it contain any other element that would not be appropriate where the \input{pref} command falls—between the \tableofcontents and \include{ch1} commands.

Summary

- LaTeX allows you to split a large document into several files, and process those files one at a time, if desired.

- The processing is controlled from the root file, which contains the `\documentstyle` and `\begin-` and `\end{document}` commands.

- The root file also contains one `\includeonly` command and an `\include` command for each file belonging to the document.

- The `\includeonly` command, which must go in the preamble, takes an argument that is a list of files to be processed in this run.

- The `\include` commands each take one argument: the name of one file.

- Each `\include` command causes LaTeX to start a new page.

- There should be an `\include` command for each file in the document (not just the files being processed) every time the file is `latex`ed.

- For each file that is in the `\include` list, and not in the `\includeonly` command, LaTeX looks for an auxiliary file, and if it is present, the numbering of pages, equations, figures, etc., in that file, plus cross references to that file, will be read out of the auxiliary file and taken into account.

- The root file is the one that you `latex` and `prnt`.

- If the `\includeonly` command is omitted, all files in the `\include` list will be processed.

- The root file should also contain any commands that pertain to or affect the entire document, such as margin settings, page style settings, et cetera.

- The files called in by the `\include` and `\input` commands contain document text. They must not contain `\documentstyle`, or `\begin` and `\end{document}` commands.

- The \input command, which takes the name of a file as its argument, causes LaTeX to read and process the contents of the file as if it were present in the document and not a separate file at all.

- \input commands do not cause LaTeX to start on a new page.

- \input commands are appropriate to use for small files, such as prefaces and acknowledgements—not for large files, such as chapters and appendices.

- In \input, \include and \includeonly commands, the file extensions do not have to be given if they are the default extension (.tex).

8.3   The Text of the Document

What exactly do the individual files besides the root file look like? Well, the most important fact about them is that they *do not* contain \documentstyle, or \begin and \end{document} commands. Those are in the root file.   Assuming that each file contains one chapter, they probably start with a \chapter command and continue with the contents of the chapter.

Exercise 8.1

1. Open a new file called root.tex and enter the following lines:

```
\documentstyle{report}
\includeonly{ch1}
\begin{document}
\pagenumbering{roman}
\tableofcontents
\listoffigures
\pagenumbering{arabic}
\include{ch1}
\include{ch2}
\end{document}
```

2. Note that this root file is made to control a document that has two chapters.

3. Save that file. Now open another file called **ch1.tex** and put the following elements into the file:

    (a) a **\chapter** command

    (b) at least one paragraph

    (c) an equation or two

    (d) a figure with a caption

4. Save and exit from the editor.

5. Look on your directory and notice that you have a **ch1.tex** and a **root.tex**.

6. Now **latex root** and **prnt root**. (Remember, the root file is always the one you **latex** and **prnt**.)

7. Note that LaTeX gave the message "No File **ch1.aux**" when it was processing the root file. At the end of the run, however, it did write out a **ch1.aux** containing numbering information to be used in subsequent runs.

   NOTE: If LaTeX comes across an error and stops with a "**?**", remember—don't panic. It is probably caused by a simple typo in your input file. Type "**x**" and a carriage return to get back to the DOS prompt. Then check your file carefully for mistyped commands. If that doesn't help, refer to Appendix E for help.

8. Look on your directory again and notice that you now have **ch1.aux**, as well as other new files.

9. Note the last page number, equation number, and figure number in chapter one.

10. Open a file called **ch2.tex** and enter into it the same elements as in chapter one.

11. Change the **\includeonly** command in **root.tex** to be:

```
\includeonly{ch2}
```

12. Now `latex` and `prnt root`.

13. Notice that only chapter two is printed out, and the page number, equation number, and figure number are one greater than the last page, equation and figure in chapter one.

Summary

- The files other than the root file contain document text. They must not contain \documentstyle, or \begin and \end{document} commands.

8.4   The Index

An index can be a very useful tool in a technical manual, a text book, or any other document designed to guide or teach someone on a particular subject. LaTeX provides the `theindex` environment for making an index in a two-column format. To use the `theindex` environment, you must already know the page numbers for each index entry you wish to include.

Within the `theindex` environment, an \item command produces a main index entry. For example, LaTeXing the following file:

```
\documentstyle{book}
\begin{document}
\begin{theindex}
\item apple 5, 7
\item bear  3, 10
\item cat   1, 14
\end{theindex}
\end{document}
```

would produce an index with entries for apple, bear and cat, on the page numbers listed.

Subentries, and subsubentries may be produced with the \subitem and \subsubitem commands. Each of these types of entries is indented slightly from the previous entry level.

When making a complicated index with many entries and subentries, a little bit of vertical space before the first entry starting with a new letter helps make the index more readable. The \indexspace command creates an appropriate vertical space for this purpose.

Note that the theindex environment simply lists the items you specify, indenting the sub- and subsubitems slightly to set them off. You may use any of the LaTeX commands for bold, italic, or other fonts within the items to emphasize key page numbers or other elements.

Since theindex produces a two-column index, it is probably best to put the index into a separate file from the rest of your document, if the document is in one-column format.

Exercise 8.2

1. Open a new file called myindex.tex and enter the following lines into it:

```
\documentstyle{book}
\begin{document}
\begin{theindex}
\item  {\bf Smoke Cookery,} 135--136, 754--756
   \subitem can for smoking, 135, {\bf 135}
   \subitem Chinese oven, 136
   \subitem fish, 756
   \subitem fowl, 756
   \subitem ham, 754
\item {\bf Smorgasbord,} 65
\item {\bf Snails,} about, 378--379, {\bf 379}
   \subitem butter, 339
     \subsubitem butter substitutes, 340
   \subitem canned, 379
   \subitem mushrooms stuffed with, 282
\indexspace
\index {\bf Tequila,} 40
```

```
\item {\bf Teriyaki, Shrimp,} 377
\item {\bf Terrapin,} about, 380
  \subitem lamb, 229
\item {\bf Terrines,} 435
\item {\bf Tetrazzini,} chicken; turkey; seafood, 198
\end{theindex}
\end{document}
```

2. Notice that the \bf command is used to bold the main entries and some of the key page numbers. Also, remember that the "en" dash (--) should be used for number ranges, such as the page ranges above.

3. latex and prnt the file.

4. Notice that an index comes out with the heading "Index" at the top of the page, and with the entries as specified in the \item, \subitem and \subsubitem commands.

8.4.1   Creating the Index Entries

It is possible to compile an index by hand, by looking through each page of a manuscript and noting each occurrence of a word along with the page number. This is a valid way to put together index entries for a document.

However, LaTeX provides a tool for automatically recording the page numbers of selected words in a document. The \index command, which takes the word to be indexed as its argument, records the word and the present page number in a special file called the ".idx" file. The .idx file has the same first name as the .tex file containing the \index commands.

An \index command should be placed immediately following each occurrence of each word that you wish to include in the index.

Additionally, a \makeindex command must be present in the preamble (before \begin{document}) in order for the .idx file to be created. This way, even if you are processing a file that contains \index commands, you can still omit the index by leaving out the \makeindex

command. You can save time by not running the index when you don't
need to. So, in the presence of a \makeindex command, each \index
command produces an entry in the .idx file. As an example, if the
word "flute" occurs on page 51 of your document, and you index it as
follows:

```
This is a sentence with the word
flute\index{flute} in it.
```

the following line will appear in the .idx file:

```
\indexentry{flute}{51}
```

Exercise 8.3

1. Consider the following paragraph:

> Singing is perhaps the most personal of the perform-
> ing arts. When performing, a good singer makes each
> member of the audience feel as if he or she is receiving
> a generous and loving gift. Only in singing is there a
> direct, unhindered path between the music in the per-
> former's heart and the listener's senses.

Let us suppose that the words "singing", "music", and "audience"
are to be included in the index to this document.

2. Open a new file called indtoo.tex and enter the following lines:

```
\documentstyle{book}
\begin{document}
Singing\index{singing} is perhaps the most
personal of the performing arts. When performing,
a good singer makes each member of the
audience\index{audience} feel as if he or
she is receiving a generous and loving gift.
Only in singing\index{singing} is there a
direct, unhindered path between the
music\index{music} in the performer's heart
```

```
and the listener's senses.
\end{document}
```

3. Note that *all* occurrences of each word to be indexed must be marked with the \index command. This assures that all pages containing the word are included in the .idx file.

4. latex the file indtoo.tex and prnt it.

5. Notice that the \index commands don't have any effect on the output.

6. Notice also that latexing this file did not create an .idx file. That is because it does not contain a \makeindex command.

7. Now put a \makeindex command into indtoo.tex, before the \begin{document}, and latex the file again.

8. Using your text editor, look at the file indtoo.idx.

9. Notice that there is an entry in indtoo.idx corresponding to each \index command in indtoo.tex.

10. Also notice that there are duplicate entries in the .idx file: Since this paragraph is all on one page, there two identical entries for "singing" as follows:

```
\indexentry{singing}{1}
\indexentry{singing}{1}
```

Such duplicates can easily be weeded out of the .idx file.

8.4.2   From .idx Entries to Actual Index

Once you have an .idx file full of \indexentry commands, you can take the following steps to make it into an actual index:

- Use a text editor to sort the entries alphabetically.

- Manually change the \indexentry commands into \item, \subitem, or \subsubitem commands, using the page number information supplied.

- Combine multiple entries for the same word when the page numbers are different, and delete them when the page numbers are duplicates.

- Add \begin{theindex} and \end{theindex} commands before and after the list of index entries.

A competent TEX programmer would be able to write a macro to handle the contents of the .idx file in many different ways. But a discussion of that would be beyond the scope of this manual. For the LATEX user who has no knowledge—or limited knowledge—of TEX, the \index and \makeindex commands are simply useful for automatically listing the page numbers corresponding to words that you wish to index, in the form of \indexentry commands.

LATEX also supplies a file called idx.tex that can help you see what is in an .idx file. Running LATEX on idx.tex gives a listing of the contents of the .idx file, page by page.

Exercise 8.4

1. Type the following line at your DOS prompt:

   `latex idx`

2. Hopefully, `idx.tex` has been installed in such a way that all you have to do is type this command from anywhere on your computer to run it. If this doesn't work, search your directories for the file `idx.tex`, then move it to your working directory, and then type `latex idx`.

3. When you see the prompt "Enter .idx file's first name:", enter `indtoo` and a carriage return.

4. Now type `prnt idx`.

5. Notice the four words listed under the heading "Page one" on the output.

8.5   The Bibliography

It is often desirable in a large document to refer to—or cite—other publications. One way to do this is to include a numbered list of such publications in the document, and then to refer to them by number. The `thebibliography` environment and the `\cite` command make this easy in LaTeX.

The `thebibliography` environment is not unlike the **enumerate** environment described in Section 3.10.2. Each item is created with a `\bibitem` command, which takes a key for an argument. Thus, the `\bibitem` command and its argument work like the **enumerate** environment's `\item` and `\label` commands combined.

The default label for a bibliography item is an integer enclosed in square brackets. Therefore,

```
\bibitem{key1} X. Ample. {\it Bibliography Entry.}
    How To Press, Janetown, 1991.
\bibitem{key2} U. Getit. {\it This is the Title.}
    See Press, Hahnville, 1991.
```

would produce the following entries

[12] X. Ample. *Bibliography Entry.* How To Press, Janetown, 1991.
[13] U. Getit. *This is the Title.* See Press, Hahnville, 1991.

As an alternative to the default label, you may specify a label of your choice in an optional argument to the `\bibitem` command. For example,

```
\bibitem[Ample]{key1} X. Ample. {\it Bibliography Entry.}
    How To Press, Janetown, 1991.
\bibitem[Getit]{key2} U. Getit. {\it This is the Title.}
    See Press, Hahnville, 1991.
```

would produce the following:
[Ample] X. Ample. *Bibliography Entry.* How To Press, Janetown, 1991.
[Getit]   U. Getit. *This is the Title.* See Press, Hahnville, 1991.

Note that the keys for these entries are still **key1** and **key2**. Now, however, where you have `\cite{key1}` in your text, you will get "[Ample]" instead of "[12]".

The \begin{thebibliography} command requires an argument that indicates, by its own width, the width of the widest label in the bibliography. For example, if you know you have between 10 and 99 publications, and you are using the default labels, you should start your bibliography with

\begin{thebibliography}{99}

or use any two digit number in the argument, since all numerals are the same width. If you are using customized labels, and "Longname" is the longest label, then simply type

\begin{thebibliography}{Longname}

To cite a publication from the bibliography in the text, use the \cite command, which takes a key for an argument. It is analogous to the \ref command described in Section 3.10.3. However, the argument to \cite may be one key, or two or more keys, separated by commas. For example,

```
This is how to cite a publication.\cite{key1}
This is how to cite multiple
publications.\cite{key1,key2}
```

would produce

This is how to cite a publication. [Ample] This is how to cite multiple publications. [Ample,Getit]

You may also add a note to your citation, such as a page number, by using an optional argument to the \cite command. Whatever text appears in this argument will be placed within the square brackets, after the number, or the label, if customized labels are being used. For example,

```
This is how to cite a publication.\cite[page 21]{key1}
```

would produce

This is how to cite a publication. [Ample, page 21]

Exercise 8.5

1. Open a new file called `bibtst.tex` and enter the following lines:

```
\documentstyle{article}
\begin{document}

\section{Practice Using a Bibliography}
I love Ice Cream. (See \cite{iscream}.)
I also have a good friend who adores
the stuff. (See \cite[pages 1--10]{uscream}.)
In fact, I can't think of anyone who really
doesn't like it!
(See references \cite{iscream,uscream}.)

\begin{thebibliography}{99}
\bibitem{iscream} I. Scream. {\it For Ice-cream.}
  Yum-yum Publishing Co., Nuts.

\bibitem{uscream} U. Scream. {\it We All Scream.}
  Hot Fudge Publishing Co., Nuts.
\end{thebibliography}
\end{document}
```

2. `latex bibtst.tex` twice and then `prnt` it.

3. Note that citations, like references made with the `\ref` command, are only correct after you LaTeX twice.

4. Notice that the `\cite` command puts out the number(s) of the publication(s) being cited enclosed in square brackets, with a note after the "Uscream" citation.

5. Notice also that the `thebibliography` environment produces a "References" title, and then the list of publications with numbers in brackets as labels.

6. Now edit `bibtst.tex` and change the document style from `article` to `book`.

7. At the same time, change the \bibitem commands, using optional arguments to put in labels of your choice. Don't forget to put the longest label in the argument to
\begin{thebibliography}.

8. latex twice and prnt the file again and notice that the bibliography now starts on a separate page. If you change the document style again to report, you will notice that the bibliography starts on a *right hand* page, as well as starting on a new page.

9. Also notice that the labels in the bibliography—and the citations—now are the customized labels that you put in.

8.6 Preventing Output To Auxiliary Files

During a LaTeX run, information is written into many auxiliary files. Exactly which files depends on the input. For example, if there is a \tableofcontents command in the input, a .toc file will be created. The same applies to .lof, .lot, and .idx files when there are \listoffigures, \listoftables, and \makeindex commands, respectively.

Since the compiling and writing of these files is a task that significantly increases LaTeX's memory and time requirements, you may want to use the \nofiles command to suppress them. \nofiles also suppresses the .aux file. This way, you can save time when running LaTeX on a large document if there is no new information for the Table of Contents, etcetera, or if you don't need to create auxiliary files for one reason or another, for example, in the early stages of debugging.

The \nofiles command must be placed in the preamble—that is, between the \documentstyle and \begin{document} commands.

NOTE: It is a common mistake to forget to remove the \nofiles command, so this is something to look for if the Table of Contents, List of Figures, etcetera, don't look right.

Appendix A

Defining Your Own Commands

The ability to define your own commands is useful in many situations, including when

- A piece of text, such as a company name, is repeated many times in a document

- The same series of commands is repeated many times in a document

- You wish to abbreviate existing commands.

A.1 Defining New Commands

A.1.1 Simple Text

Most word processors have user definable macros that allow the user to accomplish several functions with just a few keystrokes. LaTeX provides the \newcommand command for defining customized commands. It takes two arguments: the first is the new command's name; and the second is the text of the command. Say, for instance, that your company's name is "Aunt Jane's Healthy Cookie Company." Supposing you would like to type \ajhcc instead of the whole name. Then you could define your command by typing

`\newcommand{\ajhcc}{Aunt~Jane's Healthy Cookie Company}`

Now every time you type `\ajhcc`, it will be replaced with

Aunt Jane's Healthy Cookie Company

Notice the use of the "~" to keep Aunt and Jane on the same line.

Remember the rule that says that a space following a command is not printed out by LaTeX? Well that rule applies to your new command. Therefore if you want a space following your company name, you must type it as `\ajhcc\ `; that is, `\ajhcc` followed by backslash-space.

You must be careful to pick a command name that is not already used by LaTeX or TeX. This may be difficult, since you don't know what the TeX commands are, but don't worry: LaTeX will give you an error message that says "Command name already used" if the command name is already in use. The best thing to do is to make the command's name reflect what it does.

A.1.2   A Series of LaTeX Commands

Supposing your document has many examples in it and each one is preceded by

⌐EXAMPLE¬

You could produce this by typing

```
\begin{center}
\fbox{\large EXAMPLE}
\end{center}
```

each time you have an example, or you could define a command, `\expl`, to do it, as follows:

```
\newcommand{\expl}{\begin{center}
                   \fbox{\large EXAMPLE}
                   \end{center}}
```

Then you would only need to precede your examples with `\expl`, instead of typing all those commands every time. You see, once you have defined a command using `\newcommand`, typing the command is just like typing the elements in the definition of the command.

A.1.3 Abbreviations for LaTeX Commands

Some LaTeX commands are very long, since they are designed to be descriptive of what they do. If you don't want to type them out, you can define shorter commands of your own. For example, consider

- \newcommand{\be}{\begin{equation}} and
  \newcommand{\ee}{\end{equation}}

- \newcommand{\bi}{\begin{itemize}} and
  \newcommand{\ei}{\end{itemize}}

- \newcommand{\ds}{\displaystyle}

With these new commands defined, your document may look something like this:

```
Here is a numbered, displayed equation:
\be
x + y = z
\ee

Now an itemized list:
\bi
\item first item
\item second item
\item etc.
\ei

How about an integral in the text, with the larger
integral symbol normally used in displayed equations:
 $\ds \int_0^10 f(x)$
```

You can see how to save yourself typing by using this "shorthand" technique for *commonly used* commands.

WARNING: The definitions of the new commands (the \newcommand statements) should be in an obvious place in your document, such as the preamble, so that a person reading through the input file can easily find them. After all, that person may be you, five months later. Imagine how frustrating it would be to come across a bunch of commands whose meaning you couldn't figure out!

A.2 Redefining Old Commands

The \renewcommand command works exactly the same as \newcommand except that it lets you redefine previously defined commands. These may be commands that you defined with \newcommand, or they may be existing TₑX or LATₑX commands. For example, \be and \ee from the preceding example could be redefined as follows:

```
\renewcommand{\be}{\begin{enumerate}}
\renewcommand{\ee}{\end{enumerate}}
```

As another example, suppose you aren't happy with \bigskip, \medskip and \smallskip and want to make them skip more space than they normally do. You could type

```
\renewcommand{\bigskip}{\vspace{2.in}}
\renewcommand{\medskip}{\vspace{1.in}}
\renewcommand{\smallskip}{\vspace{.75in}}
```

and those commands would have your new meanings.

NOTE: With \renewcommand, there is the danger of accidently redefining an existing TₑX or LATₑX command. This can produce very strange results, so be sure you know the meaning of the command you are redefining.

WARNING: Although command definitions may contain other commands, they must never contain the command being defined. Suppose, for example, you want to make \bigskip leave twice as much space as it presently does. You might be tempted to say

```
\renewcommand{\bigskip}{\bigskip\bigskip}
```

This would be incorrect, since it would send TₑX into a tailspin trying to figure out the meaning of \bigskip. You would have to measure the space left by \bigskip, and redefine it using \vspace to leave two times that amount of space to accomplish this.

A.3   Defining Commands That Take Arguments

You can also define commands that have arguments using the **\newcommand** and **\renewcommand** commands. They each take an optional argument that gives the number of arguments for the new command. (The maximum number of arguments is nine.) Suppose that you are doing short biographies of the employees in your department, and you want each biography to start on a new page, with the person's name in large bold letters at the top of the page. You could define a command named **\biog** to do this for you. The person's name would have to be an argument to **\biog**, since it is different for each employee. You could define your command as follows:

```
\newcommand{\biog}[1]{%
   \clearpage
   \begin{center}
   \large\bf #1
   \end{center}
   \bigskip}
```

The [1] says that \biog will take one argument. Then, within the definition, the #1 will be replaced with the argument. To use the command, you would type

```
\biog{John Doe}
```

and you would get

John Doe

at the top of a new page. You would start each biography this way.

Notice the percent sign (%) following the first line of the definition. This is a handy trick for starting a new line in the input file without introducing a space in the output. (See Section 2.11 for usage of "%" to produce comments.) Remember from Section 2.5 that a single carriage return is normally interpreted as a word space by LaTeX. If the percent sign were not present in this definition, the first character in the definition would be a carriage return, which would be interpreted as a space.

We don't want a space to be the first character produced by the \biog command, and the percent sign prevents this from happening.

Now let's modify this command to take two arguments. The first will still be the employee's name, and the second will be his position. The employee's position will be centered below the name in normal size type.

```
\newcommand{\biog}[2]{%
  \clearpage
  \begin{center}
  \large\bf #1 \\
  \normalsize\bf #2
  \end{center}
  \bigskip}
```

The [2] says that the command takes two arguments. The #1 will be replaced by the first argument, and the #2 will be replaced by the second argument. Now to use the command you would type

```
\biog{John Doe}{Programmer}
```

and

John Doe
Programmer

would appear at the top of a new page. Using command definitions this way you not only save typing but can be sure that all the biographies look the same. And by sharing such commands among users, you can have a standard format for many users.

The \renewcommand command works the same way. Say you wanted to change the definition of \biog later in the document to place the name and position against the right margin. You could type

```
\renewcommand{\biog}[2]{%
  \clearpage
  \begin{flushright}
  \large\bf #1 \\
```

```
\normalsize\bf #2
\end{flushright}
\bigskip}
```

and the command would have the new meaning.

Also, with **\renewcommand**, you can redefine existing LaTeX commands that take arguments. Only a LaTeX expert should attempt to redefine LaTeX commands. In fact, you should not change the meaning of a LaTeX command unless you are sure you know its original meaning. If you are very familiar with TeX and LaTeX, you can find out the original meaning by looking in the style guide, or if it's not there, look in the file `latex.tex` that was provided with your LaTeX software.

A.4 Defining New Environments

The **\newenvironment** command allows you to define a new environment. It takes three arguments: the first is the name of the environment; the second is the text (and/or commands) that begins the environment; and the third is the text (and/or commands) that ends the environment. You use the new environment with the **\begin** and **\end** commands, just as with any LaTeX environment. New environments are often defined in terms of existing environments.

For example, suppose you want to have a numbered list that begins with the title "Mylist", and whose items are all in the bold typeface. You could do it using the **enumerate** environment, like this:

```
\underline{Mylist}
\begin{enumerate} \bf
\item First item
\item Second item
\end{enumerate}
```

If you were using this over and over again, you might want to define a new environment called **boldenum** as follows:

```
\newenvironment{boldenum}%
        {\underline{Mylist}\begin{enumerate} \bf}%
        {\end{enumerate}}
```

Note that the first argument is the name, the second argument contains the commands used in the example to start the special environment, and the third argument contains the commands used in the example to end the environment. Now to use it you would type:

```
\begin{boldenum}
\item First item
\item Second item
\end{boldenum}
```

and you would get the following result:

Mylist

1. **First item**

2. **Second item**

You can also define environments that take arguments. To do this, use an optional argument to \newenvironment that gives the number of arguments. For example, if you want the title to be a variable instead of "Mylist" you can define the environment as follows:

```
\newenvironment{boldenum}[1]%
        {\underline{#1}\begin{enumerate} \bf}%
        {\end{enumerate}}
```

The [1] means there is one argument, and the #1 is where the argument is placed. To make the typeface a variable instead of \bf you could use a second argument, like this:

```
\newenvironment{boldenum}[2]%
        {\underline{#1}\begin{enumerate} #2}%
        {\end{enumerate}}
```

Then to use the boldenum environment with a title "Jane's Folly" and a slanted typeface, you would type

```
\begin{boldenum}{Jane's Folly}{\sl}
\item First item
\item Second item
\end{boldenum}
```

and you would get the following results:

Jane's Folly

1. *First item*

2. *Second item*

Be sure to provide two arguments for a command or environment that
you have defined to take two arguments. Otherwise, LATEX may interpret something as an argument that is not meant to be one at all, and
this can produce strange results.

You may use `\renewenvironment` to redefine an existing environment. Again, be very careful not to redefine an environment unless you
know exactly what you are doing!

WARNING: When defining or redefining environments with arguments, you may not use any arguments in the text that ends the
environment—the third argument to `\renewcommand`.

A.5   The `list` Environment

The `list` environment allows you to define your own list, if neither of
the three pre-defined lists meets your needs. With it, you can set up
your own counters or other list labels. You can also define formatting
parameters for the list, such as margins, separation between items, label
width, et cetera.

You invoke the environment with `\begin{list}` and two arguments, the first being the default label for items in the list, the second
being a set of statements specifying the list formatting. Any formatting
parameter not specified in the second argument will receive a default
value determined by the document style. See Section C.6 under the
heading "Lists" on page 232 for a complete set of list formatting parameters.

Each item in the list is made with an `\item` command, just as in
other list environments. If a label other than the default label defined
in the first argument to `\begin{list}` is desired for this item, then

the desired label may be given in an optional argument to the \item command. An \end{list} command ends the list.

As an example, suppose you want a list that has dagger symbols as labels and default formatting otherwise. You would type

```
\begin{list}{\dag}{}
\item First item
\item Second item
\end{list}
```

Notice the \dag in the first argument to \begin{list} that defines the default label. Also, since all default values are desired for the formatting, the second argument is simply left empty. The result would be

† First item

† Second item

Now, if you want to specify that the separation between items should be very small, you could set some formatting parameters in the second argument. The separation between items in a list is controlled by two parameters called \itemsep and \parsep. Therefore the list could be redefined as follows:

```
\begin{list}{\dag}{\itemsep 0in  \parsep 0in}
\item First item
\item Second item
\end{list}
```

The second argument to \begin{list} sets \itemsep to be 0 inches, and \parsep to be 0 inches. Now the result would be

† First item
† Second item

See Table C.1 on Page 225 for the default settings for list (and other) style parameters.

You may set up a customized counting system in a list by defining a new counter, and then using the counter in the list as follows:

```
\newcounter{mycount}
\begin{list}{--\arabic{mycount}--}%
{\usecounter{mycount} \itemsep 0in  \parsep .1in}
\item First item
\item Second item
\end{list}
```

Here the new counter is defined with the \newcounter command; then the first argument to \begin{list} specifies that the items should be labelled with the value of mycount in arabic style surrounded by dashes. The \usecounter command in the second argument specifies that each item will increment the value of mycount by one. \usecounter also sets the initial value of mycount to zero. The results are

–1– First item

–2– Second item

(See Section B.5 on page 221 for a description of the \newcounter command.)

This list may be used over and over in a document. The counter will be reset to 0 by the \begin{list} command each time, as long as the second argument says \usecounter{mycount}.

Appendix B

Customizing Counters

B.1 What is a Counter?

LaTeX automatically counts certain document elements for you, such as figures, tables, equations, and pages. The numbers for these elements are kept in variables called *counters*. Each counter has a unique name, and the value of the counter at any time is the number of the element it is counting.

For example, the chapter counter is called (not surprisingly) `chapter`. Before the first `\chapter` command is encountered, the chapter counter has a value of 0. Each time a `\chapter` command comes along, the counter is incremented by 1, so that the first `\chapter` command causes the value of `chapter` to be 1, the second `\chapter` command causes the value of `chapter` to be 2, and so on.

The following is a list of all the pre-defined counters that LaTeX uses:

part	paragraph	figure	enumi
chapter	subparagraph	table	enumii
section	page	footnote	enumiii
subsection	equation	mpfootnote	enumiv
subsubsection			

215

Notice that many of the counters have familiar names. This is because they have the same names as the commands or environments that involve them, except without the \. The strangers in the list, the `enumi`, `enumii`, etc., are used in the `enumerate` environment to count the first, second, third, and fourth level items, respectively. The `mpfootnote` counts footnotes within a `minipage` environment.

The value of a counter must be a single integer. In the number you see printed for a section, such as 4.3, the 4 is the value of the `chapter` counter, and the 3 is the value of the `section` counter.

B.2 Setting a Counter

The \setcounter command allows you to set the value of a counter to be what you want it to be. It takes two arguments: the first is the name of the counter; and the second is the desired value for the counter. For example,

```
\setcounter{chapter}{2}
```

would set the chapter number to 2,

```
\setcounter{page}{4}
```

would set the page number to 4, et cetera. One thing you have to be aware of when setting counters is that many commands or environments will increment a counter *first*, and then output it. Therefore you must set the value of the counter to be one less than the desired value. In other words, say you want to start your document with Chapter 3. You must set the chapter counter to 2, and then use a \chapter command to start Chapter 3, as follows:

```
\setcounter{chapter}{2}
\chapter{This Is Chapter Three!}
```

As another example, to force an equation to be Equation 10, you would type the following commands:

```
\setcounter{equation}{9}
\begin{equation}
x = y
\end{equation}
```

and that equation would be equation 10.

Another way of saying this is that the value of the chapter, equation, figure, table, or footnote counter at any given time is the number of the *last* chapter, equation, figure, or footnote.

There is an exception to this rule, and that is the page counter. The value of the page counter is the present page's number. So, saying

```
\setcounter{page}{10}
```

will cause the present page to be page number ten.

B.2.1 Adding to a Counter

The \addtocounter command allows you to add a number to the value of a counter. It takes two arguments: the first is the name of the counter; and the second is the number to be added to the counter. This way you can increase the value of a counter by 1 (or any other number) without knowing the value of the counter. For example,

```
\addtocounter{equation}{5}
```

would increment the equation counter by 5. So, if the last equation was Equation 5, the next one will be Equation 11. Remember, the equation environment itself increments the counter by 1 before outputting it. That's why the next equation is 11 instead of 10.

You may also add a negative amount to a counter. For example, for a figure that is continued on a second page you would use two figure environments. If you want a caption on each page, you would normally get two consecutive figure numbers, such as Figure 1 and Figure 2. Consider the following solution:

```
\begin{figure}[p]
\vspace{6.5in}
\caption{This is the caption of a two-page figure}
```

```
\end{figure}
\addtocounter{figure}{-1}
\begin{figure}[p]
\vspace{6.5in}
\caption{This is the caption of a two-page figure (cont'd)}
\end{figure}
```

The result of this example would be two figure pages in a row, both having the same figure number.

NOTE: If you do something like this, you may have to edit the `.lof` file to delete the second caption from the List of Figures.

B.3   Printing a Counter

The following commands cause LaTeX to print the value of the indicated counter:

Command	Counter	Command	Counter
\thechapter	chapter	\thefigure	figure
\thesection	section	\thetable	table
\thesubsection	subsection	\thefootnote	footnote
\thesubsubsection	subsubsection	\thempfootnote	mpfootnote
\theparagraph	paragraph	\theenumi	enumi
\thesubparagraph	subparagraph	\theenumii	enumii
\thepage	page	\theenumiii	enumiii
\theequation	equation	\theenumiv	enumiv

For example, you could type

```
We are now on page \thepage\ of Appendix \thechapter\
   in the \LaTeX\ book.
```

And you would get
We are now on page 218 of Appendix B in the LaTeX book.

And this example answers a question that may have been bothering you: how are appendices counted? The `chapter` counter doubles as the appendix counter. (see Section 3.5.1 on page 47 for instructions on making appendices.)

B.4 Styles of Counters

In most cases the commands described above print the value of a counter as an arabic number. Exceptions are `\thepage` when `\pagenumbering{roman}` has been specified, and `\thempfootnote` which prints letters, the counters for inner levels of the `enumerate` environment, and the `chapter` counter after and `\appendix` command has been encountered.

You can change the style in which a counter is printed by redefining the command that prints it. This is done using the following commands, each of which takes an argument that is the name of the counter to be affected:

`\arabic{figure}`	prints the `figure` (or other) counter as an arabic number.
`\roman{page}`	prints the `page` (or other) counter as a lowercase roman numeral.
`\Roman{chapter}`	prints the `chapter` (or other) counter as an uppercase roman numeral.
`\alph{table}`	prints the `table` (or other) counter as a lowercase letter.
`\Alph{chapter}`	prints the `chapter` (or other) counter as an uppercase letter.

You may use the above commands, or combinations of them, to redefine the numbering commands and change the numbering style of a figure, table, chapter, or other numbered element. For example, if you want your chapters numbered with uppercase roman numerals, you would type

```
\renewcommand{\thechapter}{\Roman{chapter}}
```

Then the next time the \thechapter command is invoked, (e.g. by the \chapter command,) the number will come out as an uppercase roman numeral. This does not have any effect on the *value* of the counter—only the style of the counter changes.

As another example, suppose you want your figure numbers to be a combination of the chapter number in uppercase roman numerals and the figure number as a letter, such as Figure IIc, for the third figure in chapter 2. You could type

```
\renewcommand{\thefigure}{\Roman{chapter}\alph{figure}}
```

and the next captioned figure would be numbered that way. Note that the numbering style of chapters is not changed by the definition of \thefigure in this example; only the numbering of the figures and the \thefigure command are affected.

You can include any words or characters in your definitions of numbering commands. See the examples below.

```
\renewcommand{\thefigure}{\arabic{chapter}.\Alph{figure}}
\setcounter{chapter}{2}
\setcounter{figure}{3}
\begin{figure}[ht]
\vspace{.5in}
\caption{This is a sample figure with a
    customized number including a period.}
\end{figure}
```

would produce

Figure 2.D: This is a sample figure with a customized number including a period.

and

```
\renewcommand{\thepage}{\Roman{chapter}--\arabic{page}}
This is page \thepage.
```

would produce
This is page II–220.

B.4.1 Marking Footnotes with Symbols

The following series of nine symbols may be used for marking footnotes:

* † ‡ § ¶ ‖ ** †† ‡‡

The command to print the footnote counter, \thefootnote, must be redefined as follows to print these symbols:

\renewcommand{\thefootnote}{\fnsymbol{footnote}}

If you use this option, be sure that the footnote counter doesn't go above nine. You may have up to nine footnotes in each chapter, since the footnote counter is set to 0 at the beginning of each chapter.

B.5 Creating Your Own Counter

You may create your own counter—with a name of your choice—by using the \newcounter command. For example,

\newcounter{orange}

defines a counter called **orange**. It has all the properties of other counters, such as **chapter**, **page**, **figure**, etc.. In other words, you may set it to any value using the \setcounter command, as in

\setcounter{orange}{5}

Also, you may print the value of the counter. When you define **orange** with the \newcounter command, LaTeX automatically defines a command \theorange that prints the value of the counter. For example,

The value of orange is \theorange.

would produce:
The value of orange is 5.

And if you wish to add to the counter, or print it in a different style, the \addtocounter and \renewcommand commands may be used as well on the counter **orange** as follows:

```
\addtocounter{-2}{orange}
\renewcommand{\theorange}{\Roman{orange}}
Now the value of orange is \theorange!
```

with the following results:

Now the value of orange is III!

Appendix C

Style Parameters

When LATeX is formatting a document, it needs to know certain information about page layout, such as margin settings, paragraph indentation, the size of footers and headers, and many other things. This information is kept in several *style parameters*. The style parameters are given default values by LATeX, and the user can change the values if he or she so desires.

C.1 Length Parameters

Most of the style parameters have length values, such as a left margin of 1 inch, or a paragraph indentation of .5 inch. To change the value of a style parameter, you just have to know the name of the parameter, and know the length that you want to set it to. Then you can use the `\setlength` command. Say you want to set the paragraph indentation to .75 inch. The parameter's name is **\parindent**, and the value is `.75in`. You would type

`\setlength{\parindent}{.75in}`

and that would assign a length of .75 inch to the **\parindent** parameter.

C.2   Counter Parameters

Some of the style parameters are actually counters, which have a single integer value. They do not begin with a backslash (\\), and that is how you distinguish them from a length. They must be set with a `\setcounter` command. For example, the maximum number of floats allowed on a text page is called `totalnumber`, and its default number is 3. If you wanted to set it to 10, you could type

`\setcounter{totalnumber}{10}`

C.3   Default Settings for Parameters

LaTeX has 42 style parameters that can be changed by the user. The default values of most of these parameters are set by the document style (and the document style options). Some parameters are also temporarily changed within certain environments; for example, the paragraph indentation within a `\parbox` is set to zero.

Since knowing the default value of the parameter is helpful in deciding how to change it, Table C.1 is provided to give the default values of each style parameter for the `report`, `book`, `article`, and `letter` styles, assuming the default point size of 12 points is used. (See Section 3.1.1 for information on other available point sizes.) When you look at this table, you will notice that many parameters are the same in the `report` and `article` styles, whereas the `book` and `letter` styles are quite unique.

As you can imagine, the values of many of the parameters would be slightly smaller with the 10pt or 11pt document style option.

C.4   Rubber Lengths

Some of the parameters that provide spacing in the document must be flexible. For example, the spacing between words must be flexible in order for paragraphs to be right justified. Likewise the spacing between paragraphs must be flexible for the length of each page to be exactly the same.

Table C.1: Default values for style parameters in Report, Book, Article, and Letter styles, assuming the default point size of 12 points.

Parameter	Report	Book	Article	Letter
\oddsidemargin	.29in^A, .55in^B	.25in	.29in^A, .55in^B	.74in
\evensidemargin	.82in^A, .55in^B	1.25in	.82in^A, .55in^B	.74in
\textwidth	5.42in	5.in	5.42in	5.07in
\topmargin	.38in	.73in	.38in	.38in
\headheight	.17in	.17in	.17in	.17in
\headsep	.35in	.275in	.35in	.63in
\textheight	7.39in	7.39in	7.39in	7.01in
\topskip	.14in	.14in	.14in	.14in
\footheight	0in	0in	0in	.17in
\footskip	.42in	.42in	.42in	.35in
\parindent	1.5em†	1.5em†	1.5em†	0in
\baselineskip	.2in	.2in	.2in	.21in
\baselinestretch	1	1	1	1
\parskip	0in	0in	0in	.1in
\footnotesep	.12in	.12in	.12in	.17in
secnumdepth	2	2	3	N/A
tocdepth	2	2	3	N/A
\columnsep	.14in	.14in	.14in	.14in
\columnseprule	0in	0in	0in	0in
\marginparwidth	1.18in^A, .94in^B	1.in	1.18in^A, .94in^B	1.25in
\marginparsep	.14in	.1in	.14in	.15in
\marginparpush	.1in	.1in	.1in	.07in
\topsep	.125in	.125in	.125in	.4em†
\partopsep	.04in	.04in	.04in	0in
\itemsep	.06in	.06in	.06in	.4em†
\parsep	.06in	.06in	.06in	0in
\leftmargin	2.5em†	2.5em†	2.5em†	2.5em†
\rightmargin	0in	0in	0in	0in
\listparindent	0in	0in	0in	0in
\itemindent	0in	0in	0in	0in
\labelsep	.5em†	.5em†	.5em†	.5em†
\labelwidth	2em†	2em†	2em†	2em†

A. This value for two-sided printing.
B. This value for one-sided printing.
†An **em** is roughly the width of a capital M in the selected font.

(continued)

Table C.1: *(Continued)* Default values for style parameters in Report, Book, Article, and Letter styles, assuming the default point size of 12 points.

Parameter	Report	Book	Article	Letter
\jot	.04in	.04in	.04in	.04in
\mathindent	0in	0in	0in	0in
\abovedisplayskip	.17in	.17in	.17in	.17in
\belowdisplayskip	.17in	.17in	.17in	.17in
\abovedisplayshortskip	0in	0in	0in	0in
\belowdisplayshortskip	0in	0in	0in	0in
topnumber	2	2	2	2
\topfraction	.7	.7	.7	.7
bottomnumber	1	1	1	1
\bottomfraction	.3	.3	.3	.3
totalnumber	3	3	3	3
\textfraction	.2	.2	.2	.2
\floatpagefraction	.5	.5	.5	.5
dbltopnumber	2	2	2	2
\dbltopfraction	.7	.7	.7	.7
\floatsep	.19in	.19in	.19in	.17in
\textfloatsep	.28in	.28in	.28in	.28in
\intextsep	.19in	.19in	.19in	.17in
\dblfloatsep	.19in	.19in	.19in	.17in
\dblfloatpagefraction	.5	.5	.5	.5
\dbltextfloatsep	.28in	.28in	.28in	.28in
\arraycolsep	.07in	.07in	.07in	.07in
\tabcolsep	.08in	.08in	.08in	.08in
\arrayrulewidth	.006in	.006in	.006in	.006in
\doublerulesep	.03in	.03in	.03in	.03in
\arraystretch	1	1	1	1
\fboxrule	.006in	.006in	.006in	.006in
\fboxsep	.04in	.04in	.04in	.04in

Lengths that are flexible like this are called *rubber lengths*. They usually have a length assigned to them (a *natural length*), plus an amount that they can stretch, and an amount that they can shrink. LaTeX keeps these lengths as close to their natural length as possible, stretching or shrinking them as needed. When reading the definition of a parameter, watch for whether it is a rubber length or not. If it is, then be aware that the value that LaTeX uses for that parameter may vary slightly from the assigned value.

C.5   When to Change a Parameter

Some parameters, such as the margin-setting parameters, affect the overall formatting of the document, and should be set only once for the entire document. When this is the case, put the definition in the preamble (before `\begin{document}`), so that it can be easily seen.

Many parameters, however, may be changed anywhere in the document. Unless it is specifically noted in the definitions below that the parameter may only be changed in the preamble, assume that it can be changed anywhere.

C.6   Parameter Definitions

Page Formatting

`\oddsidemargin` The position of the left margin relative to a 1-inch margin. If `twoside` document style option is selected, it only affects odd pages, otherwise it affects all pages. *Change in preamble only.* Sample usage:

`\setlength{\oddsidemargin}{0in}` would give a 1-inch left margin.

`\setlength{\oddsidemargin}{.25in}` would give a 1.25-inch left margin.

`\setlength{\oddsidemargin}{-.25in}` would give a .75-inch left margin.

`\evensidemargin` In `twoside` document style option, the position of the left margin relative to a 1-inch margin for even pages. *Change in preamble only.* Sample usage:

`\setlength{\evensidemargin}{0in}` would give a 1-inch left margin.

`\setlength{\evensidemargin}{.25in}` would give a 1.25-inch left margin.
`\setlength{\evensidemargin}{-.25in}` would give a .75-inch left margin.

`\textwidth` The width of text between the left and right margins for a normal paragraph. *Change in preamble only.* Sample usage:

`\setlength{\textwidth}{6.5in}` would give 6.5 inches between the left and right margins.

`\topmargin` The position of the top of the page's head, relative to 1 inch from the top edge of the paper. *Change in preamble only.* Sample usage:

`\setlength{\topmargin}{.5in}` would leave 1.5 inches of white space above the page's head. (NOTE: If the head is empty, the total white space at the top of the page may be greater than 1.5 inches.)

`\setlength{\topmargin}{-.5in}` would leave .5 inch of white space above the page's head.

`\setlength{\topmargin}{0in}` would leave 1 inch of white space above the page's head.

`\headheight` The height of the space reserved for the page's head. *Change in preamble only.* Sample usage:

`\setlength{\headheight}{.5in}` would reserve .5 inch of vertical space for a header on each page.

`\headsep` The vertical distance between the head and the body of text. *Change in preamble only.* Sample usage:

```
\setlength{\topmargin}{0in}
\setlength{\headheight}{.4in}
\setlength{\headsep}{.1in}
```

would give a 1-inch top margin, a .4-inch space for the header, and .1 inch of white space, so the text would begin 1.5 inches from the top edge of the paper.

`\textheight` Height of the body of the text. *Change in preamble only.* Sample usage:

`\setlength{\textheight}{8.in}` would make the body text 8 inches high.

\footheight The height of the space reserved for the footer. *Change only in preamble.* Sample usage:

\setlength{\footheight}{.15in} would leave space for a .15-inch-high footer.

\footskip The vertical distance from the bottom of the body text to the *bottom* of the foot. *Change only in preamble.* Sample usage:

```
\setlength{\footheight}{.1in}
\setlength{\footskip}{.2in}
```

would leave room for a .1-inch footer, with .1 inch of blank space between the body and the top of the footer.

\parindent Paragraph indentation. Sample usage:

\setlength{\parindent}{.5in} would cause paragraphs to be indented .5 inch.

\baselineskip The *minimum* space between baselines in a paragraph. (The baseline is where the *bottoms* of letters without descenders— a, e, i, for example—fall on the line of text. g, y, and p are examples of letters with descenders.) LaTeX adjusts line spacing appropriately for lines containing tall characters. Only one setting may be used in any one paragraph—the last one encountered. Sample usage:

\setlength{\baselineskip}{20pt} would make 20 points the minimum distance between baselines.

\topskip Like **\baselineskip**, only applies just to the first line of the body text. *Change only in preamble.* Sample usage:

\setlength{\topskip}{\baselineskip} would set the minimum distance from the top of the body to the bottom of the first line of text equal to \baselineskip.

\setlength{\topskip}{14pt} would set this parameter to 14 points.

\baselinestretch A factor that increases or decreases the line spacing everywhere. The space between baselines is multiplied by this factor, which is normally 1. It is changed with **\renewcommand**.

Any change must be made before \begin{document}, otherwise *it doesn't take affect until the next typesize changing command is encountered.* Sample usage:

\renewcommand{\baselinestretch}{2} would create double-spacing.

\renewcommand{\baselinestretch}{1.15} would increase line spacing by 15%.

\renewcommand{\baselinestretch}{.90} would decrease line spacing by 10%.

\parskip Spacing between paragraphs. *This is a rubber length.* Sample usage:

\setlength{\parskip}{.15in} would cause a .15-inch space to appear between paragraphs.

Footnotes

\footnotesep The height of an invisible rule at the beginning of each footnote. Causes the distance between footnotes to be the value given plus the normal white space between lines. Sample usage:

\setlength{\footnotesep}{.25in} would cause the space between footnotes to be slightly more than .25 inch.

Section Levels

secnumdepth A counter that contains the level of the lowest sectional unit to be numbered. Sections are level 1; subsections are level 2, et cetera. In **report** and **book** styles, chapters are level 0, and parts are level -1. *May only be set in preamble.* Sample usage:

\setcounter{secnumdepth}{3} Subsections and above would be numbered; paragraphs and below would not.

\setcounter{secnumdepth}{1} Sections and above would be numbered; subsections and below would not.

tocdepth A counter that contains the level of the lowest sectional unit to be included in the Table of Contents. *Set in preamble only.* Sample usage:

\setcounter{tocdepth}{2} Everything down to subsections is listed in the

Table of Contents.

`\setcounter{tocdepth}{0}` Only chapters are listed in the Table of Contents.

Two-column Format

`\columnsep` The space between columns of text when the `twocolumn` document style option is used. Sample usage:

`\setlength{\columnsep}{.25in}` Causes a .25-inch space between columns of text.

`\columnseprule` The width of a vertical line between text columns when the `twocolumn` document style option is used. (Default is 0 inch.) Sample usage:

`\setlength{\columnseprule}{.01in}` would make a fine line appear between columns.

`\setlength{\columnseprule}{.03in}` would make a heavy line appear between columns.

Marginal Notes

`\marginparwidth` The width of marginal notes. *Change in preamble only*. Sample usage:

`\setlength{\marginparwidth}{.5in}` would cause marginal notes to be .5 inch wide.

`\marginparsep` The space between the edge of the body of text and marginal notes. *Change in preamble only*. Sample usage:

`\setlength{\marginparsep}{.1in}` would cause marginal notes to be separated from body of text by .1 inch.

`\marginparpush` The minimum vertical space allowed between two marginal notes. *Change in preamble only*. Sample usage:

`\setlength{\marginparpush}{.25}` would cause at least a .25-inch vertical space to appear between successive marginal notes.

Lists

\topsep Vertical space in addition to paragraph spacing separating a
list from surrounding text. *It is a rubber length.* May be set in
a `list` environment (within second argument to \begin{list}).
Sample usage:
\begin{list}{...}{\topsep .25in} would cause this list to be .25 inch
from surrounding text.

\partopsep More vertical space added between a list and surrounding
text if the list is preceded by a blank line. *It is a rubber length.*
May be set in a `list` environment. Sample usage:
\begin{list}{...}{\partopsep .1in \topsep .25in} would cause
.35 inch (.1 inch plus .25 inch) to be placed between the list and surrounding
text if the list is separated from text by a blank line. Otherwise, just .25
inch of separation would come out.

\itemsep The separation between list items, added to \parsep. *This
is a rubber length.* May be set in a `list` environment, or within
an `itemize`, `enumerate`, or `description` environment. Sample
usage:
\begin{list}{...}{\itemsep 0in} would make the list items only separated by the \parsep amount. Or
\begin{enumerate}\itemsep 1.in would start an enumerated list with items
separated by 1 inch plus paragraph separation.

\parsep The vertical spacing between paragraphs within an item. *It
is a rubber length.* May be set in a `list` environment. Sample
usage:
\begin{list}{...}{\parsep .1in} would cause paragraph spacing to be
.1 inch within an item. This amount, added to \itemsep, would be the
separation between items.

\leftmargin The left margin of an item's text (not including the label) relative to the left margin of surrounding text. It cannot be
negative. May be set in a `list` environment. Sample usage:
\begin{list}{...}{\leftmargin .5in} would create a list with a left margin that is indented .5 inch from surrounding text.

\rightmargin The right margin of the list relative to the right margin of the surrounding text. It cannot be negative. May be set in a list environment. Sample usage:

\begin{list}{...}{\rightmargin .25in} would create a list with a right margin that is indented .25 inch from surrounding text.

\begin{list}{...}{\rightmargin \leftmargin} would create a list with a right margin that is the same as its left margin.

\listparindent The paragraph indentation of all paragraphs but the first within an item. May be set in a list environment. Sample usage:

\begin{list}{...}{\listparindent .125in} would indent paragraphs .125 inch within each item.

\itemindent The amount of indentation before the label of each item. (Default is zero.) It may be a negative value. It may be set in a list environment. Sample usage:

\begin{list}{...}{\itemindent .5in} would cause the label of each item to be indented by .5 inch.

\begin{list}{...}{\itemindent -.5in} would cause each item to have a hanging indent of .5 inch.

\labelsep The separation between the box containing the label and the text of the item. May be set in a list environment. Sample usage:

\begin{list}{...}{\labelsep .1in} would put a .1-inch separation between the label's box and the text.

\labelwidth The width of a box containing the label of each item. The label is placed flush-left within the box. If the width of the label's box plus \labelsep equals \leftmargin, then the labels will be flush with the left margin of surrounding text. If the width of the label's box plus the \labelsep is less than \leftmargin, then the labels will be indented from the surrounding text. May be set in a list environment. Sample usage:

\begin{list}{...}{\leftmargin .5in \labelsep .2in \labelwidth .3in} would place labels in a .5-inch-wide box flush with the left margin of surrounding text.

\begin{list}{...}{\leftmargin .5in \labelsep .1in
\labelwidth .3in} would place labels in a .5-inch-wide box, .1 inch indented from the left margin of surrounding text.

Math

\jot Extra vertical space added between rows of an **eqnarray** environment. Sample usage:

\setlength{\jot}{.2in} would cause a .2-inch space to appear between **eqnarray** rows, in addition to the normal space.

\mathindent The amount that displayed equations are indented from the left margin when the **fleqn** document style option is selected. (Default is 0 inch.) Sample usage:

\setlength{\mathindent}{.5in} would cause all displayed equations to be indented .5 inch if **fleqn** were used.

\abovedisplayskip The extra vertical space left above a long displayed equation. (When **fleqn** document style option is in effect, \topsep, a list parameter, is used.) An equation is considered a long equation if its left end is further to the left than the end of the last line of text. Example:

This is a long equation:

$$x = a + b + c + d + e + f + g + h + i + j + k + l + m + n$$

This is a rubber length. Sample usage:

\setlength{\abovedisplayskip}{.25in} would leave .25 inch of space, plus paragraph spacing, above long displayed equations.

\belowdisplayskip The extra vertical space left below a long displayed equation. (When **fleqn** document style option is in effect, \topsep, a list parameter is used.) *It is a rubber length.* Sample usage:

\setlength{\belowdisplayskip}{.15in} would leave .15 inch of space, plus paragraph spacing, below long displayed equations.

\abovedisplayshortskip The extra vertical space left above a short displayed equation. (When **fleqn** document style option is in effect, \topsep, a list parameter, is used.) An equation is considered a short equation if its left end is further to the right than the end of the last line of text. Example:

This is a short equation:

$$x = a$$

This is a rubber length. Sample usage:
`\setlength{\abovedisplayshortskip}{.15in}` would leave .15 inch of space, plus paragraph spacing, above short displayed equations.

`\belowdisplayshortskip` The extra vertical space left below a short displayed equation. (When `fleqn` document style option is in effect, `\topsep`, a list parameter, is used.) *It is a rubber length.* Sample usage:
`\setlength{\belowdisplayshortskip}{.1in}` would leave .1 inch of space, plus paragraph spacing, below short displayed equations.

Floats

`topnumber` The maximum number of floats allowed at the top of a text page. It is a counter. Sample usage:
`\setcounter{topnumber}{3}` would allow a maximum of three floats to appear at the top of a text page.

`\topfraction` The fraction of a text page's space allowed for floats at the top of a page. It is changed with `\renewcommand`. Sample usage:
`\renewcommand{\topfraction}{.5}` would allow as much as half of the page to be filled with floats at the top.

`bottomnumber` The maximum number of floats allowed at the bottom of a text page. It is a counter. Sample usage:
`\setcounter{bottomnumber}{2}` would allow a maximum of two floats to appear at the bottom of a text page.

`\bottomfraction` The fraction of a text page's space allowed for floats at the bottom. It is changed with `\renewcommand`. Sample usage:
`\renewcommand{\bottomfraction}{.333}` would allow as much as one third of the page to be filled with floats at the bottom.

totalnumber The maximum number of floats allowed to appear on any page, no matter what their positions. It is a counter. Sample usage:

`\setcounter{totalnumber}{5}` would restrict the number of floats on a page to five.

\textfraction For a page containing floats and text, this fraction of the page must be filled with text. The rest of the page may contain text or floats. It is changed with **\renewcommand**. Sample usage:

`\renewcommand{\textfraction}{.5}` specifies that at least one half of a page containing a combination of text and floats must contain text.

\floatpagefraction This fraction of a float page must be occupied with floats. The rest of the page may be floats or white space. It is changed with **\renewcommand**. Sample usage:

`\renewcommand{\floatpagefraction}{.75}` specifies that at least 75% of a float page must be occupied by floats.

dbltopnumber Same as **topnumber**, except it applies to double-column floats in two-column style.

\dbltopfraction Same as **\topfraction**, except it applies to double-column floats in two-column style.

\dblfloatpagefraction Same as **\floatpagefraction** except it applies to double-column floats in two-column style.

\floatsep The amount of separation between floats on a text page. *It is a rubber length.* Sample usage:

`\setlength{\floatsep}{.25in}` would cause floats to be separated by .25 inch.

\textfloatsep The vertical space between top or bottom placed floats and adjacent text. *This is a rubber length.* Sample usage:

`\setlength{\textfloatsep}{.1in}` would cause top or bottom placed floats to be separated from text by .1 inch.

\intextsep The vertical space between floats that appear in the middle of the page and the surrounding text. *This is a rubber length.*

Sample usage:

`\setlength{\intextsep}{.2in}` would cause floats in the middle of the page to be separated from text by .2 inch.

`\dblfloatsep` The same as `floatsep`, except it applies to double-column floats in two-column style.

`\dbltextfloatsep` The same as `textfloatsep`, except it applies to double-column floats in two-column style.

Tabular and Array

`\tabcolsep` Blank space at the left and right sides of each `tabular` column. It prevents two adjacent columns from running into each other. The space between two columns would be twice this amount. Sample usage:

`\setlength{\tabcolsep}{.1in}` would cause .1 inch of white space at each side of all columns, therefore .2 inch of white space would appear between columns.

`\arraycolsep` Blank space at the left and right sides of each `array` column. It prevents two adjacent columns from running into each other. The space between two columns would be twice this amount. Sample usage:

`\setlength{\arraycolsep}{.25in}` would cause .25 inch of white space at each side of all columns, therefore .5 inch of white space would appear between columns.

`\arrayrulewidth` For `tabular` and `array` environments, the width of vertical lines produced by a | character in the argument to `\begin{tabular}` or `\begin{array}`. Also, the width of horizontal lines produced by `\hline` and `\cline` commands. Sample usage:

`\setlength{\arrayrulewidth}{.02in}` would cause vertical and horizontal lines in `array` and `tabular` environments to be .02 inch wide.

`\doublerulesep` For `tabular` and `array` environments, the amount of space between double vertical lines produced by two successive

| characters or by two successive \hline or \cline commands. Sample usage:

\setlength{\doublerulesep}{.1in} would cause .1 inch of white space between double horizontal and vertical lines.

\arraystretch A factor that increases or decreases the spacing between rows in tabular and array environments within its scope. The normal space between rows is multiplied by this factor, which is normally 1. It is changed with \renewcommand. Sample usage:

\renewcommand{\arraystretch}{2} would double the space between rows.

\renewcommand{\arraystretch}{.8} would decrease the spacing to 80% of the normal amount.

Boxes

\fboxrule The width of the lines of the box produced by an \fbox or a \framebox command. (Does not affect \framebox within the picture environment.) Sample usage:

\setlength{\fboxrule}{.02in} would cause the boxes produced by \fbox and \framebox to be .02 inch thick.

\fboxsep The amount of white space left between the box produced by \fbox and \framebox commands and the text inside the box. (Does not affect \framebox within the picture environment.) Sample usage:

\setlength{\fboxsep}{0in} would allow the text inside a box to be touching the box, when \fbox or \framebox is used.

\setlength{\fboxsep}{.1in} would cause .1 inch of white space between text and the surrounding box.

Appendix D

The Picture Environment

The `picture` environment allows you to draw simple pictures in your LaTeX documents. To use it, you must be able to visualize your picture drawn on an imaginary grid. Then each object in the picture will be given a position in the grid.

D.1   Defining the Picture Area

The first step is to decide how fine or course this imaginary grid will be. The default size of a grid step is 1 point. That is very small (1/72 inch) and may be useful for pictures requiring high resolution. Let us experiment with a grid step size of one half-inch, since it is easier to visualize. To specify this size we would type the following command before entering the `picture` environment:

`\setlength{\unitlength}{.5in}`

In other words, whatever length is assigned to `\unitlength`, that length will be the grid step size. (If no `\unitlength` command is encountered, LaTeX uses the default length of 1 point.) The `\unitlength` may only be changed *outside* of the `picture` environment, typically just before beginning the environment.

The next step is to decide how many grid cells the picture will have in the horizontal direction and how many grid cells it will have in the vertical direction. In other words, how big is the overall picture, in terms of grid steps? Let us say we want a picture that is 8 cells wide and 4 cells high. We would invoke the `picture` environment as follows:

`\begin{picture}(8,4)`

In this case, where `\unitlength` is one half-inch, the picture will be eight times a half-inch wide by four times a half-inch high, or 4 inches wide by 2 inches high. The lower left corner of the rectangle described here is called the *origin*.

Notice that the argument to the `\begin{picture}` command is enclosed in parentheses instead of braces. This argument and all other arguments specifying the positions or dimensions of objects in the picture will be enclosed in parentheses. Also, the horizontal direction will be called the *x* direction, and the vertical direction will be called the *y* direction. Note that any position in the grid may be specified with a pair of numbers, the first number being the distance from the the lower left corner (the origin) in the horizontal direction (the *x* direction), and the second number being the distance from the origin in the vertical direction (the *y* direction). These pairs of numbers describing a position in the grid are called *coordinate pairs*.

Figure D.1 shows our 8×4 grid and some points on the grid for study. Note that when the *x* coordinate is an integer, the position falls on an *x* grid line, but when it is not an integer, for example, when it is 4.5, the position is not on an *x* grid line. The same is true with *y* coordinates and *y* grid lines.

The grid lines shown in Figure D.1 will not be visible in your picture unless you actually draw them within the `picture` environment. They are shown here to help illustrate how the `picture` environment works. All the `\begin{picture}(8,4)` command really does is cause LaTeX to save the right amount of space for your picture. In this case it would save a space 4 inches wide by 2 inches high.

D.2   Putting Objects in the Picture

To put objects into the picture, use the `\put` command. The `\put` command takes two arguments: the first is a coordinate pair specifying the position of the object; and the second is the object itself. An object

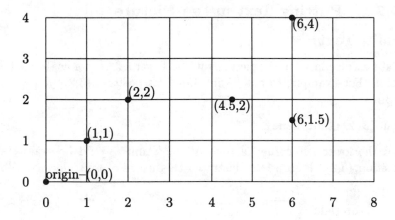

Figure D.1: Sample grid.

may be plain text, a shape such as a circle or rectangle, or a combination of text and a shape. The commands to produce various picture objects are described in the following sections. As you learn these commands, remember that they will be used in the second argument to the \put command.

Each object, whatever its size or shape, has an anchor point that is placed exactly on the position specified by the first argument to \put.

WARNING: Be sure not to put extra spaces in the second argument to the \put command, as this could affect the placement of the object. It may take a little practice to be able to determine the correct coordinates for placing objects correctly in the picture. One method that will make this easier is to draw the picture on graph paper. Perhaps the \unitlength for your picture can be made to match the grid on the graph paper. Then, finding the correct position for an object would be as simple as counting lines on the graph paper.

D.2.1   Putting Text in the Picture

Plain Text

Plain text is placed in the picture with its lower left corner as the anchor point. For example, to put "Aunt Jane" at position (3,2), you would type

`\put(3,2){Aunt Jane}`

and the lower left corner of the "A" in "Aunt" would be exactly at position (3,2). Figure D.2 illustrates this usage of text placement, as

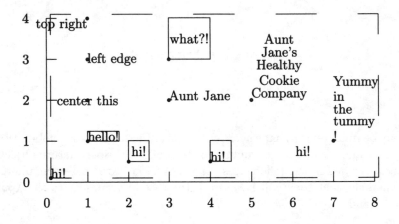

Figure D.2: Text-placing commands in the Picture environment.

well as several other examples. You may want to keep a marker on Figure D.2 so that you can refer to it often as you read on. Note that the dots in Figure D.2 are meant to show where the anchor point is for each object. The commands illustrated do not actually put out those dots.

Framebox

You can place a frame around some text on the picture with the `\framebox` command. In the `picture` environment, the `\framebox` command has a special form as follows: the first argument is a coordinate pair giving the width and height of the frame; the second argument is the text. For example,

`\put(2,.5){\framebox(.5,.5){hi!}}`

would put the word "hi!" into a .5 by .5 frame, and place its anchor point at position (2,.5). The anchor point for the frame is the lower left corner.

By default the text will be centered in the frame. But an optional argument changes the orientation of the text within the frame, by specifying top (t), bottom (b), left (l), or right (r). A combination of two letters may be used. For example, t would mean center the text at the top, but tr would mean place the text at the top right corner.

As another example,

`\put(4,.5){\framebox(.5,.5)[bl]{hi!}}`

would put a .5 by .5 frame with "hi!" at its bottom left corner into the picture at position (4,.5), as in Figure D.2.

Makebox

The \makebox command also has a special form within the `picture` environment that is the same as \framebox, except it does not draw the frame. For example,

`\put(6,.5){\makebox(.5,.5){hi!}}`

would center the word "hi!" in an invisible box of dimensions .5 by .5 with its lower left corner at position (6,.5). See Figure D.2.

Another important feature of the \makebox command is that it may also be used to center text at a position, by making the first argument (0,0). For example,

`\put(1,2){\makebox(0,0){center this}}`

would vertically and horizontally center "center this" at position (1,2). By using \makebox(0,0) with an optional positioning argument, you can also place one edge or corner of a piece of text at a position. In other words, the positioning argument should be

- **l** to put the left edge of the text on the anchor point

- **r** to put the right edge of the text on the anchor point

- **b** to put the bottom edge of the text on the anchor point

- **t** to put the top edge of the text on the anchor point

Two letters are used to indicate one corner of the text; for example,

- **tr** for the top right corner

- **tl** for the top left corner

- **br** for bottom right corner

- **bl** for the bottom left corner.

As an example, if you type

`\put(1,3){\makebox(0,0)[l]{left edge}}`

the left edge of "left edge" will appear at position (1,3). Again, see Figure D.2. Or if you type

`\put(1,4){\makebox(0,0)[tr]{top right}}`

the top right corner of "top right" will appear at position (1,4).

Newsavebox, Savebox and Usebox

The `\savebox` command also has a special form and meaning inside the `picture` environment. It is used to define a box containing text that will be used many times over within a picture. This box is invisible, unlike the frame of the `\framebox` command. First the box's name, which you will make up, must be reserved with the `\newsavebox` command as follows:

`\newsavebox{\mybox}`

This tells LaTeX that you are going to define a box named \mybox. Of course, you may use any name—\mybox is just an example.

Then the \savebox command is used to define the box. It takes three arguments. The first is the name of the box being defined, which you have made up and reserved with a \newsavebox command. The second is a coordinate pair specifying the size of the box, and the third is the text inside the box. For example, if your picture needs to have the words "Healthy Cookies" repeated at many different locations, you would type

```
\savebox{\mybox}(3,1){Healthy Cookies}
```

Now \mybox is equivalent to \makebox(3,1){Healthy Cookies}. You can use this new box with the \usebox command as follows:

```
\put(2,3){\usebox{\mybox}}
\put(1,1){\usebox{\mybox}}
```

and so on, as many times as you need to use the box. This would be equivalent to typing

```
\put(2,3){\makebox(3,1){Healthy Cookies}}
\put(1,1){\makebox(3,1){Healthy Cookies}}
```

and so on.

Recall that you had to first reserve the box's name with the \newsavebox command. That only has to be done once, before the first definition of the box. If you wish to redefine the box, you can change the contents of \mybox with another \savebox command at any time. For example,

```
\savebox{\mybox}(3,1){Aunt Jane's Cookies}
```

would change the contents of \mybox to "Aunt Jane's Cookies".

The \savebox command may be used to define a box that will be used many times within one picture, by putting it *within* the picture environment. It can also be used *outside* the picture environment, in its special form, to define a box that will be used in more than one picture. Using \savebox has the advantage of saving time in drawing many copies of the same thing. However, it does take up some of

LaTeX's memory space, so it must be used cautiously. If you have defined a box with \savebox, and you are not going to use it anymore, you may free up the memory it is taking by saying

`\sbox{\mybox}{}`

using the appropriate box name in place of \mybox.

Frame

The \frame command also puts a frame around some text, but the size of the frame is just big enough to fit around the text. The anchor point is the lower left corner of the frame. In other words,

`\put(1,1){\frame{hello!}}`

would put a tight-fitting frame around "hello!" and place the lower left corner at position (1,1). (See Figure D.2 on page 242.)

Dashbox

The \dashbox command is similar to \framebox except that the frame is drawn dashed. The length of the dashes must be an *integer multiple of* \unitlength, and is provided in an additional first argument. For example,

`\put(.1,.1){\dashbox{1}(8,4)[bl]{hi!}}`

would put an 8 by 4 box with "hi!" in the bottom left corner at position (.1,.1), only the box would be drawn with half-inch long dashes. The length of the dashes is .5 inch because that is one times \unitlength. As you can see, to make good-looking dashed boxes, \unitlength must rather small, since the dashes themselves will be at least as long as \unitlength. (See Figure D.2.)

Shortstack

The \shortstack command places a stack of words or phrases into the picture. The lower left corner of the stack is the anchor point, and it will be placed on the position specified in the \put command. The \shortstack command takes one argument, which contains the text to be stacked, with rows separated by \\. By default the stack will be centered, but an optional argument changes the justification to left (l) or right (r). For example,

\put(5,2){\shortstack{Aunt\\Jane's\\Healthy\\Cookie\\Company}}

would make a centered stack out of the five words in the argument, and put the bottom left corner of the stack at position (5,2). (See Figure D.2.) Also,

\put(7,1){\shortstack[l]{Yummy\\in\\the\\tummy\\!}}

would make a left-justified stack out of the words in its argument, and place the bottom left corner of the stack at position (7,1), as in Figure D.2.

D.2.2 Putting Shapes into the Picture

The \framebox command may be used with an invisible argument, such as \hspace{1in} or \rule{2.5in}{0.in}, to produce an empty frame, or a rectangle, on the picture. Additionally, lines, vectors (or arrows), circles, disks, and ovals may be drawn into a picture.

Lines

The \line command draws straight lines. It takes two arguments: the first argument defines the slope (or direction) of the line; and the second argument defines the length of the line. Horizontal and vertical lines are the simplest to draw.

To draw a horizontal line, the first argument to \line should be (1,0) for a line going to the right, or (−1,0) for a line going to the left. The second argument to \line is the length of the line. The starting point of the line is the first argument to the \put command. For example,

\put(1,4){\line(1,0){3}}

would produce a line that starts at position (1,4) and moves 3 cells to the right, ending at position (4,4).

For a vertical line, the first argument to the \line command should be (0,1) for a line going up, or (0,−1) for a line going down. The second argument is the length of the line. And the starting point is the first argument to the \put command. For example,

\put(4,3){\line(0,-1){2}}

would produce a line that starts at position (4,3), moves downward 2 cells, and ends at position (4,1). See Figure D.3. For lines that are not

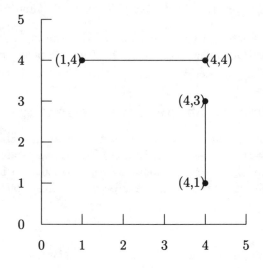

Figure D.3: Sample horizontal and vertical lines.

horizontal or vertical, the coordinate pair in the first argument to the \line command defines the slope of the line in the following way. If the coordinate pair is (x,y) as in

\put(0,0){\line(x,y){10}}

start at the starting point of the line (in this example (0,0)), and move x cells to the right (or left if x is negative). Then move y cells up (or down if **y** is negative). The line starts at the starting point and goes toward this new point you have reached (or through it, if the line is long enough.)

In other words, imagine that the starting point of the line is position (0,0), and the first argument to the \line command is (1,2), as in

\put(0,0){\line(1,2){2}}

This line would start at (0,0) and move 1 cell to the right and 2 cells up to get to position (1,2), and the line would be drawn toward that point. If the first argument to the \line command is (−3,1), and the starting point is (5,1), as in

\put(5,1){\line(-3,1){4}}}

then you would start at (5,1) and move 3 cells to the *left* and 1 cell up to get to position (2,2), and the line would go in that direction.

The length argument, which is the second argument to the \line command, is not exactly the length of the line. Rather, it is the distance in the horizontal direction that the line travels. In other words,

\put(0,0){\line(1,2){2}}

produces a line that starts at (0,0) and goes through (1,2) (or towards it) until its shadow on the horizontal axis is 2 units long. Also,

\put(5,1){\line(-3,1){2.5}

produces a line that starts at (5,1) and goes in the direction of (2,2) until its shadow on the horizontal axis is 2.5 units long. See Figure D.4. Horizontal and vertical lines are the only lines whose length argument is the actual length of the line.

If you need a line to be a certain length, and you can't come close enough by eyeballing it to see how long the shadow should be on the horizontal axis, you can use this formula to calculate the horizontal length h of the line:

$$h = \frac{d \cdot a}{\sqrt{a^2 + b^2}}$$

where (a, b) is the slope of the line (the first argument to the \line

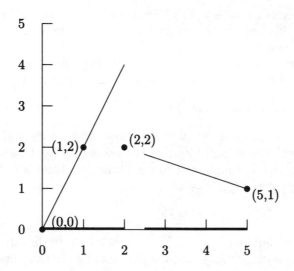

Figure D.4: Illustration of length argument to line command.

command,) and d is the desired length of the line. In other words, to get a line of length d, and slope (a,b), you would calculate h with the formula above and type

```
\put(0,0){\line(a,b){h}}
```

Of course you could put the line at any position—it doesn't have to be (0,0). See Figure D.5 for more examples of lines.

LaTeX has a finite set of line slopes to chose from. The pair of numbers that defines the slope (the numbers in the first argument to the \line command), must both be integers between −6 and +6, and they must not have a common divisor larger than 1. For example, (4,6) is illegal, but (2,3) is legal; also (7,2) is illegal because 7 is not in the legal range.

Figures D.6 through D.9 show lines of all possible slopes. Each line is labelled with the slope that defines it.

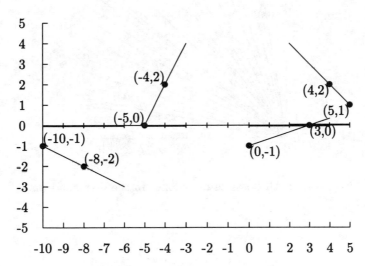

- `\put(-10,-1){\line(2,-1){4}}`

- `\put(-5,0){\line(1,2){2}}`

- `\put(0,-1){\line(3,1){4}}`

- `\put(5,1){\line(-1,1){3}}`

Figure D.5: More examples of lines.

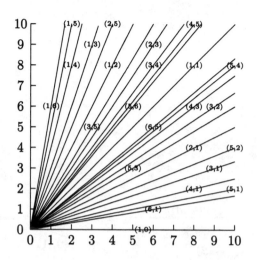

Figure D.6: All possible line slopes in the first quadrant.

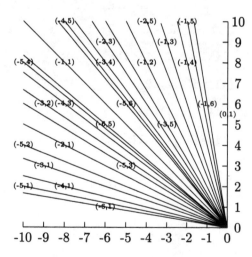

Figure D.7: All possible line slopes in the second quadrant.

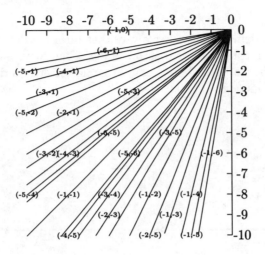

Figure D.8: All possible line slopes in the third quadrant.

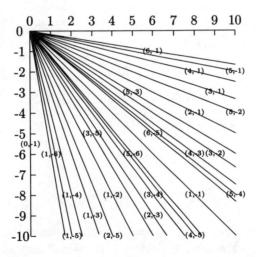

Figure D.9: All possible line slopes in the fourth quadrant.

Arrows

Arrows are defined in the same way that lines are defined, only using the \vector command. An arrow is just a line with an arrowhead at the end. Figure D.10 shows some examples of arrows drawn with the \vector command.

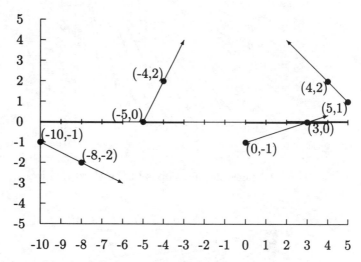

- \put(-10,-1){\vector(2,-1){4}}

- \put(-5,0){\vector(1,2){2}}

- \put(0,-1){\vector(3,1){4}}

- \put(5,1){\vector(-1,1){3}}

Figure D.10: Sample arrows.

The slopes available for arrows are slightly more limited than the slopes available for lines. For arrows, the pair of numbers defining the slope must be integers between -4 and $+4$, and must not have a common divisor greater than 1. You can still use Figures D.6 through D.9 to pick a slope, but just pick from the lines whose slopes are in this range. In other words, any slope that does not contain a 5 or 6, or a −5 or −6, is legal.

Circles

The \circle command draws a circle. Its one argument is the desired diameter for the circle. The anchor point is the center of the circle. Since LATEX has a limited set of circles it can draw, it draws the one closest to the desired diameter. The largest possible circle varies from installation to installation, but is probably around 1/2 inch in diameter. For example:

\put(3,3){\circle{.25}}

would draw a circle with a diameter of .25 unit, and place its center at position (3,3). Another circle could be drawn on top of it with a larger diameter as follows:

\put(3,3){\circle{.5}}

Another example of \circle is

\put(2,1){\circle{.3}}

which would draw a circle of diameter .3 unit at position (2,1). A disk, or a filled in circle, may be drawn with the \circle* command. As with the \circle command, its argument is the diameter of the disk, and the anchor point is the center of the disk. The largest disk available is somewhat smaller than the largest circle—around 1/4 inch. All of the points in the previous examples were drawn with the \circle* command. An example would be

\put(1,2){\circle*{.125}}

to put a disk of diameter .125 unit centered at position (1,2). A circle and its center point could be drawn as follows:

\put(4,1){\circle{.4}}
\put(4,1){\circle*{.2}}

Figure D.11 illustrates these examples.

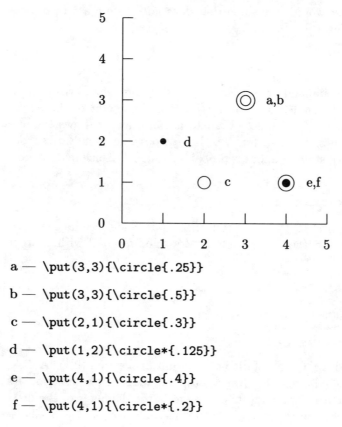

a — `\put(3,3){\circle{.25}}`

b — `\put(3,3){\circle{.5}}`

c — `\put(2,1){\circle{.3}}`

d — `\put(1,2){\circle*{.125}}`

e — `\put(4,1){\circle{.4}}`

f — `\put(4,1){\circle*{.2}}`

Figure D.11: Sample circles and disks.

Ovals

The `\oval` command produces an oval, which is really a rectangle with rounded corners. Its argument is a pair of numbers that specifies the width and height of the oval. The center of the oval is the anchor point. In other words,

`\put(3,2){\oval(4,1)}`

would put an oval shape that is 4 units wide and 1 unit high centered at position (3,2). Or

`\put(1,3){\oval(2,.75)}`

would produce an oval that is 2 units wide by .75 unit high centered at position (1,3).

Here is an example of putting text inside an oval shape:

`\put(4,4){\oval(3,1.5)}`
`\put(4,4){\makebox(0,0){HELLO THERE}`

An optional argument to the `\oval` command allows you to draw only one half or one quarter of an oval. The half ovals would be defined by t for top half, b for bottom half, l for left half, and r for right half. The quarter oval would be defined by combining two letters to indicate a corner of the oval, such as `tr` for top-right, or `bl` for bottom-left. For example,

`\put(3,1.5){\oval(4,1)[b]}`

would draw the bottom half of an oval, and

`\put(3.5,4.5){\oval(3,1.5)[tl]}`

would draw the top left corner of an oval. Figure D.12 illustrates these examples of the use of the `\oval` command.

Repeated Patterns

If a picture contains many copies of the same object, at *regularly spaced intervals* on the page, the `\multiput` command may be used instead of many `\put` commands. The `\multiput` command takes four arguments. The first argument is the position for the first copy of the object. The second argument is another coordinate pair specifying the distance in the horizontal and vertical directions to move before putting each additional copy of the object. The third argument is the number of copies to make, and the fourth argument is the object itself.

For example, look at the circles in Figure D.13. The first circle is at position (0,0). That's the first argument to `\multiput`. The other

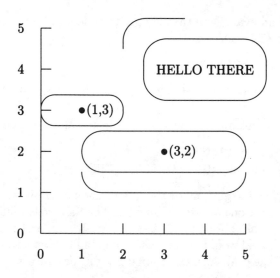

Figure D.12: Sample oval shapes.

circles are each 1 cell over and 1 cell up from the last, making the second argument (1,1). There are five circles altogether, so the third argument is 5. And the \circle command that draws the circle is the fourth argument. Therefore the command to draw these circles is

\multiput(0,0)(1,1){5}{\circle{.25}}

Just as another example, the command

\multiput(0,0)(1,2){3}{\framebox(2,1){cookie}}

would produce the result illustrated in Figure D.14.

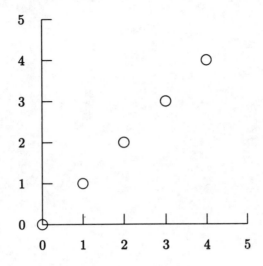

Figure D.13: Multiple circles drawn with the multiput command.

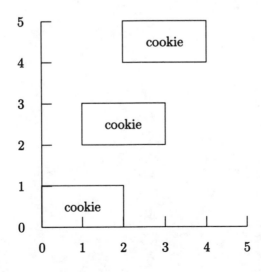

Figure D.14: Multiple frameboxes drawn with the multiput command.

Appendix E

Errors

E.1 When LaTeX Encounters an Error

When LaTeX is processing a document, it writes messages onto the screen to let you know what it is doing. For a normal run with no errors, the messages give you information such as

- The version numbers of the TeX and LaTeX software being used

- The names of files being read in and written out during the run

- The page numbers of completed pages of the resulting document

- Any warning messages that occur

For most error-free runs, this information is incidental and can be forgotten. It simply lets you know that LaTeX is doing what it is supposed to be doing.

Occasionally, however, LaTeX encounters something in an input file (a `.tex` file) that it cannot process. Here are some things that will cause LaTeX to stop with an error:

- A misspelled command name, such as "`\underine`"

- A command used where it doesn't make sense, such as `\theta` outside of math mode, or `\opening` in any document besides a letter

- A command given without its arguments, such as `\begin{tabular}` without the second argument that specifies the columns

When LaTeX does detect an error, it prints a message on the screen and stops, then it waits for a response from you. When this happens, you must make a decision as to what to tell LaTeX to do. The choices are as follows:

What To Do	Keystrokes
Recover from the error as well as possible and go on with the run	`<CR>`
Insert text into the input and go on with the run	`i text <CR>`
Write as much as possible to the .DVI file and then stop	`i\stop <CR>`
Stop the run now	`x  <CR>`

E.1.1   Continuing On With the Run

Notice that LaTeX can continue to run after encountering an error if you type `<CR>`. In most cases this is the smartest thing to do, since this way many errors can be detected in one run, and only one LaTeX run and one editing session are needed to correct those errors. Otherwise—if, for example, you type x to stop the run on the first error encountered every time you run LaTeX—you have to run LaTeX, stop, and edit your input file for each error, and that takes a lot of extra time.

However, for some errors it won't work to just keep typing `<CR>` every time LaTeX stops with an error message. This is because certain errors cause an infinite number of other errors to follow. In this case you could keep typing `<CR>` all night and you would never get through the run. So, if you find that you are running into an unreasonable number of errors in approximately the same spot in your input file, then it's time to type x and stop the run.

E.1.2 Inserting Text and Continuing

As you will see in the following sections, LaTeX indicates where it was in the input file when it found the error. Knowing this, it is sometimes possible to fix the error by using the i option to insert text.

For example, if you typed in a command incorrectly, such as "\smalskip," LaTeX would give an error message and wait for your response. You could then type i\smallskip, and LaTeX would read this as if it were in your file and go on. Note that the i command does *not* insert text into the input file; you have to go into the editor and make the change after the run is done.

E.1.3 Writing as Much as Possible to the .DVI File

LaTeX always tries to write a .DVI file, even when it encounters an error and the run is terminated with an x command. In other words, you can still print the document—it will simply be incomplete. However, LaTeX writes one complete page at a time to the .DVI file, and the last page worked on is lost when you use the x command.

Since the current page may contain a clue as to the cause of the error, it is preferable to try using i\stop if you must terminate the run. This causes LaTeX to write out as much as it can of the current page to the .DVI file, and then stop. This may simply bring on more error messages, in which case you just have to stop the run with x.

E.1.4 Missing \end{document}

If you forget to put an \end{document} in your file, LaTeX will process the file normally until it gets to the end, and then it will stop and prompt you with an asterisk. When you see this asterisk, you must respond by typing

```
\end{document}
```

Only then will LaTeX complete the processing and write the output files.

E.1.5   File Not Found

LaTeX stops the run in one more situation, and that is when it can't find a file it is trying to read. For example, if you have the following line in your file:

```
\input{myfile}
```

but there is no file `myfile.tex` on your disk, LaTeX stops and prompts you with the following message:

```
! I can't find file 'myfile.tex'.
\@iinput #1->\@@input #1

l.3 \input{myfile}

Please type another input file name:
```

In response to this, you may type the correct file name. Or, if you don't know what name to type, and you want to get past this prompt, type nul and a carriage return. This causes LaTeX to just go on with the run without reading in any file.

E.2   Interpreting Error Messages

The length of error messages varies, depending on exactly what TeX and LaTeX were trying to do at the time of the error. But two elements are always present: the *error indicator* and the *error locator*. Using these two tools, most errors can be quickly understood and corrected in the three following steps:

1. Read the error indicator.

2. Examine the line in the input file indicated by the error locator.

3. Correct any errors detected on that line or adjacent lines.

E.2.1   The Error Indicator

The error indicator is a brief sentence that defines the error. *It always starts with an exclamation point.* Here are three examples of error indicators:

```
!  Can be used only in preamble
!  Counter too large
!  Missing \begin{document}
```

The error indicator can come from LaTeX, in which case it will be one of a set of the 24 error messages explained in Section E.5. Or it can come from TeX. Many of TeX's most common error indicator messages are explained in Section E.6.

E.2.2   The Error Locator

The error locator gives the line number and the actual contents of the line in the input file where LaTeX found the error. Further, if the error occurred somewhere in the middle of the line, the error locator indicates that fact by breaking the line immediately after the point where the error occurred. For example, say your file contains the following line:

```
The baby is right next to my \chair in his playpen.
```

LaTeX would produce the following error message when processing this file:

```
! Undefined control sequence.
l.5 The baby is right next to my \chair
                                        in his playpen.
?
```

The first line of this message, which says "! Undefined control sequence." is the error indicator; the error locator is the next two lines. The "1.5" (that's the letter l, not a number 1) means the error is on line 5, and the text following is what appears on line 5 of the input file. Notice the last thing that is printed before the line break. Obviously, \chair is not a legal command, and that is what caused the error. The portion of the line following the error appears one line lower.

E.2.3   Examples of Error Messages

Here is a list of several commonly made mistakes and the error messages
that result from them:

Error: Forgetting to put a backslash before a pound sign (or other special
symbol); for example,

```
The first is
always tab #1, the second is always
tab \#2, etc.
```

Message: ! You can't use 'macro parameter character #' in horizontal mode.
1.7 always tab #
                            1, the second is always
?

Note that the line is broken right after the offending "#".

Error: Misspelled or mismatched environment names; for example,

```
\begin{enumerate}
\item ...
\item ...
\end{itemize}
```

Message: LaTeX error. See LaTeX manual for explanation.
                        Type H <return> for immediate help.
! \begin{enumerate} ended by \end{itemize}.
\@latexerr ...for immediate help.}\errmessage {#1}

\@checkend ...empa \@currenvir \else \@badend {#1}
                                                         \fi \def \@c...

\end ...tempa \relax \fi \endgroup \@checkend {#1}
                                                        \@gtempa \if...
1.19 \end{itemize}

?

Now, even though this error message has a lot of scary-looking
stuff in the middle of it, all you have to do is focus on two things:

1. The error indicator, which is marked with an exclamation point, and which describes the problem; for example,

   `! \begin{enumerate} ended by \end{itemize}.`

2. The error locator, which begins with a line number, and contains a line from the input file; for example,

   `1.19 \end{itemize}`

Notice that the error locator puts you on the last line of the badly nested environment. The information between the error indicator and the error locator is low-level TeX coding that only a TeXpert could understand, so you may just ignore it.

Error: Extra alignment tabs (&); for example,

```
\begin{tabular}{lrcr}
Left-justified & Right-Justified &
 Centered & Right-Justified\\
one & two & three & four\\
1 & 2 & 3 & 4 & \\
i & ii & iii & iv
\end{tabular}
```

Message:
```
! Extra alignment tab has been changed to \cr.
<recently read> \endtemplate

1.27 1 & 2 & 3 & 4 &
                     \\
?
```

This message is not hard to interpret once you learn that TeX calls the ampersands "alignment tabs".

Error: Missing units on a measurement; for example,

```
\begin{tabular}{lrcr}
Left-justified & Right-Justified &
 Centered & Right-Justified\\
one & two & three & four\\ [.25]
```

```
1 & 2 & 3 & 4 & \\
i & ii & iii & iv
\end{tabular}
```

Message: `! Illegal unit of measure (pt inserted).`
`<to be read again>`
`                 >`
`\@argtabularcr [#1]->\ifnum 0='{\fi }\ifdim #1>`
`                                             \z@ \unskip \@x...`
`1.35 one & two & three & four\\ [.25]`

`?`

Again, focus on the two important elements:

1. the error indicator:

   `! Illegal unit of measure (pt inserted).`

2. the error locator:

   `1.35 one & two & three & four\\ [.25]`

Since the input line given in the error locator is not broken, the error must be at the very end, and sure enough, the problem is the `[.25]` which has no units. It should be `[.25in]` (or `[.25cm]` or any other legal unit of measure). LATEX says "illegal unit of measure" because it reads the very next thing in the file and tries to interpret it as units. Since what it finds on the next line is "1," it is not happy.

E.3   The .log File

By now you are very familiar with the way LATEX reads an ASCII input file, processes the file, and writes the resulting output to the `.dvi` file. Along the way, LATEX also produces an `.aux` file, and possibly some other files, depending on the commands in the input file. One very important output file produced by every LATEX run is the `.log` file. This file contains information about the run, such as the version numbers of the TEX and LATEX programs, the names of all input and output files, and perhaps most importantly, it contains any error messages produced during the run. In fact, everything that appears on the screen during the LaTeX run is also written into the `.log` file. This information can be very useful in debugging a LaTeX document.

Take the following very simple LaTeX document:

```
1.  \documentstyle[12pt]{article}
2.  \begin{document}
3.  \section{Cat Food}
4.  \Each cat owner must decide what kind of food
5.  his or her cat will eat. There are many brands
6.  of cat food sold in grocery stores, as well as
7.  the more expensive--and probably more
8.  healthy---scientifically formulated foods
9.  available from veterinarians.
10. \end{document}
```

The line numbers printed above are for reference only, and are not actually in the file. Notice the error, "\Each", On line 4. Running LaTeX on this file produces the following `.log` file:

```
+ 1.  This is TeX, Version 2.1 (preloaded format ...
+ 2.     (PCTeX 2.10, (c)Personal TeX, Inc 1987. S/N 11586)
+ 3.  **&lplain exer1
+ 4.  (D:\JANE\BOOK\EXER1.TEX
+ 5.  LaTeX Version 2.09 <15 Sep 1987>
+ 6.  (C:\PCTEX\TEXINPUT\ARTICLE.STY
+ 7.  Document Style 'article' <12 Oct 87>.
+ 8.  (C:\PCTEX\TEXINPUT\ART12.STY)
  9.  \c@part=\count78
 10.  \c@section=\count79
 11.  \c@subsection=\count80
 12.  \c@subsubsection=\count81
 13.  \c@paragraph=\count82
 14.  \c@subparagraph=\count83
 15.  \c@figure=\count84
 16.  \c@table=\count85
 17.  )
+18.  No file exer1.aux.
+19.  ! Undefined control sequence.
+20.  l.4 \Each
```

```
+21.             cat owner must decide what kind of food
+22.  ?
+23.
+24.  Overfull \hbox (1.09114pt too wide) in paragraph ...
+25.  \twlrm expensive--and prob-a-bly more healthy...
+26.  ds avail-
 27.
 28.  \hbox(8.33333+2.33333)x390.0, glue set - 1.0
 29.  .\twlrm e
 30.  .\twlrm x
 31.  .\twlrm p
 32.  .\kern0.33333
 33.  .\twlrm e
 34.  .etc.
 35.
+36.  [1] (D:\JANE\BOOK\EXER1.AUX)
 37.  Here is how much of TeX's memory you used:
 38.    140 strings out of 1596
 39.    1332 string characters out of 13943
 40.    25885 words of memory out of 65535
 41.    2082 multiletter control sequences out of 3000
 42.    18419 words of font info for 72 fonts, out of 23023 for ...
 43.    14 hyphenation exceptions out of 307
 44.    12i,4n,15p,154b,84s stack positions out of 200i,40n,60p,...
 45.
+46.  Output written on D:\JANE\BOOK\EXER1.DVI (1 page, 624 byt...
```

Lines marked with a "+" also appear on the screen during the run. The information in lines 9–17, 28–34, and 37–44 contain information that is useful to a TeX expert, but probably not to the average user. Especially notice that lines 19–22 contain a record of the error that occurred during the run. Since LaTeX writes all error information into the .log file, there is no need to stop after each error to make a correction. Rather, you may run LaTeX on a file and carriage-return past all the errors without even trying to remember what they all are. After the run is finished, you may print the .log file with a simple DOS print command, or you may use your ASCII editor to look into it, since it is an ASCII file.

E.4 Helpful Hints for Finding Errors

Many errors may be found and corrected by using the three-step method mentioned above:

1. Read the error indicator.

2. Examine the line in the input file indicated by the error locator.

3. Correct any errors detected on that line or on adjacent lines.

When this does not work, there are several other techniques that can help.

E.4.1 Look Before the Indicated Line

If you cannot see anything wrong with the line given in the error locator, then look at the 4–5 lines just above that line for an error. Something may have gone wrong there, but not wrong enough to stop LATEX.

For example, some math errors will cause LATEX to stop on the \end{equation} line, when the error is within the equation environment. See the following example:

```
\begin{equation}
x = e^{\alpha-\beta
\end{equation}
```

Notice that the closing brace is missing on the superscript. This produces the following error message:

```
! You can't use '\eqno' in math mode.
\endequation ->\eqno
                     \@eqnnum $$\global \@ignoretrue
\end #1->\csname end#1\endcsname
                                  \if@endpe \global \let \@gtem...
1.9 \end{equation}

?
```

This is a message from TEX that is not very helpful to the LATEX user who has no idea what `\eqno` means! What this message usually indicates is that LATEX got to the end of the equation (i.e., it was trying to put on the equation number), then detected something wrong. Even though the error locator gives the `\end{equation}` line, that line is plainly not where the error is. By looking carefully at the lines above that line, you would be able to see the missing brace.

If you carriage return past this error message, the following error comes up:

```
! Missing } inserted.
<inserted text>
                        }
<to be read again>
                          $
\endequation ->\eqno \@eqnnum $
                               $\global \@ignoretrue
\end #1->\csname end#1\endcsname
                                \if@endpe \global \let \@gtem...
l.9 \end{equation}
```

This is more helpful, since it tells you exactly what is wrong with the equation; but it does not tell you where the error is. All you will know is that the error was in that particular equation.

E.4.2   Incidental Error?

In the above example, there were two error messages, but only one error. This is not uncommon. So, one of the first steps to take in debugging an error is to make sure this error message does not stem from an earlier error that you have already understood.

Many times, when more than one error message comes up for the same error, the error locator will display the same line number over and over. That is a good indication that there is only one error.

Of course, if it turns out that an error message is referring to an error that you have already debugged, then that message may be disregarded.

E.4.3 Which Input File?

If your document is spread out into many different files—one for each chapter, for instance—and you are using \input or \include commands with a root file to LaTeX your document, then you must determine which file LaTeX is reading when it encounters the error. Otherwise, the line number in the error locator will not be very useful in finding the error.

LaTeX prints out, on the screen and in the .log file, the name of each file that it reads or writes. When it opens a file to read it, it prints an open parenthesis followed by the file name. Then, when it is done reading that file, it prints a close parenthesis. Look again at the sample .log file from Section E.3:

```
1. This is TeX, Version 2.1 (preloaded format ...
2.   (PCTeX 2.10, (c)Personal TeX, Inc 1987. S/N 11586)
3. **&lplain exer1
4. (D:\JANE\BOOK\EXER1.TEX
5. LaTeX Version 2.09 <15 Sep 1987>
6. (C:\PCTEX\TEXINPUT\ARTICLE.STY
7. Document Style 'article' <12 Oct 87>.
8. (C:\PCTEX\TEXINPUT\ART12.STY)
9. \c@part=\count78
10. \c@section=\count79
11. \c@subsection=\count80
12. \c@subsubsection=\count81
13. \c@paragraph=\count82
14. \c@subparagraph=\count83
15. \c@figure=\count84
16. \c@table=\count85
17. )
18. No file exer1.aux.
19. ! Undefined control sequence.
20. l.4 \Each
21.            cat owner must decide what kind of food
22. ?
23.
24. Overfull \hbox (1.09114pt too wide) in paragraph ...
25. \twlrm expensive--and prob-a-bly more healthy...
26. ds avail-
27.
28. \hbox(8.33333+2.33333)x390.0, glue set - 1.0
```

```
29.  .\twlrm e
30.  .\twlrm x
31.  .\twlrm p
32.  .\kern0.33333
33.  .\twlrm e
34.  .etc.
35.
36.  [1] (D:\JANE\BOOK\EXER1.AUX)
37.  Here is how much of TeX's memory you used:
38.   140 strings out of 1596
39.   1332 string characters out of 13943
40.   25885 words of memory out of 65535
41.   2082 multiletter control sequences out of 3000
42.   18419 words of font info for 72 fonts, out of 23023 for 1...
43.   14 hyphenation exceptions out of 307
44.   12i,4n,15p,154b,84s stack positions out of 200i,40n,60p,1...
45.
46.  Output written on D:\JANE\BOOK\EXER1.DVI (1 page, 624 byte...
```

While processing this run, LaTeX read input from three files:

exer1.tex the LaTeX input file

article.sty the main style file for `article` style

art12.sty the portions of `article` style having to do with the 12pt document style option.

Line 4 indicates that it is beginning to read `exer1.tex`. Line 6 says that it is beginning to read `article.sty` (but `exer1.tex` is still open). Line 8 says that it opens, reads, and closes (note the closing parenthesis) `art12.sty`. The closing parenthesis on line 17 indicates that it is done with `article.sty`. And the `.log` file doesn't contain the closing parenthesis for `exer1.tex`.

If you start at line 19, where the error occurs and search backwards for the last file that was opened, but not closed, you will come to `exer1.tex`, which is the file containing the error.

Let's take a slightly more complex example. Say you have a root file named `root.tex`, and in it you have `\include` statements that call in three files named `ch1.tex`, `ch2.tex`, and `ch3.tex`—say each one of these files contains a chapter. So `root.tex` might look like the following:

```
\documentstyle{report}
\includeonly{ch1,ch2,ch3}
\begin{document}
\pagenumbering{roman}
\tableofcontents
\pagenumbering{arabic}
\include{ch1}
\include{ch2}
\include{ch3}
\end{document}
```

Now, say that you misspelled the \tableofcontents command and
typed "\talbeofcontents" instead. If you LaTeX the file, typing a
carriage return after the error, your .log file would look something like
this:

```
1.  This is TeX, Version 2.1 ...
2.   (PCTeX 2.10, (c)Personal TeX, Inc 1987. S/N 11586)
3.  **&lplain root
4.  (D:\JANE\BOOK\ROOT.TEX
5.  LaTeX Version 2.09 <15 Sep 1987>
6.  (C:\PCTEX\TEXINPUT\REPORT.STY
7.  Document Style 'report' <12 Oct 87>.
8.  (C:\PCTEX\TEXINPUT\REP10.STY)
9.  \descriptionmargin=\dimen99
10. \c@part=\count78
11. \c@chapter=\count79
12. \c@section=\count80
13. \c@subsection=\count81
14. \c@subsubsection=\count82
15. \c@paragraph=\count83
16. \c@subparagraph=\count84
17. \c@figure=\count85
18. \c@table=\count86
19.  (C:\PCTEX\TEXINPUT\TITLEPAGE.STY))
20. No file root.aux.
21. ! Undefined control sequence.
22. 1.5 \talbeofcontents
23.
24. ?
25. (D:\JANE\BOOK\CH1.TEX
26. Chapter 1.
```

27.) [1
28.
29.
30.
31.] (D:\JANE\BOOK\CH2.TEX
32. Chapter 2.
33.) [2
34.
35.
36.
37.] (D:\JANE\BOOK\CH3.TEX
38. Chapter 3.
39.) [3
40.
41.
42.
43.] (D:\JANE\BOOK\ROOT.AUX (D:\JANE\BOOK\CH1.AUX)
                              (D:\JANE\BOOK\CH2.AUX):
44. \JANE\BOOK\CH3.AUX))
45. Here is how much of TeX's memory you used:
46.   191 strings out of 1596
47.   1662 string characters out of 13943
48.   26328 words of memory out of 65535
49.   2099 multiletter control sequences out of 3000
50.   19025 words of font info for 74 fonts, out of 23023 for 1...
51.   14 hyphenation exceptions out of 307
52.   12i,4n,15p,170b,94s stack positions out of 200i,40n,60p,1...
53.
54. Output written on D:\JANE\BOOK\ROOT.DVI (3 pages, 884 byte...

LATEX opens root.tex on line 4. In lines 6–19 it opens and closes
report.sty, rep10.sty, and titlepage.sty, which are all parts of
the document style. Then the error occurs on line 21 of the .log file.
The last file opened but not closed was root.tex, so the error locator
is talking about line 5 in root.tex.

Now let's correct that error and see what happens if there is an
error in one of the chapter files, ch1.tex, ch2.tex, or ch3.tex. The
.log file from this new run looks like the following:

1. This is TeX, Version 2.1 (preloaded format=lplain 88.6.16)...
2.   (PCTeX 2.10, (c)Personal TeX, Inc 1987. S/N 11586)
3. **&lplain root
4. (D:\JANE\BOOK\ROOT.TEX

```
 5. LaTeX Version 2.09 <15 Sep 1987>
 6. (C:\PCTEX\TEXINPUT\REPORT.STY
 7. Document Style 'report' <12 Oct 87>.
 8. (C:\PCTEX\TEXINPUT\REP10.STY)
 9. \descriptionmargin=\dimen99
10. \c@part=\count78
11. \c@chapter=\count79
12. \c@section=\count80
13. \c@subsection=\count81
14. \c@subsubsection=\count82
15. \c@paragraph=\count83
16. \c@subparagraph=\count84
17. \c@figure=\count85
18. \c@table=\count86
19.  (C:\PCTEX\TEXINPUT\TITLEPAGE.STY))
20. (D:\JANE\BOOK\ROOT.AUX (D:\JANE\BOOK\CH1.AUX) (D:\JANE\BOO...
21. (D:\JANE\BOOK\CH3.AUX))
22. No file root.toc.
23. \tf@toc=\write3
24. [1
25.
26.
27. ] (D:\JANE\BOOK\CH1.TEX
28. Chapter 1.
29. ) [2
30.
31.
32. ] (D:\JANE\BOOK\CH2.TEX
33. Chapter 2.
34. ! Undefined control sequence.
35. l.3 This is a very \short
36.                          chapter with only one sentence i...
37. ?
38. ) [3
39.
40.
41.
42. ] (D:\JANE\BOOK\CH3.TEX
43. Chapter 3.
44. ) [4
45.
46.
47.
48. ] (D:\JANE\BOOK\ROOT.AUX (D:\JANE\BOOK\CH1.AUX)
```

```
                              (D:\JANE\BOOK\CH2.AUX) (D :
49.  \JANE\BOOK\CH3.AUX))
50.  Here is how much of TeX's memory you used:
55.  1212 strings out of 1596
52.  1767 string characters out of 13943
53.  27112 words of memory out of 65535
54.  2102 multiletter control sequences out of 3000
55.  19025 words of font info for 74 fonts, out of 23023 for ...
56.  14 hyphenation exceptions out of 307
57.  12i,4n,15p,170b,94s stack positions out of 200i,40n,60p,...
58.
59.  Output written on D:\JANE\BOOK\ROOT.DVI (4 pages, 984 byte...
```

The first 19 lines are identical to the previous example. LaTeX has opened `root.tex`, and it has opened and closed `report.sty`, `rep10.sty`, and `titlepage.sty`. Now, in lines 20 and 21, you see it opening and closing `root.aux`, `ch1.aux`, `ch2.aux`, and `ch3.aux` (four open parentheses, four closing parentheses). These files are there now because this is the second time we have LaTeXed `root.tex`. But they don't have any errors.

LaTeX opens `ch1.tex` on line 27 and closes it on line 29—still no errors. Then on line 32 it opens `ch2.tex`, and right after that, before it has closed it, the error comes up. Ah HAH! The error must be, and in fact is, on line 3 of `ch2.tex`.

Anyway, sometimes you will recognize the text in the error locator line and know which of your files it is in. But in case you don't, this gives you a way of figuring out which file LaTeX is talking about.

E.4.4   Checking Output for Anomalies

As was mentioned in Section E.1.3, LaTeX attempts to write out a .DVI file even if the run is terminated with an x after an error. Therefore, it is sometimes helpful to print out the output and look for something unexpected. This can sometimes give a clue as to what and where the error is.

For example, take the following paragraph:

```
Here is some text in which the author uses
$\theta without a closing dollar sign.
```

```
Then he uses the $\theta$ command correctly,
but \LaTeX\ reports an error on that line.
```

`latexing` this text would produce the following error message:

```
! Missing $ inserted.
<inserted text>
                        $
<to be read again>
                        \theta
1.6 Then he uses the $\theta
                            $ command correctly,
?
```

There is no error on the line indicated in the error locator, line 6. The error happened before that. It is easy to see what went wrong by looking at what LaTeX does with this paragraph:

> Here is some text in which the author uses
> $\theta withoutaclosingdollarsign.Thenheusesthe\theta$ command cor-
> rectly, but LaTeX reports an error on that line.

Notice that the first dollar sign begins math mode, therefore the text following it is italicized, because LaTeX never received the signal to get out of math mode.

E.4.5 Isolate the Error

When all of the above methods fail, there is still a good way to debug a subtle error. Start by taking a section of the file that is near the line indicated by the error locator, or near where you think the error is. Put this section of the file into a separate file, add \documentstyle, \begin{document} and \end{document} commands, and latex the new file.

Keep trying different sections until you get the error to occur with the small file. Then gradually remove little bits from the small file, and latex again each time you remove something to see if you still get the error message. This can save a lot of time, since it is faster to latex a small file than a big one. Also, if you get the file down to a few lines and the error still comes up, you should be able to see what is causing the error.

E.5 LaTeX's Error Messages

What follows is an alphabetical list of all of LaTeX's error messages. With each message is a brief explanation, and an example of what would cause the error. If you get an error and you cannot find it in this list, see Section E.6 for a list of TeX's most common error messages.

- ! Bad \line or vector argument.

  The first argument to a \line command is an illegal slope. The coordinate pair that defines the slope of a line must be two integers between −6 and +6, and they must not have a common divisor larger than one.

  For example, \line(7,1){5} is illegal, but \line(6,1){5} is legal; \line(4,6){3} is illegal, but \line(2,3){3} is legal. See Section D.2.2 for a full explanation of the \line command.

- ! Bad math environment delimiter

  LaTeX found a \[(begin a displayed, unnumbered equation) command when it thought it was already in math mode, or else it found a \] (end displayed, unnumbered equation) command when it did not think it was in math mode.

  This could be caused by a forgotten—or an extra—\[or \] command, causing mismatched math mode delimiters. For example, take the following lines:

  ```
  Here's an equation with an extra backslash-bracket:

  \begin{equation}
  x = y
  \end{equation} \]
  ```

And here's one with a forgotten backslash-bracket:

```
a = b \]
```

LATEX would give the following error messages when processing this file:

```
LaTeX error.  See LaTeX manual for explanation.
            Type  H <return>  for immediate help.
! Bad math environment delimiter.
\@latexerr ...for immediate help.}\errmessage {#1}

\]...finner \@badmath \else $$\fi \else \@badmath
                                              \fi \ignores...
1.5 \end{equation} \]

?
LaTeX error.  See LaTeX manual for explanation.
            Type  H <return>  for immediate help.
! Bad math environment delimiter.
\@latexerr ...for immediate help.}\errmessage {#1}

\]...finner \@badmath \else $$\fi \else \@badmath
                                              \fi \ignores...
1.9  a = b \]

?
```

- ! Bad use of \\.

A \\ (end-of-line) command appears on a line by itself in a centering or flushing environment. For example, see the following lines:

```
The wrong way to leave space after a line:

\begin{center}
Suppose you want space after this line\\
\\
The above double-backslash all alone on a line
```

```
    is incorrect\\
\end{center}
```

The right way to leave space after a line:

```
\begin{center}
Use vspace after the double-backslash\\ \vspace{.25in}
Or use double-backslash followed by
                    a length in brackets\\ [.25in]
\end{center}
```

LaTeX would give the following error message when processing this file:

```
LaTeX error.  See LaTeX manual for explanation.
            Type H <return>  for immediate help.
! Bad use of \\.
\@latexerr ...for immediate help.}\errmessage {#1}

\\->\ifhmode \unskip \else \@badcrerr
                                      \fi \par \@ifstar {\pena...
1.5 \\

?
```

Do not try to leave space *between lines*, rather, think in terms of leaving space *after a line*, where needed. Study the correct examples in this sample file. This way you will not run into problems.

- ! \begin{enumerate} ended by \end{itemize}

  LaTeX found an \end{itemize} where it was expecting an \end{enumerate}. Either you simply typed the wrong environment name, or you left out an earlier \end{enumerate}. This message can contain any mismatched environment names. Examples:

  ```
  ! \begin{itemize} ended by \end{document}
  ! \begin{description} ended by \end{itemize}
  ```

Check for matching \begin and \end commands in your file. For
an example, look at the following lines:

```
\begin{enumerate}
\item This is the first
\item This is the second
\end{emunerate}
```

Running LATEX on this will produce the following error:

```
LaTeX error.  See LaTeX manual for explanation.
               Type  H <return>  for immediate help.
! \begin{enumerate} ended by \end{emunerate}.
\@latexerr ...for immediate help.}\errmessage {#1}

\@checkend ...empa \@currenvir \else \@badend {#1}
                                                  \fi \def \@c...

\end ...tempa \relax \fi \endgroup \@checkend {#1}
                                               \@gtempa \if...
1.4 \end{emunerate}

?
```

Note that the environment name is misspelled in the \end statement.

- ! Can be used only in preamble.

  One of these commands appears after \begin{document}:

```
\documentstyle
\nofiles
\includeonly
\begin{document} (a duplicate)
```

These commands may only appear in the preamble (between the
\documentstyle command and the \begin{document}).

- ! Command name \mycommand already used

Where **\mycommand** is an existing LaTeX command, or a command you have previously defined with **\newcommand**. This helps prevent you from accidentally redefining an existing command that may be important.

This error message also appears if you attempt to define an existing environment with **\newenvironment**, an existing box with **\newsavebox**, or an existing counter with **\newcounter**. The solution is to choose a different name for the command, environment, box, or counter. Or, if you are sure you want to give a command or environment a new definition, use one of the following commands:

\renewcommand
\renewenvironment

The following lines are an example of defining a command, and then trying to define it again:

`\newcommand{\ajc}{Aunt Jane's Cookies}`

`The best cookies in the world are \ajc.`

`\newcommand{\ajc}{Aunt Jane's Crackers}`

`And the best crackers in the world are \ajc!`

Running LaTeX on this file would produce the following error:

```
LaTeX error.  See LaTeX manual for explanation.
             Type  H <return>  for immediate help.
! Command name 'ajc' already used.
\@latexerr ...for immediate help.}\errmessage {#1}

\@ifundefined ...me #1\endcsname \relax #2\else #3
                                                  \fi
1.5 \newcommand{\ajc}{Aunt Jane's Crackers}

?
```

To correct the error, change line 5 to read:

```
\renewcommand{\ajc}{Aunt Jane's Crackers}
```

- **! Counter too large.**

  A counter that prints out as a letter—such as the second level items in an enumerated list—has gotten larger than 26 (or z). This can happen if you accidentally set a letter-style counter too large with \setcounter, or if you simply have more than 26 of something that is being counted with letters; e.g., 27 appendices.

  For example, you could define the page number to be a capital letter, and then try to print a page 30:

```
\renewcommand{\thepage}{\Alph{page}}
This is page one, but the page number
    will come out ''A''.
\clearpage
Now I set the page counter to 30
\setcounter{page}{30}
but it won't work because there's no
    corresponding letter.
```

  latexing this file produces the following error:

```
LaTeX error.  See LaTeX manual for explanation.
            Type  H <return>  for immediate help.
! Counter too large.
\@latexerr ...for immediate help.}\errmessage {#1}

\@Ialph ...or V\or W\or X\or Y\or Z\else \@ctrerr
                                                \fi
\@Alph ...#1\or A\or B\or C\or D\else \@Ialph {#1}
                                                \fi
\@oddfoot ->\rm \hfil \thepage
                            \hfil
\@outputpage ...le \let \index \@gobble \@thefoot
                                            }}}\global \...
```

```
\@opcol ...lumn \@outputdblcol \else \@outputpage
                                                    \global \@co...
<output> ...specialoutput \else \@makecol \@opcol
                                                    \@floatplace...

\newpage ->\par \vfil \penalty -\@M

\clearpage ->\newpage
                         \write \m@ne {}\vbox {}\penalty -\@Mi
\enddocument ->\@checkend {document}\clearpage
                                                    \begingroup \if...
\end #1->\csname end#1\endcsname
                                        \if@endpe \global \let \@gtem...
1.34 \end{document}

?
```

This is a good example of how important it is to focus on the error indicator, marked with an exclamation point, and the error locator, marked with a question mark. All those lines of jibberish in between the two indicate that T_EX was way down into the guts of the program when it tried to produce the page number and bombed.

- ! Environment () undefined

  where "()" can be any name that LAT_EX does not recognize to be a defined environment. You probably mistyped the environment name in a \begin statement. For example,

```
\begin{iemize}
\item The first item
\end{itemize}
```

would produce the following error message:

```
LaTeX error.  See LaTeX manual for explanation.
              Type  H <return>  for immediate help.
! Environment iemize undefined.
\@latexerr ...for immediate help.}\errmessage {#1}
```

```
1.34 \begin{iemize}
```

```
?
```

To correct the problem (only for this one run), you could now type

```
i\begin{itemize}
```

and LATₑX would throw away the `\begin{iemize}` and use the `\begin{itemize}` that you inserted. You also would need to edit your input file and correct the error permanently.

- `! Float(s) lost.`

  This error message occurs when LATₑX finds a `figure` or `table` environment in one of the following places:

  - a `minipage` environment
  - the contents of a `\parbox` command
  - a footnote
  - a `figure` or `table`

  It seems obvious why a `figure` or `table` should not be found in these situations. For an example, see the following file:

```
\begin{minipage}{3.in}
A float in a minipage doesn't make
sense---where can the float float to?!
\begin{figure}
\vspace{2.in}
\caption{Here is the caption}
\end{figure}
\end{minipage}
```

latexing this file produces the following error:

```
LaTeX error.  See LaTeX manual for explanation.
                Type  H <return>  for immediate help.
! Float(s) lost.
\@latexerr ...for immediate help.}\errmessage {#1}

\@doclearpage ... \@latexerr {Float(s) lost}\@ehb
                                                    \gdef \@curr...

\@specialoutput ...penalty > -\@Mii \@doclearpage
                                                    \else \ifnum...
<output> ... \outputpenalty <-\@M \@specialoutput
                                                    \else \@make...

\clearpage ...rite \m@ne {}\vbox {}\penalty -\@Mi

\enddocument ->\@checkend {document}\clearpage
                                                    \begingroup \if...
\end #1->\csname end#1\endcsname
                                    \if@endpe \global \let \@gtem...
l.46 \end{document}

?
```

- ! Illegal character in array arg.

This means that LaTeX found something in the argument to
\begin{array} or \begin{tabular} that it couldn't understand.
This is the argument that specifies the columns. Legal characters
for array arguments are:

l	—Left-justified column
r	—Right-justified column
c	—Centered column
p{*width*}	—Paragraph-wrapping column of width *width*
|	—Vertical line the length of the table
@{*expression*}	—Insert *expression* in every row

Any character other than those listed above will cause this error.
The same error message applies for illegal characters in the sec-

ond argument of a \multicolumn command, which specifies the justification of the multi-column entry.

The following example has an illegal character ("a") in a tabular argument:

```
\begin{tabular}{lcar}
a & b & c & d \\
e & f & g & h
\end{tabular}
```

latexing this tabular would give the following error message:

```
LaTeX error.  See LaTeX manual for explanation.
                Type  H <return>  for immediate help.
! Illegal character in array arg.
\@latexerr ...for immediate help.}\errmessage {#1}

\@testpach ...else \if #1p3 \else \z@ \@preamerr 0
                                                 \fi \fi \fi ...
<argument> \@testpach \@nextchar
                                 \ifcase \@chclass \@classz \o...

\@nextwhile ...let \@nextwhile =\@fornoop \else #4
                                                  \relax \let ...

\@tfor ...else \@tforloop #2\@nil \@nil \@@ #1{#3}
                                                  \fi
\@mkpream ...@classv \fi \@lastchclass \@chclass }
                                                 \ifcase \@la...

\@array ... \dp \strutbox width\z@ }\@mkpream {#2}
                                                 \edef \@prea...
1.51 \begin{tabular}{lcar}

?
```

- **! Missing \begin{document}**

Either the \begin{document} command is missing from the file, or there is some text or command before it that will cause LATEX to print something.   Normally, all the things before the

`\begin{document}` are declarations and definitions for the run, *not* printable text.

Examine the file below:

```
\documentstyle{report}
\newcommand{\ajhc}{Aunt Jane's Healthy Cookie}s
\begin{document}
\chapter{Cookies}

Everyone should eat \ajhc, because they are so good!
\end{document}
```

Notice that the closing brace on the definition of `\ajhc` is before the final "s" instead of after it. Now look at what happens when LaTeX processes this file:

```
LaTeX error.  See LaTeX manual for explanation.
                Type  H <return>  for immediate help.
! Missing \begin{document}.
\@latexerr ...for immediate help.}\errmessage {#1}

<to be read again>
                  s
1.2 ...command{\ajhc}{Aunt Jane's Healthy Cookie}s

?
```

- **! Missing p-arg in array arg.**

  This error occurs if you try to define a p-column in a **tabular** or **array** environment, but you forget to specify the width for the column. For example, if you tried to **latex** the following table,

```
\begin{tabular}{lp}
Hammer & A tool used for putting in nails \\
Screwdriver & A tool used for putting in screws \\
\end{tabular}
```

  you would get the following error:

```
LaTeX error.  See LaTeX manual for explanation.
               Type  H <return>  for immediate help.
! Missing p-arg in array arg.
\@latexerr ...for immediate help.}\errmessage {#1}

\@mkpream ... \@preamerr \@ne \or \@preamerr \tw@
                                                 \or \or \@ac...
\@array ... \dp \strutbox width\z@ }\@mkpream {#2}
                                                 \edef \@prea...
1.8 \begin{tabular}{lp}

?
```

- ! Missing @-exp in array arg.

This is similar to the previous error. A **tabular** or **array** is defined with an **@** in the column-defining argument, but no expression is given after the **@**. See the example below:

```
\begin{tabular}{lr@}
```

A \begin{tabular} command like this would produce the following error:

```
LaTeX error.  See LaTeX manual for explanation.
               Type  H <return>  for immediate help.
! Missing @-exp in array arg.
\@latexerr ...for immediate help.}\errmessage {#1}

\@mkpream ...class \@acol \or \or \@preamerr \@ne
                                                 \or \@preame...
\@array ... \dp \strutbox width\z@ }\@mkpream {#2}
                                                 \edef \@prea...
1.8 \begin{tabular}{lr@}

?
```

This error only occurs if the **@** sign is the last thing in the argument. Otherwise, the character immediately following the **@** sign will be taken for the **@**-expression. In other words,

```
\begin{tabular}{lr@ll}
```

would be interpreted as

```
\begin{tabular}{lr@{l}l}
```

- ! No such counter

  This error can occur if you don't put all your \newcounter commands in your preamble, and you process a portion of a document
  using the \includeonly and \include commands.

  It also occurs if you attempt to use a \setcounter, or
  \addtocounter command on a counter that is not previously
  defined. For instance, if you accidentally put

  ```
  \setcounter{pag}{30}
  ```

  in your file, you will get the following error:

  ```
  LaTeX error.  See LaTeX manual for explanation.
              Type  H <return>  for immediate help.
  ! No such counter.
  \@latexerr ...for immediate help.}\errmessage {#1}

  \@ifundefined ...fx \csname #1\endcsname \relax #2
                                              \else #3\fi
  l.13 \setcounter{pag}{30}

  ?
  ```

- ! Not in outer par mode

  This has a very specific meaning: LaTeX found a figure or table
  environment or a \marginpar command in math mode. Or it
  found one of these commands inside a \parbox.

  For example, typing

  ```
  This is a figure in math mode:
  $x=y \begin{figure} big mistake \end{figure}$
  ```

would produce the following error message:

```
LaTeX error.  See LaTeX manual for explanation.
                Type  H <return>  for immediate help.
! Not in outer par mode.
\@latexerr ...for immediate help.}\errmessage {#1}

\@xfloat ...ef \@captype {#1}\ifinner \@parmoderr
                                                \@floatpenal...
<to be read again>
                  b
l.17 $x=y \begin{figure} b
                        ig mistake \end{figure}$
?
```

- **! Something's wrong--perhaps a missing \item.**

  You have a list environment with no items in it. This can happen if you forget the backslashes on the \item commands. For example,

```
\begin{itemize}
item   blah, blah, blah
\end{itemize}
```

would produce this error message:

```
LaTeX error.  See LaTeX manual for explanation.
                Type  H <return>  for immediate help.
! Something's wrong--perhaps a missing \item.
\@latexerr ...for immediate help.}\errmessage {#1}

\endtrivlist ->\if@newlist \@noitemerr
                                \fi \if@inlabel \indent...

\end #1->\csname end#1\endcsname
                                \if@endpe \global \let \@gtem...
l.21 \end{itemize}

?
```

- ! Tab overflow

You have a line in a **tabbing** environment that contains more tab stops— that is, more \= commands—than LaTeX allows.

- ! There's no line here to end.

LaTeX is telling you that you have used the \\ or the \newline command improperly. This message comes up if one of these commands appears between paragraphs. For example, if you are trying to leave extra space between paragraphs and you type

```
Here is a paragraph. We want extra space after it.

\\
Another paragraph following the first one.
```

you will get

```
LaTeX error.  See LaTeX manual for explanation.
              Type  H <return>  for immediate help.
! There's no line here to end.
\@latexerr ...for immediate help.}\errmessage {#1}

\newline ->\ifvmode \@nolnerr
                              \else \unskip \hfil \penalty -\@...
<to be read again>
                  A
1.26 A
      nother paragraph following it.
?
```

To leave extra vertical space after a paragraph, use a \vspace command.

- ! This may be a LaTeX bug.

This may be the culmination of a long string of error messages produced by one error. If so, then ignore it and pay attention to the earlier messages about the bug. If this is the first message a file produces, then call a LaTeX expert. You may have found a bug in the LaTeX program.

- ! Too deeply nested.

You tried to nest a list environment more than four levels deep. Four is the maximum. For example, if you input:

```
\begin{itemize}
 \item Here's the item
 \begin{itemize}
  \item Here's the item
  \begin{itemize}
   \item Here's the item
   \begin{itemize}
    \item Here's the item
    \begin{itemize}
     \item Here's the item
    \end{itemize}
   \end{itemize}
  \end{itemize}
 \end{itemize}
\end{itemize}
```

LATEX will give you this message:

```
LaTeX error.  See LaTeX manual for explanation.
            Type  H <return>  for immediate help.
! Too deeply nested.
\@latexerr ...for immediate help.}\errmessage {#1}

\itemize ->\ifnum \@itemdepth >3 \@toodeep
                                          \else \advance \@it...
1.36     \begin{itemize}

?
```

- ! Too many unprocessed floats.

If you give LATEX a string of several full page floats when it is halfway through filling a page it can have this error. You see, it has to hold on to the portion of the page that it has so far, plus all the floats you give it, and it has to keep reading in stuff from your input file until it can fill up the rest of the page. It can run out of memory doing this.

Try moving the floats to the end of a page and preceding them with a \clearpage command. If you have very many floats together, you may also have to place \clearpage commands after every 5th float or so.

- ! Undefined tab position.

  LaTeX found a \> command in a tabbing environment when there were no more tab stops to go to. The following example sets up two tab stops and then tries to go to three tab stops:

```
\begin{tabbing}
Here is \= stop one and \= stop two \\
That's all there are \\
Go to \> stop one and \> stop two and
    \> stop three which doesn't exists
\end{tabbing}
```

LaTeX gets the following error trying to process this:

```
LaTeX error.  See LaTeX manual for explanation.
             Type  H <return>  for immediate help.
! Undefined tab position.
\@latexerr ...for immediate help.}\errmessage {#1}

\>...global \advance \@curtab \@ne \else \@badtab
                                                  \fi \@tempdi...
l.48    \>
           stop three which doesn't exists
?
```

E.6   Some of TeX's Error Messages

Below is a list of some common errors encountered by TeX, and hints on how to correct them. You can tell if an error message is from TeX and not from LaTeX, because it does not contain the following two lines, which all LaTeX errors have:

```
LaTeX error.  See LaTeX manual for explanation.
              Type  H <return>  for immediate help.
```

Otherwise, TEX errors act just like LATEX errors.

- ! `Double subscript.`

  Check the indicated formula for correctly nested braces on subscripts to subscripts. For example, T_{X_I} is produced by `$T_{X_I}$`, not `$T_X_I$`.

- ! `Double superscript.`

  Same as above, only applies to superscripts to superscripts.

- ! `Extra alignment tab has been changed to \cr.`

  Check for a line in a `tabular` or `array` that has too many ampersands. Perhaps the previous line is missing the `\\`.

- ! `Extra }, or forgotten $.`

  Check the last formula for a missing dollar sign or brace, or for missing math mode delimiters such as `\[, \]`.

- ! `Illegal unit of measure (pt inserted).`

  Look for a length argument where you forgot to put the units, such as `\vspace{.25}`.

- ! `Missing { inserted.`

  Look for mismatched braces anywhere before the message occurred.

- ! `Missing $ inserted.`

  Look for an in-text formula where you forgot the beginning or ending dollar sign. TEX detects the error when it gets to the end of the paragraph.

- ! `TeX capacity exceeded, sorry.`

  Try putting `\clearpage` commands after your floats, if there are very many of them. Or look for a `\begin{figure}` or `\begin{table}` command with no matching `\end` command.

- ! Undefined control sequence.

  Look for a misspelled command name.

Appendix F

Examples

F.1 Eqnarray and Array

Delimiters in Eqnarray and Array

Question: How do you get large delimiters to work when the left one is in one column of an `eqnarray` or `array` and the right one is in another column? Example:

$$\{x \quad = \quad y + z\}$$
$$\{y \quad = \quad x - z\}$$

Answer: Use the `\right.` and `\left.` to make invisible matching delimiters in each column containing a delimiter. *You may not have a `\left` without a matching `\right` or a `\right` without a matching `\left` in any column entry.* Solution:

```
\begin{eqnarray*}
\left\{ x \right. & = & \left. y+z \right\} \\
\left\{ y \right. & = & \left. x - z \right\}
\end{eqnarray*}
```

Question: What if one column entry is taller than the other and the delimiters don't want to come out the same size? Example:

$$\begin{aligned} \{x &= \frac{y+z}{y-z}\} \\ \{y &= \frac{x+z}{x-z}\} \end{aligned}$$

Answer: You have to use a `\rule` in both columns containing delimiters to make LATEX think the two column entries are the same size. The rule should be just a little bit taller than the bigger column entry. Solution:

```
\begin{eqnarray*}
\left\{ \rule{0in}{.25in} x \right. & = &
    \left. \rule{0in}{.25in} \frac{y+z}{y-z} \right\} \\
\left\{ \rule{0in}{.25in} y \right. & = &
    \left. \rule{0in}{.25in} \frac{x+z}{x-z} \right\}
\end{eqnarray*}
```

and the result is

$$\left\{ x \;=\; \frac{y+z}{y-z} \right\}$$

$$\left\{ y \;=\; \frac{x+z}{x-z} \right\}$$

Rules that are used in this way to reserve space are sometimes called *struts.*

Single-column Arrays

Question: How can one get the following equation:

$$\mathrm{PEAK} = \frac{\mathrm{MAX}}{\mathrm{T}}$$

?

Answer: The `array` environment can be used with one centered column for the right hand side of the equation. SOLUTION:

```
\[ \rm PEAK = \begin{array}{c}
            \rm MAX \\
            \rm T
        \end{array}
\]
```

Eqnarray with More than Three Columns

Question: How do you get a multi-line formula that has equation numbers on each line and *more than three columns*? Example:

$$x = \frac{1}{y} + \frac{2}{z} \quad , \quad x \leq 100, y, z \neq 0 \qquad \text{(F.1)}$$

$$a + b = 2y + 2z \quad , \quad x \leq 100, y, z = 0 \qquad \text{(F.2)}$$

Answer: It takes some work, since **eqnarray** only sets up three columns for you. Use **eqnarray**, and create some extra columns within the third column by using boxes. SOLUTION:

```
\begin{eqnarray}
x& = & \makebox[1.in][l]{$\displaystyle
                \frac{1}{y}+\frac{2}{z}$}
    , \quad x \leq 100, y,z \neq 0 \\
a+b & = & \makebox[1.in][l]{$2y + 2z$}
    , \quad x \leq 100, y,z = 0
\end{eqnarray}
```

Note that the **\makebox** commands on each line place their contents in a one inch wide box. This causes the commas to line up. Also, the **\makebox** command's third argument will be set in text mode, so the dollar signs are needed to set the argument in math mode.

Vertical Bars

Question: How could the following formulas be typeset?

$$\ell_{xk} \;=\; \ell_x \frac{G_{ux}G_{vy}}{G_{uy}}\bigg|_k$$
$$\ell_{yk} \;=\; \ell_y \frac{G_{ux}G_{vy}}{G_{ux}}\bigg|_k$$

Answer:

```
\begin{eqnarray*}
\ell_{xk} & = &
   \displaystyle \left.
                 \ell_x \frac{G_{ux}G_{vy}}{G_{uy}}
                 \right|_k \\
\ell_{yk} & = &
   \displaystyle \left.
                 \ell_y \frac{G_{ux}G_{vy}}{G_{ux}}
                 \right|_k
\end{eqnarray*}
```

Usage of Array

Question: What is wrong with the following input?

```
This is text before an array.

\begin{array}{ll}
 a & b \\
 c & d
\end{array}
This is text after the array.
```

Answer: The array should be placed within a math environment, either dollar signs or one of the displayed math environments. See the following example of an array in a displayed math environment:

| Commands | Result |

```
\[
 \left\{
  \begin{array}{ll}
       a & b \\
       c & d
  \end{array}
 \right.
\]
```

$$
\left\{
\begin{array}{ll}
a & b \\
c & d
\end{array}
\right.
$$

Complicated Array

Question: How could you code the following structure?

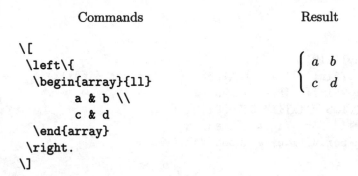

$$N_1 = |f(t)|_{\max} \qquad \text{Peak Value} \qquad \text{AMPLITUDE}$$

$$N_2 = |df/dt|_{\max} \qquad \text{Peak Derivative} \qquad \text{VARIATION}$$

$$N_3 = \left| \int_0^t f(x)dx \right|_{\max} \qquad \text{Peak Impulse}$$

$$N_4 = |\int_0^\infty f(x)| \, dx \qquad \text{Rectified Impulse} \qquad \left.\right\} \text{CONTENT}$$

$$N_5 = \left\{ \int_{\int}^\infty [f(x)]^2 \, dx \right\}^{1/2} \qquad \text{Root Action Integral}$$

Answer: This is very difficult, because the tall left brace before "CON-TENT" can't simply be placed between array columns; therefore the last three lines are a separate displayed equation from the first two lines, consisting of a two column array, followed by the brace, and the single word "CONTENT" in an \mbox. The first two lines can be put into a three-column array. The big problem is getting the columns of the two arrays to line up, and this must be done by forcing the columns to be the right width with \makebox commands. At the same time, the overall width of both equations must be the same, so that when LaTeX centers both equations, they line up with each other.

SOLUTION:

```
\[
\begin{array}{llr}
 \makebox[1.75in][l]{$N_1 = \left|f(t) \right|_{\max}$} &
 \makebox[1.75in][l]{Peak Value} &
 \makebox[1.125in][l]{AMPLITUDE} \\ [2mm]
N_2 = \left| df/dt \right|_{\max} &
 \mbox{Peak Derivative} & \mbox{VARIATION}
\end{array}
\]
\[
\left. \begin{array}{llr}
\makebox[1.75in][l]{$N_3 =
             \left| \int_0^t f(x) dx \right|_{\max}$} &
   \makebox[1.75in][l]{Peak Impulse} & \\ [2mm]
N_4 = \left| \int_0^\infty f(x) \right| dx &
   \mbox{Rectified Impulse} & \\ [2mm]
N_5 = \left\{\int_)^\infty
    \left[f(x)\right]^2 dx \right\}^{1/2} &
   \mbox{Root Action Integral} &
     \end{array}
\right\} \makebox[1.in][l]{CONTENT}
\]
```

F.2   General Math

Special Matrices

Question: What is a simple way to code the following matrix?

$$M = \begin{array}{c} \\ C \\ I \\ C' \end{array} \begin{pmatrix} C & I & C' \\ 1 & 0 & 0 \\ B & 1-b & 0 \\ 0 & a & 1-a \end{pmatrix}$$

Answer: There is a TeX command called \bordermatrix that allows you to do this. Example:

```
$$ M = \bordermatrix{   & C & I   & C' \cr
                   C & 1 & 0   & 0   \cr
                   I & B & 1-b & 0   \cr
                   C' & 0 & a   & 1-a \cr} $$
```

Since this is a T_EX command (not L^AT_EX) it looks different from what we are used to. To get this matrix with an equation number, put it in an **equation** environment and drop the double dollar signs:

```
\begin{equation}
 M = \bordermatrix{   & C & I   & C' \cr
                   C & 1 & 0   & 0   \cr
                   I & B & 1-b & 0   \cr
                   C' & 0 & a   & 1-a \cr}
\end{equation}
```

Non-italic Math

Question: How can one get all formulas and equations to come out in roman type instead of the default math italic font?

Answer: Use T_EX's **\everymath** and **\everydisplay** commands in the preamble. Example

```
\documentstyle[12pt]{report}
\everymath{\rm}
\everydisplay{\rm}
\begin{document}

\chapter{MATH IN ROMAN TYPE}

The following equation, and all equations in this
document will be in roman type:
\begin{equation}
f(x) = \frac{x + \pi}{x - \pi}
\end{equation}
\end{document}
```

Manual Control of Equation Numbers

Question: Is it possible to force an equation to have a certain number?
Answer: Yes. Use the `\setcounter` command just before the equation to set the `equation` counter to one less than the desired number. EXAMPLE:

```
Say the last equation was \#10, and we want the
next one to be \#20. Here's what we do...
\setcounter{equation}{19}
\begin{equation}
x = y
\end{equation}
Voila! See, it works!
```

which will produce the following results: Say the last equation was #10, and we want the next one to be #20. Here's what we do...

$$x = y \tag{F.20}$$

Voila! See, it works!

F.3 Footnotes

Symbol Markers

Question: How can one get footnotes with symbols instead of numbers as markers?
Answer: Use the `\renewcommand` command to redefine the style of the footnote counter. SOLUTION:

```
\renewcommand{\thefootnote}{\fnsymbol{footnote}}
```

F.4   Table of Contents, Lists of Figures and Tables

Page Numbers in T. O. C. Off by a Consistent Amount

Question: I have a `\tableofcontents` command in my root file, immediately followed by several chapters. Why are all the page numbers in the Table of Contents off by the same amount in my document? I `latex`ed the file twice!

Answer: Because the Table of Contents is more than one page long. When this is the case, the page numbers will not be right until you have `latex`ed at least *three* times. The first time you `latex`, the resulting Table of Contents is a blank page with a heading on it. It is just one page long. During the run, Chapter 1 will start on page two. LaTeX writes entries for chapters and sections into the `.toc` file, and the page numbers are assigned assuming that the Table of Contents is one page long. The second time you process, the resulting Table of Contents comes from what was written out to the `.toc` file during the first run, so it will have incorrect page numbers, but it will be the right length, say, two pages long. During this second run, Chapter 1 will fall on page three, and the entries written to the `.toc` file will all be correct.

SOLUTION: `latex` three times to get the resulting Table of Contents to be correct. See the table below:

LATEX Run	.toc File Used	Resulting Table of Contents
First	None exists.	One page. Has a heading and nothing else.
Second	From the first run. Thinks the Table of Contents is one page long. Therefore thinks the first chapter is on page two.	Two pages. Wrong page numbers for chapter one, et cetera.
Third	From the second LATEX run. Takes into account the two page Table of Contents.	Two pages. Correct page numbers for chapter one, et cetera.

F.5   Style

Double-spacing

Question: Exactly how do you get a document double-spaced?
Answer: Use a `\renewcommand{\baselinestretch}{2}` command in your preamble. EXAMPLE:

```
\documentstyle[12pt]{dnatest}
\renewcommand{\baselinestretch}{2}
\begin{document}
This will be a double-spaced document.
\end{document}
```

Now my document is double-spaced, but the tables done with `tabular` environment look funny. How can I force them to stay single-spaced?
Answer: Use a `\renewcommand{\arraystretch}{.5}` command in your preamble to counteract the double-spacing that is in effect.
EXAMPLE:

```
\documentstyle[12pt]{dnatest}
\renewcommand{\baselinestretch}{2}
```

```
\renewcommand{\arraystretch}{.5}
\begin{document}
This will be a double-spaced document. BUT, arrays
and tabulars will be SINGLE-SPACED.
\end{document}
```

Changing the Top Margin

Question: Is it possible to move the top of the text closer to the top of the page?

Answer: Yes, it can be done by making \topmargin smaller than the default value for the style guide being used, or even making it negative. EXAMPLE:

```
\documentstyle[12pt]{dnatest}
\topmargin -.75in
\textheight 9.5in
\begin{document}
The top margin on this document will be higher
than normal.
\end{document}
```

To make the text on a particular page start higher than the other pages of a document, start the page with a \vspace*{-.5in}, replacing the -.5in with an appropriate measurement.

Switching to Right-Justification from Ragged Right

Question: How can you get a paragraph of right-justified text within a flushleft environment?

Answer: Use a minipage environment that is the width of the text column. Example:

```
{\raggedright
Here is some text that will not be flush-right because
of the ragged right declaration. Following this, we
may want a paragraph that will be flush-right. How do
we do it?
```

```
\begin{minipage}{\hsize}
The minipage environment does the trick. if you
make it the right width.
This paragraph will be flush-right, and the
margins will be the width of the rest of the
document. Hsize is a variable that equals Textwidth.
\end{minipage}
```

Defining Page Numbering Style

Question: I have a
`\renewcommand{\thepage}{\arabic{chapter}--\arabic{page}}`
command in my file, but the pages come out with plain arabic page
numbers. Why?

Answer: If you have a `\pagenumbering{arabic}` command *after* the
definition above, it will override the definition. That's because the
`\pagenumbering{arabic}` command is a macro that expands to
`\renewcommand{\thepage}{\arabic{page}}` plus some other things.
To correct this problem, simply put your definition *after* the
`\pagenumbering{arabic}` command.

Controlling line breaks in Section headings

Question: How do you control line breaks in the section headings, captions etc., and in the corresponding entries in the table of contents and
list of figures?

Answer: Use the `\newline` or the `\linebreak` command to break the
line where you want to. Since section headings and captions are moving
arguments, (see Section 2.12), you must use the `\protect` command to
carry the line break over into the Table of Contents, List of Figures, or
List of Tables. Or you may use the optional argument to the sectioning command or the `\caption` command to specify an entry for the
front matter that is different from the caption or section heading. (See
Section 3.5.4.) For example, suppose you have the following section
heading:

THIS IS A SAMPLE SECTION HEADING WITH AN UN-DESIRABLE LINEBREAK

You may want to break the line before "UNDESIRABLE" to get rid of the hyphenation. To do this, and to have the line break carry over to the Table of Contents, you would type

```
\section*{THIS IS A SAMPLE SECTION
          HEADING WITH A VERY \protect\newline
          UNDESIRABLE LINEBREAK}
```

Keep in mind that the `\newline` command ends the line without right-justifying it, whereas the `\linebreak` command would end the line and right-justify.

F.6   Tabular Environment

Controlling Column Widths

Question: How do you make all of the columns in a tabular 1 inch wide?

Answer: Use p-columns that are one 1 inch wide. NOTE: If you specify a p-column and don't make any entries in that column, LaTeX will not leave the space you requested for the column. You can still make an empty column of a certain width by using a p-column specification and putting something invisible in the column (like a rule with 0-inch height). For example, to make the following table

	two
	three

you could use the following commands:

```
\begin{tabular}{|p{1.in}|p{1.in}|}\hline
\rule{.5in}{0in} & two \\ \hline
             & three \\ \hline
\end{tabular}
```

Question: If I make a `tabular` environment with three p-columns that are each 1 inch wide, why doesn't the `tabular` come out to be *exactly* 3 inches wide?

Answer: LaTeX inserts a little bit of space between rows as well as at the right and left of the entire `tabular`. This is so that text is slightly separated from vertical lines between columns and from text in adjacent columns. If two p-columns were next to each other with no space in between, you would not be able to tell where one column stopped and where the other began!

The spacing between columns is defined by a parameter called `\tabcolsep`, whose default value is 6 points. It is inserted on each side of each column. The result is that you get 6 points of white space on the left and right sides of the entire table, and you get twice that amount between columns. Example:

6	c	6	6	c	6	6	c	6
p	o	p	p	o	p	p	o	p
t	l	t	t	l	t	t	l	t
s		s	s		s	s		s
	1			2			3	

Horizontal placement of `tabulars`

Question: How can I get a `tabular` environment to come out on the left margin instead of indented?

Answer: Precede the `\begin{tabular}` command with a `\noindent` command. Example:

```
... end of previous paragraph.

\noindent\begin{tabular}{ll}
...
```

You see, when LaTeX finishes typesetting a `tabular` environment, it has a box-shaped product. This box is treated the way a single word would be treated. In other words, it will be indented like a new paragraph if it follows a blank line.

Question: How can I center a `tabular`?

Answer: Place the `tabular` environment inside a `center` environment. Example:

```
\begin{center}
\begin{tabular}{ll}
...
\end{tabular}
\end{center}
```

Headings for Tabulars

Question: How can I control the vertical spacing between a heading and a table made with the `tabular` environment?

Answer: Use the `\vspace` command, or the `\\` command with the optional length argument, such as `\\ [.25in]`. You must also decide whether the heading will be part of the `tabular`, made with a `\multicolumn` command, or entered before the `tabular` environment. See the following table, and study the three examples of how to create it:

This is the heading

One	Two	Three
Uno	Dos	Tres

Method 1:

```
\begin{center}
{\bf This is the heading} \\[.25in]

\begin{tabular}{ccc}
One & Two & Three \\
Uno & Dos & Tres
\end{tabular}
\end{center}
```

Method 2:

```
\begin{center}
{\bf This is the heading} \\
\vspace{.25in}
\begin{tabular}{ccc}
One & Two & Three \\
Uno & Dos & Tres
\end{tabular}
\end{center}
```

Method 3:

```
\begin{center}
\begin{tabular}{ccc}
\multicolumn{3}{c}{\bf This is the heading} \\[.25in]
One & Two & Three \\
Uno & Dos & Tres
\end{tabular}
\end{center}
```

Question: What causes a heading to come out to the left of a tabular instead of above it?

Answer: That happens if LaTeX thinks the heading and the tabular are supposed to be on the same line. To make the heading come out on top of the tabular, you need to put a blank line between the heading and the tabular, or, if the heading and tabular are both enclosed in a center environment, there needs to be a \\ after the heading. For example,

```
\begin{center}
\noindent{\bf Heading}
\begin{tabular}{ccc}
one & two & three \\
un & deux & trois
\end{tabular}
\end{center}
```

will produce

Heading	one	two	three
	un	deux	trois

To correct the problem, put \\ after the `\noindent{\bf Heading}`.

Controlling the Height of Rows

Question: How can I make the spacing between rows in all **tabulars** and **arrays** different from the default?

Answer: Use the `\arraystretch` parameter. It must be set with a `\renewcommand` outside of a **tabular** or **array** environment. The `\arraystretch` parameter is a factor that is multiplied by the default distance between rows to obtain a new distance between rows. To double the space between rows, for example, use the following command: `\renewcommand{\arraystretch}{2}`. To increase the spacing between rows just a little bit, use something like `\renewcommand{\arraystretch}{1.3}`.

Question: Why doesn't this work:

```
\begin{tabular}{lll}
\renewcommand{\arraystretch}{1.5}
1 & 2 & 3 \\
a & b & c \\
x & y & z
\end{tabular}
```
?

Answer: That doesn't work because the `\renewcommand{\arraystretch}{1.5}` doesn't belong inside the **tabular** environment. It should be before the `\begin{tabular}`. To confine the effect of the `\arraystretch` to this **tabular** environment, use braces around the `\renewcommand` *and* the **tabular**, as follows:

```
{  \renewcommand{\arraystretch}{1.5}
   \begin{tabular}{lll}
   1 & 2 & 3 \\
   a & b & c \\
   x & y & z
   \end{tabular}    }
```

F.7   Floats

Full-Page Figures and Tables

Question: What is the best way to input full-page figures and tables?
Answer: Use the [p] position specifier whenever you know that a figure
should fall on a page of floats, whether it is a full-page figure or not.
In other words, two figures with the [p] specifier may be placed on the
same page if they fit. Example:

```
\begin{figure}[p]
\vspace{4.in}
\caption{This is a figure that will should not
be put on a page with text.}
\end{figure}
```

Floats that Continue to a Second Page

Question: How do you get a continuation page for a table (or figure)?
Answer: Use two `table` (or `figure`) environments. For the second
page, do not use a `\caption` command, as that would make a second
entry in the List of Tables (or List of Figures). Rather, use bolding
and manual centering to make the caption on the continuation page.
Example:

```
Here comes a two-page figure:
\begin{figure}[p]
\vspace{6.5in}
\caption{Example of two-page figure.}
\label{twopage}
\end{figure}
\begin{figure}[p]
\vspace{6.5in}
\begin{center}
\bf Figure~\ref{twopage}.~~Example of two-page figure.}
\end{center}
\end{figure}
```

F.8 Page Breaks

Question: How can I keep LaTeX from making a page break where I don't want one?

Answer: This is not easy to do, since LaTeX seems to be pretty resolute about where *it* wants to break the pages. Keep in mind that once LaTeX says a page is full, that page really is efficiently packed with material.

Suppose that you have several lines in a list that you want kept together, or any block of text that you want kept together on one page. You could force a page break *before* that block of text with a \clearpage. Or you could use a combination of the \samepage, \nopagebreak, and \pagebreak commands.

Note that the \samepage command needs to be used *with braces* to show what text you want to keep on the same page. For example:

```
{ \samepage
Keep this paragraph on the same page with ...
\nopagebreak

This paragraph. }
\pagebreak
```

is correct, but

```
 \samepage
Keep this paragraph on the same page with ...
\nopagebreak
This paragraph.
\pagebreak
```

is not.

In the second example, you are actually requesting that LaTeX keep the whole rest of your document on the same page!!!

Appendix G

Making Slides with SLITEX

SliTeX is a program very similar to LaTeX that is specially designed for creating slides for presentations. With SliTeX, you may create black-and-white or color slides using a special set of suitable fonts. SliTeX contains its own commands and environments for setting up colors, annotations to slides, page styles, et cetera. Many of the LaTeX commands described in this manual are also available for creating mathematical expressions, lists, pictures and other structures to enhance your presentation.

The commands for running SliTeX are different from those used to invoke LaTeX. To learn more about using and running SliTeX, you should find the files `slides.tex` and `local.tex` in the directory containing your LaTeX style guides, run LaTeX on them, and print them.

Bibliography

1. Donald E. Knuth. *The TEXbook* Addison-Wesley, Reading, Massachusetts, 1984.

2. Leslie Lamport *LATEX: A Document Preparation System* Addison-Wesley, Reading, Massachusetts, 1986.

Index

! 5
5, 20–21
$ 5, 20–21, 25–26, 95
% 5, 20, 27, 207
& 5, 20, 112, 128
' (open singe quote, ') 5, 18–19
' ' (open quote, ") 18
' (apostrophe, ') 5, 18–19, 25–26
' ' (close quote, ") 18
" 5, 18
~ 68, 102, 142–143
(5, 98
) 5, 98
* 5, 96
, 5
- (hyphen, -) 5, 19
-- (en-dash, –) 19
--- (em-dash, —) 19
. 5
| 98, 114, 128
/ 5, 98
\ (backslash) 5, 12, 20, 97
\\ 28, 36–37, 39, 109, 112, 127, 128, 133, 142–147, 294, 313–314
: 5
; 5
< 5, 20, 98

> 5, 20, 98
<CR> (carriage return) 13, 16–18, 262
= 5
? 5, 78, 265
?? 55
@ (at-sign,) 5, 291
@-expression 119, 291
[5, 98
    \\ and 127
] 5, 98
{ 5, 12, 20, 98
} 5, 12, 20, 98
_ (underscore, _) 5, 20, 25–26, 86–88
^ (caret, ^) 5, 20, 25–26, 86–88

11pt documentstyle option 34
12pt documentstyle option 34

abbreviations
    and spacing 14
    of commands 205
accents
    foreign 77–78
    math mode 102
acknowledgements 190
acute accent 77, 102
address, in letter 36, 38

alph page-numbering style 79–
    80
Alph page-numbering style 79–
    80
ampersand
    and **array** 128
    and **tabular** 112
appendices 47–48, 219
arabic page-numbering style 79,
    310
argument
    defined 12–13
    effect of omitting 262
    moving 27–28, 310
    optional 12, 28
arrays 128–132, 299–304
    adjusting spacing in 131–132
    aligning top and bottom of
        130, 132
    and ellipses 93
    centering, with formula 130
    changing row spacing in 135,
        238
    column spacing in 237
    complicated 303–304
    delimiters with 99, 299–300
    examples of 299–304
    single-column 300
    space between double verti-
        cal lines in 237–238
    style parameters for 237
    width of vertical lines in 237
array environment. *See* envi-
        ronment, **array**. *See also*
        arrays
arrow symbols, list of 97
arrows in **picture** environment

    254
article style 16, 32
ASCII 1, 4, 5, 7
auxiliary files 5, 6
    .lof 173
    .lot 179
    .toc 49, 306, 307

b position specifier 170
backslash
    error of omitting 266
    function of 5, 12, 20
    in delimiter commands 99
bar character 98, 114, 128
bars
    horizontal, in formulas 102–
        103
    horizontal, in arrays 128–129,
        132
    horizontal in tables 113–114,
        127
    vertical 301–302
    vertical, in tables 114, 127
    vertical, in arrays 128–129,
        132
baseline spacing 229
bibliography 67–68, 198–201
binary operation symbols 96
biographies 207–208
bold type 41–42
    in math mode 105–106
book document style 32
bottomnumber 226, 235
box
    line width of 226, 238
    setting width of, in list 225,
        233

boxes 152–163
  adjusting frame thickness and
    spacing in 155, 226, 238
  centering text in 153
  defined 152
  defining for picture 244–245
  filled in with ink 157, 162
  naming 159
  putting text in 153
  raising 158, 162
  saving, for later use 158–162
  spacing between text and lines
    in 226, 238
  style parameters for 238
  text in 154
  treated as letter 152, 161
  wrapping text in 155–157
braces 12, 20, 98
  adjustable sized 98
  \\ and 127
  \boldmath command and 105
  \cal command and 95
  closing, in \rm command 45
  empty, and addresses 39
  function of, 12
  horizontal, in formulas 102–
    103
  in grouping 44, 46
  in sub- and superscripts 25–
    26, 86–89
  nested 40, 86
  typestyle-changing command
    and 44–45
  using, to form groups 44–46
breve accent 77, 102
bulleted list. *See* environment,
  itemize

c column specifier 112, 128
calligraphic letters 94–95
captions
  and moving argument 27
  in figures 171
  in tables 177–178
carbon copy, in letters 36. *See
    also* cc
caret 5, 25, 86, 88
case
  in counters 219–220
  in numbering 79
cc 37, 39
centering text. *See* text, center-
    ing
chapter counter 218–220
chapter numbers 46, 56, 216, 218,
    219
  \include and 186
chapters
  referencing 53–55, 187
  processing in separate files
    185–187
  starting 46
check accent 77, 102
circles 255–256
  multiple 257–259
closing, in letter 36–37, 39
cm (centimeters) 148
columns 34, 109–136
  controlling widths of 311–312
  in arrays 128–133
  in tables 111–128
  number of, on page 32
  paragraph 116–118
commands 1, 11
  ~ 68, 142-143

*- form 28
\ 5, 12, 20, 97, 266
\! 105, 107
\, 18–19, 105, 107
\- 57
\: 105, 107
\; 105, 107
\= 109–111, 293
\> 109–111
\@ 15
\⊔ (backslash-space) 13, 14
\# 20
\$ 20
\% 20
\& 20
\^ 20, 77
\~ 20, 77
_ 20
\{ 20
\} 20
$<$ 20
$>$ 20
$\backslash$ 20
\[28, 70
\] 28, 70
!` (¡) 77
?` (¿) 77–78
\"{o} (ö) 77
\^{o} (ô) 77
\~{o} (õ) 77
\'{o} (ó) 77
\`{o} (ò) 77
\.{o} (ȯ) 77
\={o} (ō) 77
\{ 98
\} 98
\| 97, 98

\\ 28, 36–37, 39, 109, 112,
    127, 128, 142–147, 294,
    313–314
* 28, 142
\aa 77
\AA 77, 78
\abovedisplayshortskip 226,
    234
\abovedisplayskip 226, 234
\acute{p} 102
\addcontentsline 27, 50–
    52, 173–175, 180–181
\address 38–39
\addtocounter 217, 292
\addtolength 150–152
\ae 77
\AE 77–78
\aleph 97
\alph 219
\Alph 219–220
\alpha 1, 94–95, 271
\amalg 96
\and 40
\angle 97
\appendix 47–48, 219
\approx 96
\arabic 213, 219
\arccos 98
\arcsin 98
\arctan 98
\arg 98
\arraycolsep 226, 237
\arrayrulewidth 226, 237
\arraystretch 226, 238, 315
\ast 96
\asymp 96
\author 40–41

\b{o} (ọ) 77
\backslash 20, 97–98
\bar{p} 102
\baselineskip 225, 229
\baselinestretch 225, 229–230
\begin 28, 59–60
\begin{array} 128
\begin{document} 9–11, 185, 283, 289
\begin{letter} 36
\begin{tabbing} 110
\begin{tabular} 112
\begin{verbatim} 29–30
\belowdisplayshortskip 226, 235
\belowdisplayskip 226, 234
\beta 94–95
\bf 41–42, 105
\bibitem 198, 201
\bigcap 97
\bigcirc 96
\bigcup 97
\bigodot 97
\bigoplus 97
\bigotimes 97
\bigskip 147–148, 206
\bigsqcup 97
\bigtriangledown 96
\bigtriangleup 96
\biguplus 97
\bigvee 97
\bigwedge 97
\boldmath 105–106
\bordermatrix 304–305
\bot 97

\bottomfraction 226, 235–236
\bowtie 96
\Box 97
\breve{p} 102
\bullet 96
\c{o} (ọ) 77
\cal 94–95
\cap 96
\caption 27, 171–173, 177–178, 310, 316
\cc 37
\cdot 96
\cdots 92–93
\chapter 46–47, 49, 52, 215
\chapter* 48–49
\chapter, after \appendix command 47
\check{p} 102
\chi 94
\circ 96
\circle 255
\cite 198–201
\clearpage 51, 79–80, 137, 140–141, 317
\cline 113–114, 127, 129, 132
\closing 37, 39
\clubsuit 97, 100
\columnsep 225, 231
\columnseprule 225, 231
\cong 96
\coprod 97
\copyright 77
\cos 98
\cosh 98
\cot 98

\coth 98
\csc 98
\cup 96
\d{o} (o) 77
\dag 77, 212
\dagger 96
\dashbox 246
\dashv 96
\date 38–39, 40
\dblfloatpagefraction 226, 236
\dblfloatsep 226, 237
\dbltextfloatsep 226, 237
\dbltopfraction 226, 236
\ddag 77
\ddagger 96
\ddot 102
\ddots 92, 93
\deg 98
\delta 94
\Delta 94
\det 98
\diamond 96
\Diamond 96
\diamondsuit 97
\dim 98
\displaystyle 73–74, 76
\div 96, 100
\documentstyle 9–11, 31–33, 35, 185, 283
\doteq 96
\dot{p} 102
\doublerulesep 226, 237–238
\downarrow 97, 98
\Downarrow 97, 98
\ell 97

\emptyset 97
\encl 37
\end 28, 59
\end{document} 9–11, 185, 263
\end{equation} 71
\end{letter} 37
\epsilon 94
\equiv 96
\eta 94
\evensidemargin 164, 166, 225, 227–228
\everydisplay 305
\everymath 305
\exists 97
\exp 98
\fbox 154, 161
\fboxrule 226, 238
\fboxsep 226, 238
\fill 149, 152
\flat 97, 100
\floatpagefraction 226, 236
\floatsep 226, 236
\fnsymbol 221, 306
\footheight 164, 166, 225, 229
\footnote 21–23, 27–28
\footnotesep 225, 230
\footnotesize 43
\footskip 164, 166, 225, 229
\forall 97
\frac 88–90
\frame 246
\framebox 154, 156, 161, 242–243
\frown 96
\gamma 94

\Gamma 94
\gcd 98
\geq 96
\gg 96
\grave{p} 102
\H{o} (ő) 77
\hat{p} 102
\hbar 97
\headheight 164, 166, 225, 228
\headsep 164, 166, 225, 228
\heartsuit 97, 100
\hline 113, 127, 128, 134
\hom 98
\hookleftarrow 97
\hookrightarrow 97
\hspace 146–147
\hspace* 146–147
\huge 43
\Huge 43
\hyphenation 57–59
\Im 97
\imath 97, 104, 107
\include 186–189, 273, 292
\includeonly 185–189, 283, 292
\index 194–196
\indexentry 194–197
\indexspace 193
\inf 98
\infty 85, 97
\input 188–190, 273
\int 72–73, 76, 97
\intextsep 226, 236
\iota 94
\it 41
\item 28, 61–62, 66, 70, 192,

197, 198, 211–212, 293
\itemindent 225, 233
\itemsep 212, 225, 232
\jmath 97, 104, 107
\Join 96
\jot 226, 234
\kappa 94
\ker 98
\kill 110–111
\l 77
\L 77
\label 54–57, 66, 72, 133–134, 136, 172, 177, 178, 183, 198
\labelsep 225, 233
\labelwidth 225, 233
\lambda 94
\Lambda 94
\langle 98
\large 43
\Large 43
\LARGE 43
\lceil 98
\ldots 92–93
\left 98–99, 299
\left. 99, 101
\leftarrow 97
\Leftarrow 97
\leftharpoondown 97
\leftharpoonup 97
\leftmargin 225, 232
\leftrightarrow 97
\Leftrightarrow 97
\leq 96, 100, 102, 300
\lfloor 98
\lg 98
\lhd 96

\lim 98
\liminf 98
\limsup 98
\line 247–253
\linebreak 141–143, 310
\listoffigures 172–173, 177
\listoftables 179, 183
\listparindent 225, 233
\ll 96
\ln 98
\log 98
\longleftarrow 97
\Longleftarrow 97
\longleftrightarrow 97
\Longleftrightarrow 97
\longmapsto 97
\longrightarrow 97
\Longrightarrow 97
\makebox 153, 161, 243–244, 301
\makeindex 194–196
\maketitle 34, 40–41
\mapsto 97
\marginpar 23–24
\marginparpush 225, 231
\marginparsep 225, 231
\marginparwidth 225, 231
\markboth 28, 82–84
\markright 28, 82
\mathindent 226, 234
\max 98
\mbox 101, 106, 142–143, 153, 161
\medskip 147, 206
\mid 96
\min 98
\models 96

\mp 96
\mu 94
\multicolumn 114–116, 128, 289, 313
\multiput 257–259
\nabla 97
\natural 97
\nearrrow 97
\neg 97
\neq 96
\newcommand 203–205, 207, 284
\newcounter 213, 221, 284, 292
\newenvironment 209–211, 284
\newlength 149, 151, 152
\newline 142–143, 294
\newsavebox 159, 162, 244, 284
\nofiles 201, 283
\noindent 17, 120, 312
\nolinebreak 141, 143
\nonumber 133, 134, 136
\nopagebreak 138, 139, 141, 317
\normalmarginpar 24
\normalsize 43
\nu 94
\nwarrow 97
o 94
\o 77–78
\O 77
\oddsidemargin 163, 166, 225, 227
\odot 96
\oe 77–78

\OE 77
\oint 97
\omega 94
\Omega 94
\ominus 96
\opening 36, 39
\oplus 96
\oslash 96
\otimes 96
\oval 256–257
\overbrace 103, 107
\overline 102, 107
\P 77
\pagebreak 138–141, 317
\pagenumbering 78–80, 219, 310
\pageref 55
\pagestyle 80–83
\paragraph 46, 52
\parallel 96
\parbox 155–156, 162
\parindent 223, 225, 229
\parsep 212, 225, 232
\parskip 225, 230
\partial 97
\partopsep 225, 232
\perp 96
\phi 94
\Phi 94
\pi 94
\Pi 94
\pm 96
\pounds 77
\Pr 98
\prec 96
\preceq 96
\prime 97

\prod 97
\protect 28–29, 310–311
\ps 37
\psi 94
\Psi 94
\put 240–242
\raisebox 158, 162
\rangle 98
\rceil 98
\Re 97
\ref 54–56, 66, 72, 172, 178
\renewcommand 206–209, 211, 229, 236, 284, 306, 310, 315
\renewenvironment 211, 284
\reversemarginpar 24
\rfloor 98
\rhd 96
\rho 94
\right 98–100, 299
\right. 99, 101
\rightarrow 97
\Rightarrow 97
\rightharpoondown 97
\rightharpoonup 97
\rightmargin 225, 233
\rm 41–42, 45, 88
\roman 219
\Roman 219
\rule 157, 300
\S 77
\samepage 139, 141, 317
\savebox 159, 162, 244–245
\sbox 159, 162
\sc 41
\scriptscriptstyle 74, 76
\scriptsize 43

\scriptstyle 74, 76
\searrow 97
\sec 98
\section 46–47, 49, 52
\section* 48
\setcounter 216, 285, 292, 306
\setlength 149–150, 152
\setminus 96
\settowidth 150, 152
\sf 41
\sharp 97
\shortstack 246–247
\sigma 94
\Sigma 94
\signature 37, 39
\sim 96
\simeq 96
\sin 98
\sinh 98
\sl 41, 105
\small 43
\smallskip 147, 206
\smile 96
\spadesuit 97
\sqcap 96
\sqcup 96
\sqrt 91, 92
\sqsubset 96
\sqsubseteq 96
\sqsupset 96
\sqsupseteq 96
\ss 77
\stackrel 104, 107
\star 96
\subitem 193, 194, 197
\subparagraph 46, 52

\subparagraph* 48–49
\subsection 46, 47, 49, 52
\subsection* 48–49
\subset 96
\subseteq 96
\subsubitem 193–194, 197
\subsubsection 46, 52
\subsubsection* 48–49
\succ 96
\succeq 96
\sum 72–73, 76, 97
\sup 98
\supset 96
\supseteq 96
\surd 97
\swarrow 97
\t{oo} (o͡o) 77
\tabcolsep 226, 237, 312
\tableofcontents 49, 53, 307
\tan 98
\tanh 98
\tau 94
\textfloatsep 226, 236
\textfraction 226, 236
\textheight 164, 166, 225, 228
\textstyle 73–76
\textwidth 163, 225, 228
\thanks 40
\thechapter 218–220
\theenumi 218
\theenumii 218
\theenumiii 218
\theenumiv 218
\theequation 218
\thefigure 218
\thefootnote 218

\thempfootnote 218
\thepage 218–219, 220
\theparagraph 218
\thesection 218
\thesubparagraph 218
\thesubsection 218
\thesubsubsection 218
\theta 94
\Theta 94
\thetable 218
\tilde{p} 102
\times 96
\tiny 43
\title 40
\today 40
\top 97
\topfraction 226, 235
\topmargin 164–166, 225, 228, 309
\topsep 225, 232, 234
\topskip 225, 229
\triangle 97
\triangleleft 96
\triangleright 96
\tt 41
\u{o} (ŏ) 77
\unboldmath 105
\underbrace 103
\underline 102–103, 107, 166–167
\unitlength 239–241
\unlhd 96
\unrhd 96
\uparrow 97, 98
\Uparrow 97, 98
\updownarrow 97, 98
\Updownarrow 97, 98

\uplus 96
\upsilon 94
\Upsilon 94
\usebox 159, 163, 245
\usecounter 213
\v{o} (ŏ) 77
\varepsilon 94
\varphi 94
\varpi 94
\varrho 94
\varsigma 94
\vartheta 94
\vdash 96
\vdots 92, 93
\vec 102
\vector 254
\vee 96
\vspace 146–147, 149, 172, 313
\vspace* 146, 148, 309
\wedge 96
\widehat 102, 107
\widetilde 102, 107
\wp 97
\wr 96
\xi 94
\Xi 94
\zeta 94
abbreviations for 205
and case sensitivity 12
and optional arguments 12
characters allowed 12
conventions 12–13
defined 5, 12–13
defining, that take arguments 207–209
defining your own 203–213

for running LaTeX 10–11
for recovering from errors 262
for special symbols. *See* special symbols
fragile 28–29
improper use of 261
math, in paragraph mode 85
mistyped 10
redefining old 206
sectioning 27, 46
captions
   in figures 171
   in tables 177–178
center environment. *See* environment, **center**
comment character 26–27
continuing a LaTeX run 262
coordinate pairs 240
counter parameters 224
counters
   creating 221
   customizing 212–213, 215–222
   defined 215
   incrementing 217
   listed 218
   printing 218
   setting 216
   style of 219
cross references. *See* symbolic referencing
cube root 91
customization 8, 137–167
customizing
   documents 8
   spacing in math mode 105

dagger symbol 78, 96

dashes 19–20
date
   in letter 36
   in title page 40
   today's 40
dbltopnumber 226, 236
decimal point spacing 118–119
defining commands 203
delimiters 98–101
   in **eqnarray** and **array** 299–300
   "invisible" 99–100
descriptive list. *See* environment, **description**
displayed formulas 70
   customizing of 76
displaymath environment. *See* environment, **displaymath**
display mode vs. text mode 73, 74
documents
   creating 1–2, 9–10
   customizing 8, 137–167
   double-spacing of 308–309
   preparing large 185
   printing 7
   splitting, into small files 185
   text of large 190
document environment. *See* environment, **document**
document style 13, 31–35
   and headers 82–83
   and style guide 13
   changing defaults in 8
   default parameter values in 225–226
   defined 7–8, 13

selecting 31
See also style
document style options 32–35
DOS
file name conventions 6
system prompt, returning to 10
dot accent 102
dotless i and j 104
double-spacing 308
DVI (DeVice Independent) file 5, 7
writing as much as possible to the 263

e.g. 14
editing 3
editor
ASCII 7
and index entries 196
ellipses 92–93
em (measure) 148
em dash 19–20
empty (page style) 80
en (measure) 148
en dash 19–20
enclosures, in letters 36–37, 39
enumerate environment. *See* environment, enumerate
enumerated list. *See* environment, enumerate
enumi counter 218
enumii counter 218
enumiii counter 218
enumiv counter 218
environment 59

array 128–132, 299–304. *See also* arrays
bibliography 198–201
center 144–145
defined 59
defining a new 209–211
description 68–70
displaymath 70–71, 76
document 59
enumerate 65–68, 216
eqnarray 133–136, 299–304
eqnarray* 134–135
equation 70–71, 76
figure 170–177, 183. *See also* figures
figure* 183
flushleft 145–146
flushright 145–146
itemize 61–65, 69–70
list 211–213
minipage 144, 145, 156–157, 162, 216, 309
name of, misspelled 266
picture 239–259. *See also* pictures
quotation 60–61
quote 59, 60
tabbing 109–111
table 177–183. *See also* tables
table* 183
tabular 111–128, 144–145, 146, 311–315. *See also* tables
theindex 192–197
undefined, error 286
verbatim 29–30

eqnarray. *See* environment,
     eqnarray
eqnarray*. *See* environment,
     eqnarray*
equation counter 217, 218
equation environment. *See* en-
     vironment, **equation**
equation numbers 34, 75, 76, 133–
     134, 136, 306
     \include and 186
equations
     aligned 133–136
     breaking lines in 134–135
     changing numbering of 306
     customizing displayed 76
     displayed 70–76
     \include and 186
     indenting of displayed 234
     in-line 25–26
     italic type in 305
     justifying 34, 35, 133–134
     left-justified 34–35, 75, 76
     long 234
     numbered 70–72
     placement 34
     placing and numbering 33–
          34, 76, 133–134
     referring to numbered 72
     short 234–235
     space above 234
     space below 234–235
     typesetting commands for 85–
          107, 128–136
     unnumbered 70, 76, 134
     vertical spacing of 234–235
     words in 101–102
error indicator 264–265, 267–268

error locator 264–268
error messages 10, 261, 266–270
     explained 280–298
     in TeX 296–298
     interpreting 264
     list of 280–298
     responses to 262
errors 261–298. *See also* error
          messages
etc. 14
ex (measure) 148
examples 299
     eqnarray and **array** 299
     floats 316
     footnotes 306
     general math 304
     page breaks 317
     style 308
     tables 311
     T.O.C., L.O.F., L.O.T. 307
expression 25, 118–119
extension, in file names 6

figure counter 218–220
figure environment. *See* envi-
     ronment, **figure**
figure* environment. *See* envi-
     ronment, **figure***
figures 169–177
     captions and numbering 171
     \include and 186
     labelling and referencing 172
     List of. *See* List of Figures
     numbering 53, 171–172, 176
     position of 170–171
     See also environment, **figure**
file

.aux 6, 268
.idx 194–197
input 5
.log 268–270, 273–278
.toc 49, 307–308
DeVice Independent (DVI)
    5, 6, 263
not found 264
suppressing output to a 201
file names 6
conventions in 6
fleqn document style option 33,
    34, 75, 76, 234
float. *See* floating objects 169
floating objects 169–183, 235–237,
    316
and positioning options 170–
    171, 176
continuing, to second page
    316
defined 169–170
error in number of unprocessed
    295
figures 170. *See also* figures
formatting parameters 235–
    236
fraction of page allowing 235–
    236
in two-column format 183
lost 287
number of, allowed at top of
    text 235
number of, allowed on page
    236
rules for placement of 183
spacing and 236–237
tables 177. *See also* tables

tying, to reference 169, 172,
    178
flushleft environment. *See* en-
    vironment, flushleft
flushright environment. *See*
    environment, flushright
fonts
styles of 41–42
sizes of 42–43
footers 80–83, 229
footnote counter 218, 221
footnotes 21–23
adjusting spacing of 23
and enumerated list 67
controlling numbering of 22
distance between 230
optional argument to 22
symbols for markers in 22,
    221, 306
foreign accents 77–78
foreign symbols 77–78
formatting
customizing 8, 137–167
defined 3
page 227–230
parameters, listed and defined
    223–238
formulas 25
breaking lines in 134–135
displayed 26, 70–76
in-line 25–26
style parameters for 234–235
typesetting commands for 85–
    107, 128–136
words as part of 101–102
See also equations
fractions 88–90

fragile commands 28–29
functions, special 98

grave accent 77, 102
Greek letters 94–95
    as letters or symbols 105
grid 239–241
groups 44–46

h position specifier 170
hat accent 77, 102
headers
    in tables 114–116
    page 34, 80–84, 228
    sectional 46–48, 310–311
hidden text. *See* comment character 26
horizontal space 146
hyphen 19–20
hyphenation
    automatic 16, 18
    inhibiting with `\mbox` 142–143
    user-specified 57–59

`.idx` file. *See* file, `.idx`
i, dotless 104
i.e. 14
`i\stop` 262–263
`in` (inches) 148, 152
input file 5
integrals 72, 97
in-text mode 76
indenting
    before list labels 233
    in list 233
    See also paragraph indentation

index 192–197. *See also* environment, `theindex`
input from a separate file 188
input file 4–5
    contents and structure of 9–11
    essential commands in 62
integrals 72–74, 76
italic type 41
`itemize` environment. *See* environment, `itemize`
itemized list. *See* environment, `itemize`

j, dotless 104
justification
    in tables 111–116
    of text 144–146
    switching 309

kerning 4
key, in referencing 53–57. *See also* commands, `\label`; label; labelling and referencing
Knuth, Donald 1

l column specifier 112, 128
labelling and referencing 53–57
    in `eqnarray` 133–134, 136
    of figures 172
    of numbered equations 72
    of pages 55
    of sectional units 54
    of tables 178
label, in list
    bolded 69
    other than default 61, 63, 212

setting width of box containing a 233
large documents 185
LaTeX
   commands 5, 11–13
   defined 2–3
   logo 11–13
lengths 148–152, 223
   default values for 225–226
   rubber 224, 226
`leqno` document style option 34, 75, 76
`letter` document style 36–39
letter, elements of a 36–39
ligatures 4
limits
   of integrals 72–74
   of summations 72–74
line breaks 141–143
   controlling, in section headings 310–311
   in formulas 134–135
   inhibiting 142
   protected 29
lines 247–253
   breaking, in formulas 134
   horizontal, in arrays 128
   horizontal, in formulas 102–103
   horizontal, in tables 113
   in pictures 247–253
   vertical, in array 128–129
   vertical, in tables 114
   width of, between text columns 231
   width of, in boxes and `tabular` and `array` environments 237–238
line spacing
   adjusting, in `array` and `tabular` 113, 132, 238
   adjusting, in `eqnarray` 135, 234
   adjusting, in text 15, 229–230, 308
   adjusting, with optional argument to \\ 142–143
   new 142
`list` environment. *See* environment, `list`
lists 61–70
   customized 211–213
   descriptive 68–70
   enumerated 65–68
   itemized 61–65
   missing items in 293
   nesting error in 295
   setting indent in 233
   setting left margin of 232
   setting right margin of 233
List of Figures 172–177
   alternate entry to 173
   adding a line to 173
List of Tables 179–183
   alternate entry to 179
   adding a line to 180
logo 11–13
`.log` file. *See* file, `.log`
lowercase letter 14

macros. *See* commands, defining own 203–213
marginal notes 23–25
   spacing between, and text 231

margins 163–166
  adjusting 15
  changing top 309
  defining, in list 211, 232–233
  setting 163, 227–228
math mode 25–26
  array environment and 128–129
  bolding in 105–107
  customizing spacing in 105, 234–235
  eqnarray environment and 133–136
  paragraph mode and 85
  size-controlling commands in 73–74
  switching from, to paragraph mode 25–26
  typesetting commands in 85–107
math mode accents 102
math symbols 95–100
mathematics, typesetting 85
  examples of 299–306
matrices, special 304–305
matrix 93
measurement
  error of missing units in 267
  units of 148
  See also lengths
messages. *See* error messages
minipage environment. *See* environment, **minipage**
mm (millimeters) 148
modes, error of incorrect 292
moving arguments 27–29, 310–311

mpfootnote counter 218
myheadings (page style) 81–84

nesting, error in 295
new line. *See* line breaks
  and % 207
nul 264
numbering
  extra control over sectional 51, 230
  \include and 186
  styles of 219, 220
  See also counter, counters

optional arguments 12, 28
output, checking 278
output file 5
  suppressing 201
  See also file
ovals 256–258

p position specifier 170
p-columns 116–118, 311–312
page counter 216, 218–220
pages
  elements of 163–166
  headers and footers 80–84
  labelling and referencing 55
  numbering of 78–80
  styles of 80–84
page breaks 137–141, 317
page formatting 163–166, 227
page-numbering style 78–80
page numbers
  correcting in Table of Contents 307
  default 80
  defining style of 78, 310

\include and 186
  in List of Figures 172–173
  listed, during LATEX run 261
  referring to 55
page styles 80–84
pages, labeling and referencing 55–57
paragraph column 116–118
paragraph counter 218
paragraph indentation 8, 17
  adjusting 17, 229–230
  automatic 16
  avoiding 17
  in list 233
paragraph mode 25–26
paragraphs 16–18
  in list 233
  indenting. *See* paragraph indentation
  spacing between 230, 232
parameter definitions 227–238
parameters
  changing a 227
  default values of 225–226
  definitions for 227–238
  page formatting 163–166
  See also style parameters
patterns, repeated 257
pc (picas) 148
picture environment. *See* environment, **picture**
pictures
  defining area 239
  objects in 240
  shapes in 247
  text in 242
plain (page style) 80

position specifier 316
  for figures 170–171
  for tables 177
preamble 164
prefaces 190
prime, command for 25, 97
printer processor 7
  invoking 11
printing 10–11
  of LATEX documents 7
  one- and two-sided 32–35
  one-sided, and headers 82, 83
  two-sided, and headers 83
  with DVI file 5
prnt 7, 11
P.S. 36–37
pt (points) 148
punctuation 18–20

question mark 78
quotation environment. *See* environment, **quotation**
quotations. *See* quotes; environment, **quotation**
quotes 18–19 *See also* environment, **quote**; environment, **quotation**

r column-specifier 112, 128
radical symbol 91–92
references, to list items 66–68
referencing, symbolic 53–57
  of **eqnarray** items 133–134, 136
  of equations 72
  of figures 172

of list items 66–68
of pages 55–57
of sectional units 53–55
of tables 178
relation symbols 96
repeated patterns 257
report document style 32
return address 36
roman type 41
    in sub- or superscripts 88
    in formulas and equations 305
roman page-numbering style 79
Roman page-numbering style 79
root file 185–192
roots 91–92
rows 109–136. *See also* columns
    changing spacing of 234, 238
    controlling height of 315
rubber lengths 224, 227
rules 157, 300

salutation 36
sans serif type 41
secnumdepth 225, 230
section counter 218
sections
    \include and 186
    labelling of 53–55
    starting 46
    unnumbered 48
sectioning commands 46–50
sentences 13–15
sentence space 14
    default 14
    special cases 14–15
shapes, in pictures 247

shorthand commands. *See* commands, abbreviations for
signature, in letter 36–37
single-spacing, forcing 308–309
slanted type 41
slides 319
SliTeX 319
slope
    of line 247–253
    of arrow 254–255
small caps type 41
software version numbers 261
space
    between words 13–14
    between sentences 14–15
    horizontal 146–147
    in math mode 105
    preventing, with % sign, 207
    producing a 13
    vertical 146–148
spacing 17
    above displayed equation 234
    around **array** columns 237
    around **tabular** columns 237
    baseline 229
    below displayed equation 234–235
    between box text and lines 238
    between double vertical lines 237
    between floating objects 236
    between floating object and text 236
    between label box and text in list 233
    between lines of text 229

between list and text 232
between list items 69, 232
between marginal notes and
    text 231
between paragraphs 230, 232
changing row 234, 238
customizing in math mode
    105
footer 229
header 228
horizontal 14, 146–147
in arrays 129, 131, 132
in columns of text 231
in formulas 76, 234–235
in tables 112–113, 127, 237–
    238
of **eqnarray** rows 135, 234
vertical 146–148
vertical, in line breaks 142
vertical, of displayed equa-
    tions 76, 234
with <CR> 16–17
word 13
See also rubber lengths 224
special characters 20
special functions 98
special symbols 20
square root 91–92
stacking symbols 104
stopping a LaTeX run 262
struts 157, 300
style 31, 308–311
    article 16, 32, 35
    book 32
    document. *See* document style
    letter 32, 36–39
    matters of 31–84

page-numbering 78–80
    report 32–33, 35, 48
style guide 13
style parameters 223–238
    changing 227
    counter 224
    default settings for 224–226
    for boxes 238
    for floats 235–237
    for footnotes 230
    for list 232–234
    for marginal notes 231
    for math 234–235
    for page formatting 227–230
    for section levels 230
    for tables and arrays 237–
        238
    for two-column format 231
    lengths and 223
    listed and defined 227–238
    rubber lengths and 224
style, page 80–84
subcaptions 173–175, 180–181
sublist 62–66
    levels of 70
subscripts 86–88
    command for 25
subparagraph counter 218
subsection counter 218
subsubsection counter 218
summations 72–73
superscripts 86–88
    command for 25
symbolic referencing. *See* refer-
    encing, symbolic
symbols
    arrow 97

binary operation 96
commands for 20
delimiter 98
foreign 77–79
Greek letter 94
math 95
miscellaneous 97
relation 96
special 20
stacking 104, 107
variable-sized 97, 100

t position specifier 170
tab stops 109–111
tabbing environment. *See* environment, tabbing
table counter 218–219
table environment. *See* environment, table
table* environment. *See* environment, table*
Table of Contents 49
adding a line to 50–51
changes to 49–50
entry 46
misnumbering 307–308
moving arguments and 27
sectioning commands and 49
section levels 230–231
.toc file 49, 51–53
tables 177–183
aligning, with text 120–121
as paragraphs 120
captions and numbering of 177–178
centering 121, 313

changing row spacing in 113, 238
full-page 316
headings in 114–116, 313–314
horizontal lines in 113
horizontal placement of 312
inserting expressions into 118
labelling and referencing 178
List of 179. *See also* List of Tables
multiple, on one line 120
numbering of 177–178
paragraph columns in 116
positioning options in 177
setting up 109–128
space between double vertical lines in 237–238
spacing around columns in 237
spacing between rows 113, 239, 315
style parameters for 237–238
treated as word 120
vertical lines in 114
width of vertical lines in 237
within sentence or paragraph 120
tabs 109–111
alignment, error in number of 267
error in defining position of 296
overflow error in 294
sequence of, 110
tabular environment. *See* environment, tabular. *See also* tables

TeX 1–3

text
  centering 144–145
  centering, in boxes 153
  different treatments of 59
  document, files 190, 192
  grouping 44, 46
  height of 228
  in boxes 153–163
  in list environment 232–233
  in picture 242–247
  inserting, and continuing a
      run 263
  inside ovals 257–258
  keeping, together 139–141
  of large documents 190
  setting, flush 145, 146
  spacing of first line of 229
  width of 228

text mode vs. display mode 73–
      74, 76
theindex environment. *See* en-
      vironment, theindex
tie 67–68, 142–143, 169
tilde 67–68, 102, 142–143
titlepage document style op-
      tion 33, 34
title page 33–34, 39–41
tocdepth 225, 230
.toc file. *See* file, .toc
topnumber 226, 235
totalnumber 224, 226, 236
trigonometric functions 98
twocolumn documentstyle option
      32, 34
two-column format. *See* twocolumn
      documentsytle option

twoside documentstyle option 32,
      34
two-sided printing. *See* twoside
      documentstyle option
type sizes 42–44
  and printer driver 43
  available 43, 46
  changing 42–44
  in document style options 32,
      34
typesetting 3–4
typestyles 41–42
  available 41, 46
  bold 41
  changing 41–42, 44
  changing, and braces 44–45
  italic 41
  math 74
  Roman 41
  sans serif 41
  slanted 41
  small caps 41
  typewriter 41
  underlined text 166–167
typos 10–11

underlining
  in math 102–103
  in text 166–167
underscore 20
  using, to make subscript 86–
      88
uppercase letters 15

variable-sized symbols 97, 100
\vec accent 102
verbatim text 29–30

vertical space 146

warning message 261
word processing 3–4
word space 13, 17
words, in formulas 101

x (quit LaTeX run) 262

♦ *Free* ♦
♦ *Demo* ♦

Yes, I want to know more about PC TEX Typesetting Software

Free ♦
Demo ♦

Including LATEX and A𝓜S-TEX

PC TEX is the leading personal computer implementation of the popular TEX typesetting system originally designed by Donald E. Knuth at Stanford University. PC TEX typesetting software lets you produce printed documents and books with master typesetting artistry and full control over pagination, hyphenation, justification, rule drawing, and many other professional typesetting elements. Complex mathematical papers, technical journals, theses, books, and manuals all look perfect when typeset with PC TEX. Included with PC TEX are two popular macro packages: LATEX, which includes pre-defined formats for tables, technical documents, books, and manuals; and A𝓜S-TEX, a macro set designed especially for mathematicians by the American Mathematical Society.

Name: _____

Affiliation: _____

Address: _____

City: _____   State: _____   Zip: _____

Phone: (   ) _____   Fax: (   ) _____

Please send me: □ Catalog
□ 3.5" Demo Disk
□ 5.25" Demo Disk
□ Site license information

I currently use a:
□ HP LaserJet or compatible printer
□ PostScript printer
□ HP DeskJet printer

□ Epson FX or compatible 9-pin printer
□ Epson LQ or compatible 24-pin printer
□ Other _____

Please have a representative call me □   **Add me to your mailing list** □

Return this card to Personal TEX, Inc. or call (415) 388-8853
Fax: (415) 388-8865 • 12 Madrona Street • Mill Valley, California 94941

PERSONAL
TEX
INC

PCTEX and Personal TEX are registered trademarks of Personal TEX, Inc. TEX is a trademark of the American Mathematical Society. Site licenses available to qualified organizations. Inquire about PTI distributorships. This was typeset using PCTEX with Computer Modern and Bitstream Fonts.

BUSINESS REPLY MAIL

FIRST-CLASS MAIL   PERMIT NO.28   MILL VALLEY, CA

POSTAGE WILL BE PAID BY ADDRESSEE

Personal TeX, Inc.
12 Madrona St.
Mill Valley CA 94941-9914

NO POSTAGE
NECESSARY
IF MAILED
IN THE
UNITED STATES